T.D. JAKES

SPEAKS TO MEN

Books by T. D. Jakes

Loose That Man & Let Him Go! (with workbook)
So You Call Yourself a Man?
Woman, Thou Art Loosed!
Woman, Thou Art Loosed! Devotional

T. D. Jakes Speaks to Men (3 in 1)
T. D. & Serita Ann Jakes Speak to Women (3 in 1)

SIX PILLARS FROM EPHESIANS
Celebrating Marriage
Experiencing Jesus
Intimacy With God
Life Overflowing
Loved by God
Overcoming the Enemy

Life Overflowing (6 in 1)
Life Overflowing (6 DVD set)

To contact T. D. Jakes, write:

T. D. Jakes Ministries
P.O. Box 5390
Dallas, Texas 75208

www.tdjakes.org

T.D. JAKES
SPEAKS TO MEN

THREE BESTSELLING BOOKS IN ONE VOLUME!

LOOSE THAT MAN AND LET HIM GO!

SO YOU CALL YOURSELF A MAN?

T.D. JAKES SPEAKS TO MEN

BETHANYHOUSE

a division of Baker Publishing Group
Minneapolis, Minnesota

© 1995, 1996, 1997 by T.D. Jakes

Published by Bethany House Publishers
11400 Hampshire Avenue South
Bloomington, Minnesota 55438
www.bethanyhouse.com

Bethany House Publishers is a division of
Baker Publishing Group, Grand Rapids, Michigan

Paperback edition published 2014
ISBN 978-0-7642-1287-1

Printed in the United States of America

Previously published in three volumes:
  Loose That Man and Let Him Go!
  T.D. Jakes Speaks to Men!
  So You Call Yourself a Man?

The Library of Congress has cataloged the hardcover edition as follows:
Jakes, T.D.
        T.D. Jakes speaks to men: three bestselling books in one volume!
            p.   cm.
        Summary: "Popular writer and minister T.D. Jakes exhorts and encourages men to face the
life issues that keep them from reaching their potential so that they can accomplish all God
intends for them"—Provided by publisher.
        ISBN 978-0-7642-0357-2 (hardcover)
        ISBN 10: 0-7642-0357-6 (hardcover)
        1. Christian men—Religious life. 2. Christian men—Prayer-books and devotions
English. I. Title.
BV4528.2.J35 2007
248.8'42—dc22   2006038403

Unless otherwise identified, Scripture quotations are from the King James Version of the Bible.

Scripture quotations identified NASB are from the New American Standard Bible®, copyright © 1960, 1962, 1963, 1968, 1971, 1972, 1973, 1975, 1977, 1995 by The Lockman Foundation. Used by permission.

Scripture quotations identified TLB are from *The Living Bible*, copyright © 1971. Used by permission of Tyndale House Publishers, Inc., Wheaton, Illinois 60189. All rights reserved.

Cover design by Eric Walljasper

14 15 16 17 18 19 20   7 6 5 4 3 2 1

T. D. JAKES, founder and senior pastor of The Potter's House Church in Dallas, Texas, is a celebrated speaker and author with many bestselling books to his credit. His weekly television broadcast is viewed in millions of homes nationwide. Featured on the cover of *Time Magazine,* he is known around the world for his message of freedom to be found in Christ.

T.D. JAKES

LOOSE THAT MAN AND LET HIM GO!

DEDICATION

This book is dedicated to the memory of my father, Rev. Ernest L. Jakes, Sr.; to my brother Earnest L. Jr., whose presence in this world has made life richer and fuller for me; and especially to the destiny of my three sons, Jamar, Jermaine and T.D., Jr., whose lives have been a burning blaze in my heart. I know that they are manuscripts yet to be written and songs waiting to be sung. To the world I say get ready for them, they are being printed at this very moment and soon to be published. They will be well worth reading.

CONTENTS

CHAPTER ONE

WHEN I WAS A CHILD

When I was a child, I spake as a child, I understood as a child,
I thought as a child: but when I became a man,
I put away childish things.

— 1 CORINTHIANS 13:11 —

E very man, great and ordinary, famous or forgotten, enters this world traumatically and begins to perceive his surroundings through the eyes of a child. It is during these tender years that he experiences the beginnings of his masculinity.

Our development as men is shaped by the things we encounter as children. Our masculinity is defined by our fathers and our relationships. Dysfunctions in our adulthood were also shaped or influenced by the presence—or absence—of the men who fathered us. What painful childhood memories haunted young Adolf Hitler? Who touched the life of Martin Luther King, Jr., or of Abraham Lincoln? What childhood pains or dreams framed the thoughts of Malcolm X and Mahatma Gandhi?

Our father's absence can form a sustained question in our minds, a haunting thought, *Maybe it was something I did or something I lacked that caused him to leave.* We learn the art of suppression early, deeply burying the painful questions and the native sensitivity that is so easily bruised. We suppress the natural creativity that springs from a probing mind as we encounter the pain of continually being told, "Shut up! I don't have the time to listen to you."

Our fathers are our first definition and demonstration of masculinity.

Unfortunately, our fathers' model has caused many of us to equate masculinity with absence, irresponsibility, sullen silence, or violence. All the fruits of our manhood are rooted in our childhood—our self-esteem, our inner awareness of who we are, our sexuality, our preferences. They are all deeply planted in the soil of our early memories, experiences, and definitions.

God plants an infinitely curious mind within every little child and adolescent. As they grow older, many children bend to indifference and ignorance, while others surrender to scorn and punishment, and eventually most will finally succumb to a "formal education" that will quench their natural hunger for knowledge.

Young minds never stop gathering information through their senses, and they constantly process their perceptions. What do you suppose those Judean children perceived the day the young Rabbi, Jesus, rebuked the men who were pushing the small ones away from Him? What went through their minds as the children heard Him say, "Suffer the little children to come unto me, and forbid them not" (Mark 10:14)? How many lives and destinies were changed forever by His tender embrace and unconditional love that day?

Within every man dwells the little child who preceded him. Manhood is rooted in childhood, and many of the thoughts you and I have today come from our early experiences as children. You may read these words with sadness if you are one of the thousands who involuntarily recoil at the mere sight of the words, *Father, Daddy, Papa, or Dad*. They only represent pain and loss to you.

I Spoke as a Child

My mother used to listen closely to me when I talked. Now I understand that *my mother's attention dignified my opinion*. Her actions confirmed to me that I mattered. Her careful (and patient) listening enriched my thinking process with a self-esteem that caused me to believe that my thoughts were important. Regardless of whether she agreed or didn't agree with what I said, what excited me was that she listened to me.

Jesus *spoke* when He was a child. According to Luke 2:46–47, He entered the temple and spent five days listening to and speaking with the leading doctors of the Law while He was barely an adolescent! The Bible says these scholars "were astonished at his understanding and answers" (Luke 2:47 TLB). If you want to know who someone is, listen to what he says! "For of the abundance of the heart his mouth speaketh" (Luke 6:45). Jesus started perfecting the art of expression early in His life, and even the leading teachers of the day listened to Him. What a boost that must have been to His self-esteem! There is something about expressing thoughts that airs out the mind and sorts out the closets of the intellect.

My mother stimulated my creativity by listening to my expressed thoughts. Her attention gave me respect for my own opinion, a respect that still exists today. I am concerned that in the busy world of our day, *the children know we are not listening to them, and the pressure is rising.*

Sadly, many times our parents did not listen to us. Neither have we always listened to our children or to one another. Thus we have raised a generation of angry young men. They in turn have carried their inner anger into marriages in which they believe no one is listening to them. This consuming anger has surfaced as violence, introversion, perversion, or outright self-destruction! Their self-esteem and integrity have been destroyed because they have felt muzzled all their lives. They suffer like bound and gagged prisoners in a rigid shell of outrage and despair.

As parents, pastors, and leaders, we often seem extremely stretched ourselves, but *we need to listen anyway!* Men who curse and swear or even become violent are just overgrown little boys having a tantrum because they feel out of control. They are frustrated because "life isn't listening!"

"When I was a child, I spake as a child" (1 Corinthians 13:11). We all need to be able to communicate our thoughts and express how we feel. Jesus said, "But those things which proceed out of the mouth come forth from the heart; and they defile the man" (Matthew 15:18). If there is anything worse than the rage, the frustration, and the other negative things that come out of us, it is the things that do not come out! Festering wounds are dangerous wounds. A rumbling volcano is a dangerous omen, a solemn warning of a coming eruption that could rain down destruction on everyone living in its shadow.

Many men lose their ability to communicate during childhood. As youngsters we are told what is "appropriate" to do (or is it merely *convenient?*). "Just sit over in the corner and be *quiet!*" Now, as adults, we feel the rush of unchecked adult passions, frustrations, and anger coursing through us on the inside, and we can't speak. We can't communicate. We're ready to explode, but we don't dare cry! We're hurting too bad to laugh. The only emotion we are allowed to express is *anger!* (Why is anger the primary emotion attributed to the *male gender?*)

The raging child who takes a hammer and pounds his toy into oblivion soon becomes the grown man who runs his fist through the wall and batters his wife into an early grave. Many times this kind of rage is fueled by an inability to turn thoughts into words. It is crucial for men to be able to vent emotions and frustrations safely through appropriate channels—for when they don't, everything breaks loose. No one wins but the adversary of men's souls.

I Understood as a Child

Our *understanding* is the "digestive" process of our minds. It is the stage in which we come to a resolve and draw conclusions. Paul said that when he was a child, he understood as a child. If as adults our understanding is still elementary and childish, we may come to immature conclusions. Childish wisdom can be the most dangerous of all—especially in the mind of a wounded adult.

So many children who have grown up in broken homes determine at some point in their lives that it is their fault their fathers and mothers separated. Many attempt to shoulder the blame and responsibility for their fractured upbringing and become terribly scarred because of their childhood conclusions and understandings. We court disaster when we carry childish perceptions into adult relationships.

Distorted childhood perceptions and conclusions are often a spawning bed for crippling thoughts of inadequacy. Such perceptions and conclusions produce a lifetime of insecurity. At this very moment you and I still carry the deep wounds that were incited by the cutting statements of other children who never knew that their reckless words of scorn were lethal! Even our sexuality is affected by early encounters and incidents. Many grown men are recreating scenarios from their scarred and twisted childhood in their adult fantasies. They are trapped by endless nightmares of sordid passions and insatiable lusts.

We often build protective layers of denials, lies, and illusions around our secret pains (like pearls, which are just abnormal growths of secretions layered around irritating foreign objects in the *hearts* of oysters) until something forces the issue. One day the pry bar of circumstance will force open the shell and expose the secrets for all to see.

Our needs and preferences are a composite of early childhood experiences and encounters—a glimpse of naked flesh furtively stolen from someone stepping out of a bath, a tender touch, a forbidden fondle, a feeling of fleeting pleasure. The nostalgia that shapes adult issues arises from a thirty-year-old memory of sweet-smelling cologne, the touch of warm flesh, or the gentle caress of silken hair across the face. Whether the church wants to deal with it or not, most men are involved with little boy thoughts that have escaped their childhood and entered their adulthood like steam escaping from a shower.

If sexuality is tampered with early in life, it can greatly twist and influence a man's perception of the whole issue of sex and personality.

"I *understood* as a child." What a powerful statement! What is normal for a child can be deadly for a man who still *understands* as a child. The suit is bigger and the man is bigger. He has more hair and bigger biceps, but he is no longer a baby; he's making babies. Despite his size, his childish understanding is *dwarfing* him.

"Depravation dwarfism" is a psychological concept used to describe children who have been physically dwarfed because they were not nurtured, touched, or handled. The lack of love and physical closeness literally caused their physical handicap. Millions of men are "dwarfed" in their emotions and personalities because they were deprived of love and affection as children.

Although men have "toys," many of them use them to cover their pain and shame. They have the toys as well as the contrived expressions and fanfare that go with them, but the toys are relative to culture.

Few people in our country understand that there is little difference between an executive in a business suit and tie who goes to "Joe's Place" for happy hour, then staggers home half drunk, and a derelict on the street corner in dirty blue jeans and a raggedy T-shirt sucking on a bottle in a brown paper bag. *It's the same addiction.* One addict is simply better dressed than the other. The differences are only economic, social, and cultural. One man plays on a yacht while the other plays on a basketball court. Both men may be trying to escape through the use of toys. One pays more for his toy than the other, but in the end they both fail to escape.

Now there is nothing wrong with adult toys, but we need to know what we use our toys for. Some of us use our toys for identification or to impress people, while others use their toys to escape reality.

There is a universal commonality of masculinity; we are not that different from each other. It doesn't matter whether we are Oriental, Caucasian, Hispanic, Native American, or African American. Whether we are well educated or illiterate our basic needs are the same, and our ability to express ourselves is relative to the "amount of marbles we have in the bag." If you have more marbles, you can do more things.

The book of Proverbs warns us with the passionate writings of a wise father trying to save his son from the dangers of "too much, too soon." Many of us didn't read his words in time. There wasn't a father patient enough or wise enough to save us from the pain. We became engulfed in excess. Our heads intoxicated with the swirling spirals of unchecked emotions ingested too much too early and never resolved the conflicts that raged within us.

You can't have manpower until you have boy power. Someone must save the children within us and the children we've fathered! They are being destroyed before our very eyes. They are dying in the courtrooms of our land and killing one another on the streets of our cities.

Our own broken childhoods have turned our little children's lives into unthinkable horror stories, spawning more crimes and murders in the bosoms of children than have ever been witnessed in history! The Apostle Paul warned us in Ephesians 6:4, "And, ye fathers, *provoke not your children to wrath*: but bring them up in the nurture and admonition of the Lord." Have we so abused our children that now they rise in wrath to kill us?

I Thought as a Child

Never in history have we been so afraid of our own children! Grown men are afraid to walk through crowds of pre-teen and young teenage boys in the city. Young men have become so angry that adult men are intimidated by them. Grandmothers are being killed by raging grandchildren who tie them up in basements and set them on fire! The news media report increasingly gruesome teen atrocities that sound like gothic horror fictional novels or nightmares from hell, but they're happening. We sit in our easy chairs and watch through television as thirteen-year-old boys stand trial before a judge and jury and receive a life sentence without shedding a tear. *Preoccupied by our own pain, we have created monsters in our children.* This plague transcends racial and social boundaries. From the well-to-do Menendez boys in affluent California to the "boys in the hood" of the urban ghetto, the spirit of anger transcends culture. We have become angry, frustrated men, and we have spawned a generation that is angrier than we are.

We have been given too much responsibility too fast. We have seen too much. We have heard too much. We have watched the gropings of twisted flesh on prime time television and have listened to the squeaking noises coming from our parents' rooms in the night. We have challenged childish minds with manly issues.

The mind of a child should not be stressed with harsh issues like molestation, abuse, or domestic violence. This strain produces a mental hernia that is visible in the character of the youngster for the rest of his life! Many young men have followed their fathers' footsteps into promiscuity, thinking it natural to define their masculinity by extreme sexuality. "Isn't that what Dad did?" Like so many other excesses and escapes, it is just a drug taken too often for a pain that will not go away. It only masks the symptoms without healing the source of the pain.

Nearly every problem in society becomes more inflamed by the raw anger burning out of control within our young men. Racism is on a rampage because men are angry. Violence is sweeping through our schools, our homes, and our prime time crime shows. Even the "politically correct" demands of the feminist movement have been swept aside by a new wave of raw, angry sexuality that openly exploits and degrades participants on both sides of the gender line. Whenever men are angry, they look for somebody to blame. Adam set the pattern when he blamed Eve for making him disobey God's command in the Garden of Eden. (See Genesis 3:12.) Whenever we are captured or feel trapped, we cast the blame on someone else. An entire generation has become imprisoned in a pit of anger and frustration, and somebody has to take the blame.

The people of this generation look at each other and say, "You're the reason I'm in a rut!" White men say, "Blacks are taking all the jobs and forcing the rest of us out! Just because I'm white, I can't get a job with all this Affirmative Action business. I'm angry—we should do away with these stupid programs!" Meanwhile, angry black men are saying, "White people are the reason we can't find decent work. It's white people's fault that we can't earn a living, because we have been discriminated against all those years." Immigrants are saying, "Neither of you is right. Here is the real reason. . . ." And so the arguing, blaming, and childish finger-pointing go on and on.

Everyone is angry. We wound one another in our jealous, childhood exchanges of bitter words. Our whole culture has become angry because we have provoked our sons to wrath. How does a child forget the scene that replays in his mind every day and night—the picture of his mother angrily wiping away her tears as his father mutters and throws his glass through the television screen? Did he make his father angry that afternoon? Was his mother upset because he couldn't please Dad enough to calm him down? Surely there was something he could have done to fix whatever was wrong. . . .

Who can erase the burning shame and anger of the boy who dreaded the bus ride home from school? Twenty years later he can still feel the vicious blows, the curses, the blazing hatred in the eyes of his attackers—what had he done to deserve what they did to him? Whatever the reasons, this boy, now inhabiting a frame bearing nearly 280 pounds of muscle, bone, and sinew, can't control the burning rage and hatred he feels every time he sees a member of that race. He only knows that he wants to strike back again and again until his pain goes away. That's why he is in prison.

Those feelings of buried childhood pain never leave us. They stay with us all our lives, even when the roles change. We get bigger and we learn to hide them better, but inside the little boy is still intimidated. We still feel fearful. We're still bullied and overwhelmed by people at times. The child within doesn't want to deal with the secret thoughts no one else knows about. But many times, the secret thoughts force their way to the surface and press the issue.

What prompts a forty-year-old man to suddenly discover one night as he lies in bed that *he needs to be held?* All his life he's been the "holder." All of a sudden, this macho man turns to his wife and says, "Just hold me." When the pain breaks through, we are wrestled to the ground and made to face an unsettling fact: A hurting little boy still lives within. We cannot divorce ourselves from our inner need. So how do we spell relief?

> *Society, would you give me permission to be who I am without categorizing what you see? Must I live up to some image that you created for me to conform to? Can you accept the fact that I'm a combination of many different types of dysfunctions bound together within one house?*

All that I express, speak, and understand is relative to my childhood. You will never understand the man I am on the outside until you have touched the child within me. Wife, beware. Children, beware. Pastor, beware. Boss, beware. If you never develop empathy for the little boy in me who is holding a blanket and sucking his thumb in a doorway, watching everyone leave, then you will never understand my erratic behavior as a man on the job, or in the bed, or with my own sons and daughters. "When I was a child, I spake as a child, I understood as a child, I thought as a child . . ." (1 Corinthians 13:11).

CHAPTER TWO

SUFFER THE LITTLE CHILDREN

Suffer the little children to come unto me, and forbid them not: for of such is the kingdom of God. Verily I say unto you, Whosoever shall not receive the kingdom of God as a little child, he shall not enter therein.

— MARK 10:14–15 —

Many times, buried and suppressed beneath our manly facade and pretense, our fear comes from a trembling, angry, confused child whose frustrations and insecurities are covered with muscles, sweat, and hair. Often, beneath our blustery masculinity, there are issues that must be confronted.

Where can the little child in each of us go but to God? Jesus declares that the kingdom is composed of little children, not just the chronologically young, but even the little children who live in big bodies.

"Forbid them not: for of such is the kingdom of God." Any pastor will tell you that the kingdom is one big playground filled with dysfunctional children who have found solace only in the presence of God. That does not mean that this kingdom is simply a collection of losers who couldn't keep up with winners—no, *all men* are losers in some way because we are incomplete, and we will never be healed until we come to God *like little children*.

There is no room in the kingdom for macho men in a power struggle to impress one another with their collection of "toys" or "possessions." It doesn't matter whether these toys are cars, biceps, girlfriends, church members, or certificates of deposit. We must confront the child in us before we can enjoy the man.

What Could Have Been . . .

And David said, Is there yet any that is left of the house of Saul, that I may shew him kindness for Jonathan's sake? And there was of the house of Saul a servant whose name was Ziba. And when they had called him unto David, the king said unto him, Art thou Ziba? And he said, Thy servant is he. And the king said, Is there not yet any of the house of Saul, that I may shew the kindness of God unto him? And Ziba said unto the king, Jonathan hath yet a son, which is lame on his feet. And the king said unto him, Where is he? And Ziba said unto the king, Behold, he is in the house of Machir, the son of Ammiel, in Lo-debar.

Then king David sent, and fetched him out of the house of Machir, the son of Ammiel, from Lo-debar.

2 SAMUEL 9:1–5

Mephibosheth is one of my favorite characters in the Bible. His name is a tongue-twister, but it is not nearly as twisted as his life. The Bible describes him as being lame in both of his feet. His story is tragic because *he could have been, he should have been,* king over Israel! He was the grandson of Saul, who was the first king of Israel. He should have been a strong, handsome, virile leader like Jonathan his father. Instead, when we find Mephibosheth we see a twisted, bruised, incapacitated victim whose broken ankles and twisted limbs have exiled him to a terrible place called "Lo-debar."

Rabbinic scholars say *Lo-debar,* when literally translated from the Hebrew, means "place of no communication" (*lo* means "no," and *debar* or *devar* means "word").

Mephibosheth was a deposed and maimed prince from a fallen house of kings, whisked from a royal palace to live in "a place of no communication." This wounded young man lost his birthright without uttering a single word or doing a single evil deed. He was just a frightened little five-year-old boy when he was buried in a land of silence, separated from his father and his destiny, and left to dream of what might have been!

Have you ever been to Lo-debar?

Isn't it amazing how brokenness in one area can rob us of rightful success and imprison us in a valley of regret, a silent place where no one can hear our pain or ease our sorrow?

"*I could have been. . . . I should have been . . .*" Mephibosheth *could have been* a king, but there was a problem in his life. He *would have been* great, but he had an area in his life that seemed beyond his control. There was nothing wrong with his mind. He could command his legs to walk, but there was a problem between the command and the function. He meant to do it, but he couldn't and didn't perform what he meant to perform. He was maimed and handicapped.

Maybe you and I can't relate to Mephibosheth's physical handicap, but every one of us has a certain degree of dysfunction. We can give a command in our head, but it just doesn't function in our lives. Our dysfunction can leave us in Lo-debar, gagged, hopeless, and alone, when we *could have been*—and *should have been*—kings sitting in a palace.

Mephibosheth was Jonathan's son and King Saul's grandson. He was the only surviving heir and male descendant of Israel's first royal family. He *should have been* groomed to be king over Israel, but instead his father was tragically killed in battle and he was left living like a broken-down recluse in Lo-debar—stripped of his crown and wounded in spirit, a long-forgotten prisoner of his own infirmity. Yet the only thing wrong with Mephibosheth was that he was lame in both of his feet.

Wretched Mephibosheth is a vivid picture of you and me, trying desperately to deal with our inward handicaps without letting anyone know "what really goes on inside." Mephibosheth is the model for every man who should have been *here*, but instead ended up *there*. The reason men end up in Lo-debar instead of the palace is because something occurred in their life that so traumatized them that it kept them from reaching the hope of their calling. Our handicaps—whatever form they may take—keep us from reaching our potential or fulfilling our dreams. We have stopped short of the goal because a hidden issue in our life seems to hold us back.

Carried to the Calling

> Now when Mephibosheth, the son of Jonathan, the son of Saul, was
> come unto David, he fell on his face, and did reverence. And David
> said, Mephibosheth. And he answered, Behold thy servant!
> And David said unto him, Fear not: for I will surely shew thee
> kindness for Jonathan thy father's sake, and will restore thee all the land

*of Saul thy father; and thou shalt eat bread at my table continually.
And he bowed himself, and said, What is thy servant, that thou should-
est look upon such a dead dog as I am?*

*Then the king called to Ziba, Saul's servant, and said unto him, I
have given unto thy master's son all that pertained to Saul and to all his
house. Thou therefore, and thy sons, and thy servants, shall till the land
for him, and thou shalt bring in the fruits, that thy master's son may
have food to eat: but Mephibosheth thy master's son shall eat bread
alway at my table. Now Ziba had fifteen sons and twenty servants.
Then said Ziba unto the king, According to all that my lord the king
hath commanded his servant, so shall thy servant do. As for Mephibosheth, said the king, he shall eat at my table, as one of the king's sons.
And Mephibosheth had a young son, whose name was Micha. And all
that dwelt in the house of Ziba were servants unto Mephibosheth. So
Mephibosheth dwelt in Jerusalem: for he did eat continually at the king's
table; and was lame on both his feet.*

2 SAMUEL 9:6–13

Mephibosheth is no longer a five-year-old boy when he enters the scene
in 2 Samuel 9. He is a grown man with a son of his own.

It all began when David called in Ziba, a former servant of King Saul, to
ask if there was anyone left of the house of Saul to whom David could show
kindness. This man told King David that only one descendant of his old
friend, Jonathan, was still alive—Mephibosheth, the lame man. This maimed
prince lived in another man's house in *Lo-debar,* the place of no communication, the land of lost and forgotten potential. David's answer was immediate and forceful: He sent messengers, or perhaps Ziba himself, to go "fetch"
him out.

Jonathan and David were close friends and covenant brothers. The Bible
clearly shows that they had the most intimate covenant relationship two
men could ever have as friends. David meant to keep his oath to his
deceased friend Jonathan, so his invitation to bring Mephibosheth was genuine and trustworthy.

Unfortunately, there was a problem. Although Mephibosheth was called,
he couldn't come on his own. Someone had to go get him. The real truth of
the matter is that many of us have been called, but we can't get to the place

we have been called to dwell in because we are so distracted and crippled by our own brokeness. We hear the voice but we can't get up. David sent the servant Ziba to "fetch" Mephibosheth out of the "place of no communication." In this scene, I feel that Ziba is a type of the Holy Spirit, Who comes to fetch us out of the valley of silent sorrows and oppression.

Remember, by the time Ziba comes to get Mephibosheth, he is a grown man.

When Mephibosheth arrives at the palace, he must be brought in by Ziba. This grown man is literally being carried like a child! This is a very powerful image in my mind. If I look at Mephibosheth's *presence,* I want to let him walk. But when I look at his *problem,* I realize that he must be carried. I can just see Mephibosheth falling down, clutching David's kingly robes, lying on the floor of a palace that *should have been his,* begging. This is a picture of dysfunction.

Dysfunction is desperate men clutching onto relationships, living beneath their privilege, lying on the floor of life stripped of their self-respect and integrity. They are in the right place, but they are not in the right position. They have been violated and emasculated. Some have been violently raped; others have been secretly molested. Some have been consumed by drugs, and others are lost in a sea of mind-numbing alcoholism. These would-be princes have become beggars in their own houses, lying on the floor and unable to rise to fulfill their destiny.

While Mephibosheth is lying on the floor, David says something like, "You know, I've prepared a table for you. . . ." Mephibosheth says, "Oh not me, my lord; I am a dead dog. I have no self-worth—I'm not worthy to be in this place."

This young man was born to an aristocratic, noble, good-looking, affluent, attractive, upper echelon family in Israel. He *should have been* tall like his grandfather, who was "a head and shoulders" above all men. (See 1 Samuel 9:2.) Mephibosheth *should have been* good-looking like Jonathan, the royal prince. Mephibosheth's father caused everyone to gasp when he walked by because he was handsome to look upon—so why was his son groveling on the floor of the palace in which he was born? What happened to make him a trembling, shaking, frail and fragmented, tattered and torn, emasculated and wounded would-be prince? Born with so much going for him, how could Mephibosheth now be so impoverished physically, emotionally, and spiritually?

Somebody Dropped Me!

Several things came into play to determine Mephibosheth's fate. The Bible describes an event that was destined to change Mephibosheth's life forever. At the time this event took place he was only five years old.

Everything began as usual that day. Young Mephibosheth arose from his bed to scamper around the palace and play after breakfast. His nurse carefully dressed him, perhaps hoping this would be the day the young prince's father would return with King Saul to tell of their triumph in battle. According to 2 Samuel 4:4, however, something terrible was about to happen.

> . . . [Mephibosheth] was five years old when the tidings came of Saul and Jonathan out of Jezreel, and his nurse took him up, and fled: and it came to pass, as she made haste to flee, that he fell, and became lame. And his name was Mephibosheth.

Prince Mephibosheth's nurse heard that his father and Saul had been killed. Then the Bible tells us that on the very same day that Mephibosheth lost his father and his grandfather, his nurse dropped him and maimed him for life! It wasn't fair! He didn't deserve it, but it happened to him nonetheless. Realize that *something happened to this man as a child* that he had never recovered from! *Somebody had dropped him.*

Has somebody dropped you? "I *would have been* more of a man than I am, but somebody dropped me. I apologize for not being everything you expect me to be, but *somebody dropped me.* I realize that for my age and my stage, I *should have* done more with my life, but before you determine the subtotal of all that I am, you have to *allow for* what I've been through, for I *have been dropped* in flight, in the middle of the process. I've been incapacitated."

While other children went out to play, Mephibosheth could not move. While other children climbed trees, he had to stay in the house. What damage did this situation do to his self-esteem, his emotions, his self-perception, his sexuality? No one wanted to go out with Mephibosheth the teenager. Nobody saw him as attractive. What kind of weird, perverted mentality must have begun to fester like a fungus in his mind—all because the bumbling mistake of a hurrying nurse forever had deprived him of natural growth experiences!

The Bible says that against this backdrop of broken dreams, the king commanded that Mephibosheth be carried from Lodebar, "the place of no communication," to *Jerusalem,* the "possession of peace." He moved into the king's palace on the southwestern hill of Jerusalem called *Zion,* which means "fortress." But what happened? Now that Mephibosheth had been brought out of Lo-debar, it seemed that he was "out," but his mind wasn't! His body was not "out." He was still as handicapped as before. His problem was not "out." He still didn't know who he was; he had still missed a lifetime of normality. Within this suffering man lived a suffering child.

Mephibosheth is one of the few characters in the Bible *who never got healed.* He ached all his life. He was wounded all his life. I think we have damaged a lot of men by saying, "Come to the altar, brother, and everything will be fine! Join the church, and everything will work out. Get in the choir, you'll be okay. Pay your tithes. You'll see, everything will be fine."

The truth is that some woundings stay with us all our lives. We may always be more needy, more fragile, more dependent, and more vulnerable than other people because we have experienced a serious injury. Jesus still bears the scars from the cross, and we are no different from our Master.

If I have a car wreck and crush my leg, the leg may heal and I may be able to get around, but when certain types of weather conditions occur, I will feel pain in a way you may never experience. Am I saved? Yes, I am saved. Am I healed? Yes, I am healed. But yet, I have to bear in my body a certain degree of affliction as a result of a past injury. That is something we have not been honest about, and Christianity has been disappointing in the minds of men who thought somebody could lay hands on them and wipe away their childhood injuries forever. Some things won't go away completely. They just won't disappear.

If there were an "executive boardroom" in the kingdom where representatives from every major group of stockholders met together before God, then Mephibosheth might represent us (he is a type of another scarred Son Who returned to His throne). He brings to the forefront a man who is sitting at that table with the King's kids, though he is not whole, attractive, or nice-looking. He's scarred and wounded, and he's got a problem that has to be taken care of when nobody is looking. But the good news is: *at least Mephibosheth made it to the table!*

You Belong at the Table

Even our failures are successes! They represent the miracle that you and I survived! Considering what we had to work with, though it looks like failure to us, we survived and our survival has been our success!

No matter how wounded you are, no matter how handicapped you have become, no matter how far you are from where you *could have and should have been*—you can still make it to the palace and sit at the table with the rest of the King's kids! Yes, even though you still have a "problem" tucked under the tablecloth that other people cannot see, you still belong at the table. It is the command of the King!

When Mephibosheth was finally carried to King David's table, he began to enjoy several blessings he had not experienced since his family's royal house fell. First, he began to receive food that he didn't have to labor for. There is help for the handicapped through the Holy Spirit. *God knows exactly where you are—even if you're lost in Lo-debar!* Second, Mephibosheth looked different. If you looked at him from the top side of the table, Mephibosheth was as "princely" as Absalom, with his majestic flowing hair, or Amnon, with his princely demeanor, or even Solomon, the son with the wise countenance who would ultimately ascend to David's throne.

Mephibosheth, the maimed and forgotten prince of a fallen house, the pitiful broken recluse from the land of silence, now looked like everybody else at the royal table. He was a prince among princes. That was his *position,* and hidden under the table was his *condition.* His return to the palace is good news: *Your position can overcome your condition!*

We need the freedom in the church to say, "Yes, I am in this *position,* but I still have this *condition.* Yes, I am a pastor, an elder, a deacon, a choir member; but I have this *condition* called 'being human.' I'm sorry, but I have some hidden wounds. I have some brokenness under this table. There are some childhood scars under my clerical collar that you don't see."

We have never been able to say that. The church has been hypocritical about the way it views and treats its very human leaders. Men are frustrated because we are in *positions* that do not allow us to admit that we have *conditions* with our wives, our families, and within ourselves.

We are in *positions* as husbands that do not allow us to say, "Yes, I'm married, but I'm going through a mid-life crisis, and I want my twenty-two-year-old secretary! I know my daughter is nineteen, my wife is forty, and I'm forty-five. But I'm going through this *condition*. Help me stand, help me go from *here* to *there*. The King is calling me to His table, but my ankles aren't working, and I'm growing weak."

Every time we have to silence our *conditions* because of our *positions*, our hidden wounds and problems begin to fester. We become angry and throw away everything we have. In desperation, we make permanent decisions about temporary circumstances—circumstances that we would eventually outgrow if we just had somebody we could confide in. "This is how I feel today, brother. I know it's wrong, and I want to do right, but I'm afraid. That's where I am. Help me *stand up,* brother! My ankles are hurting me again, but I've got to get to the King's table!"

CHAPTER THREE

CONFRONTING THE CHILD IN YOU

We can no longer allow our past to destroy what God has for us in the present. We must admit the hidden issues threatening our destiny and confront them. All of us have crippling wounds and disadvantages hidden within.

No one is exempt from disadvantage.

Unattractive men think attractive men are exempt from problems, and black men think, "If I were just a white man in this country, I would have it made!" Yet white men are dysfunctional also. White men look at black men and say, "You've got all the benefits in this country! If I were black, I could get a job too!"

We know something is evading us. The "something" we are grasping for is out of our reach. Although we work hard to obtain it, it keeps moving back. We blame each other, but we still know that we cannot get it. The black hand has not reached it; the white hand has not reached it. The businessman and the corporate lawyer have not reached it; those men are committing suicide right along with the junkie who is strung out on crack. The only hope any of us have is in Jesus. Only Jesus can walk us through the barrier of time to invade our past. There He can make us comfortable with our uncomfortable parts and at peace with our frailties and brokenness.

From the executive to the drug dealer, from the deacon to the doper, we have but one God to go to, yet something is standing in our way. We're in for a battle if we're serious about breaking free from that thing.

And Jacob was left alone; and there wrestled a man with him until the breaking of the day.
GENESIS 32:24

Whether you are a preacher, a deacon—black or white—a Baptist, a Methodist, a Presbyterian, or one of the "boys in the hood," one truth confronts you: *You can never become who you want to be until you can drop who you used to be.*

The Enemy Within

If you want to be free, you must be willing to challenge all definitions of your masculinity. You have to be willing to confront issues that other men run from. Freedom only comes when you challenge yourself, when you open up and say things to yourself that you might not have admitted to your wife, to your friends, or to your parents. It is time to confront old issues.

These issues are enemies of your soul.

I am not overly concerned about witches, demons, sorcery, or astrology. As bad as crime is, I am not too worried about muggers, thieves, rapists, or con artists. I don't want to be their victim, but they are not my greatest dread. Nor do I suffer anxiety thinking about a figure dressed in red with a pitchfork and a pointed tail who peers in the window making evil suggestions to me. If there is anything that I constantly fight against and wrestle with, it is *the enemy in me.* That is the one I am most concerned about—the enemy "in-a-me"!

If anything takes you back, it will be the enemy within.

The book of Romans paints a frightening picture of men who fail to confront the enemy within:

Because that, when they knew God, they glorified him not as God. . . .
And even as they did not like to retain God in their knowledge, God

gave them over to a reprobate mind, to do those things which are not convenient.

ROMANS 1:21, 28

These men once knew the Lord, but they decided not to glorify Him as God. His judgment was *to turn them over to themselves!* Some of us may have to enter a witch's house, or confront a warlock or sorcerer head on, or walk through a high-crime red light district, but the greatest danger—the greatest judgment—that could ever confront any of us is for God to turn us over to ourselves. If God ever adopts the advertising slogan that says, "Have it your way," you and I will self-destruct!

Left to our own devices, we may be surprised to discover how corrupt we really are. You and I conceal many things in us that we don't talk about. There are hidden things in us that we belittle other people for. Oh yes, we're careful to make sure no one knows what is lurking in the dark corners of our heart, but *they are there.* Under difficult circumstances, those secret weaknesses can erupt with terrible results.

You might be surprised at what you would do if you were pressed. If your hidden anger raged high enough, what would you do with that knife in the kitchen drawer? Under certain stresses, you would be shocked to learn who would rob a convenience store. Pastor, deacon, faithful husband, and provider, you keep your secret passions well hidden, but you would be dismayed to discover who you would sleep with if pressured with the wrong circumstances. How many moral and emotional land mines are buried in the depths of your soul?

If I have made you uncomfortable, I apologize, but as my brother once told me, "When you get in a fight, you may as well throw the first punch."

You would be disturbed by what is lurking in the shadows of your being. In fact, you would be shocked to know what your best friends and family members have done, but haven't told anyone.

Men can be incredibly hypocritical. We often strongly condemn others for the very things we are most guilty of ourselves.

The greatest and most lethal weapon the enemy can ever challenge you with is you.

I thank God He didn't turn me over to myself.

Thank You, for contending with me, Lord. Thank You for arguing with me, convicting me, wrestling with me, warring with me, talking to me, and challenging me. I could never find a way out of my pain if You weren't there to point the way home.

God challenges us in unique and special ways to help us know who we are, despite our handicaps. Most of us are suffering from manipulation. When we have no goals, it is easy for others to impose on us their ideas of who we are and are not, and of what we should and should not be doing. Manipulation is a result of purposelessness. Anytime we don't know and understand our purpose, or who we were created to be, we become vulnerable to manipulation.

Anybody can assign his agenda to you if you don't know who you are. Unless you confront your own frailties and map your own vulnerabilities, you will never be prepared for attacks in those areas. When you are not prepared, you will find yourself saying, "But I never thought I would do that! I never believed I could get that angry and hostile! I never ever thought I would have an affair! How could I be that weak?"

Thousands of men once believed they could never cheat on their income tax or their wives, but they did. When you do not assess the potential of sin within, you will not pray against these things. It will inevitably leave you vulnerable to the attack of the enemy.

A Seat is Reserved for You

Our salvation lies in the fact that God has put His hand on us. He has made such a costly and personal investment in each of us that He is not easily discouraged from what He said about us! He set a chair in the midst of the angels in eternity. Then He told them:

"I am going to bring that man to sit in this seat, and he shall be Mine when I make up My jewels. I'm going to bring him right here."

The angels protested, "But Holy One, the man was dropped. He isn't whole."

"That doesn't matter. I am going to bring him right here."

"But he's a liar!"

"That's all right. I'm telling you, this is his seat. I have inscribed his name on it."

"Oh, but he's a molester!"

"That's ugly, but that's all right. I'm going to bring him right here."

"But Ancient One, I heard he was a pervert."

"Even so, when it is all said and done, and I have completed My teaching, preaching, and ministering through My servants, that man is going to sit right here!"

You may be sitting in a seat that ten years ago nobody ever believed you would be sitting in right now. *They underestimated the power of God to change you.*

God "calleth those things which be not as though they were" (Romans 4:17). Why? He knows He has the power to make them become what He says they will be. He is not afraid to call you and me holy and blameless, even while we are still confused, in trouble, and in turmoil! We may be guilty of inflicting domestic violence or mental abuse, but God says, "When I get through with him, he's going to be a deacon in the church. Give him that seat!" I want to thank God for reserving that seat for me. I want to thank Him for making a reservation in my name.

God is holding a seat for you. You don't have to be jealous of anybody. God has a special, one-of-a-kind seat reserved for you, and "ain't nobody going to sit in it but you!" God has a reserved seat for you, even though your enemies never thought you would be there. Some of your friends thought you wouldn't be there, either. Sometimes, even you thought you wouldn't make it to that spot at His right hand—and you wouldn't have, except for His holy arms. Praise God, He pulled you out, even when you didn't want to come! Sometimes you were kicking and screaming, but He pulled you out anyway. Hallelujah!

God has to get you ready. You need to get ready before you can sit in that seat He has reserved for you. When you were driving down the highway drunk, God had His angels watching over you. When you were slapping your wife around and boasting that you weren't ever going to church, God protected you from yourself. He knew you were crazy. He knew He had to deal with your mind. He knew exactly how He was going to pull that bitterness out of you and bring you to your knees.

You are a miracle.

If God had dealt with you according to your sins, you would be dead. But God is merciful. He was determined to maneuver you to a place where He could minister to you. When you really belong to God, He will go to extreme measures to *get you away from people*—the cliques and clubs, spas and pubs, society or any kind of entanglement that would hinder you from hearing His voice. But when you are really listening, when you are called of God, He will orchestrate things in your life so He can have you to Himself—completely.

Alone With God

And he [Jacob] rose up that night, and took his two wives, and his two womenservants, and his eleven sons, and passed over the ford Jabbok. And he took them, and sent them over the brook, and sent over that he had.

And Jacob was left alone. . . .

GENESIS 32:22–24

Jacob wasn't necessarily lonely; he was alone. When God starts calling you away to Himself, you may want to surround yourself with people. Unless you realize what is going on, you will gather people around you so you won't be alone. That won't help. You can be surrounded by people and still be alone if God is after you. You can experience intimate relationships and still be alone.

Who are you really? Who are you when nobody is looking? That is the real you. Who are you when all the camouflage is off, when you don't have an ego to defend, when you have nothing to prove at the office? Who are you when you're not concerned about who is driving the nicest car, who owns the biggest house, or who makes the best business decisions? Who are you aside from all the imitations of life?

If you ever go through a real life-or-death situation or recover from a life-threatening disease, you will discover the "real you." You will find out that most of the things people say are "important" aren't really important at all.

I'm alone anytime I am surrounded by people *who don't know who I am.* Anytime I am in a situation where I cannot fully be myself, I am alone. Anytime I have to put on a facade or camouflage who I really am, I am alone. I am isolated. I watch people through a glass because they really don't know me.

God wants you to be alone because that is when He really operates. Nobody receives guests in the operating room. I don't care how many loved ones you have around you, when you get ready to go through surgery, the doctors put them all out—even your wife and kids. God put this book in your hands because he wants to do surgery.

"And Jacob was left alone . . ." (Genesis 32:24). Jacob was not just alone—he was *left* alone. The word *left* implies that somebody who was there departed. Somebody he thought he could depend on moved. Someone he fellowshiped with abandoned him.

"And Jacob was left *alone*. . . ." He was left alone, isolated, and separated by God for a divine purpose. ". . . and there *wrestled* a man with him until the breaking of the day" (Genesis 32:24). Are you ready? God Himself is coming down to fight with you.

God is Coming to Fight Me?

"But Lord, this was a low moment in Jacob's life. He was left alone, and it seems like You should have comforted him."

"No," the Lord says, "I didn't come to *comfort* Jacob—I came to *confront* him. I came to challenge him, to wrestle with him for mastery of his life—just as I have come to wrestle with you!"

"Not You too, Lord! Everybody is wrestling with me. My wife is wrestling with me; my children are wrestling with me; my boss is wrestling with me; my church is wrestling with me; my mind is wrestling with me; and now You!"

"You're right, but I didn't come to baby you. I didn't come to comfort you—I came to confront you. I came to challenge you. I came to wrestle you into submission to My will and purpose for your life!"

The Bible says, "Faithful are the wounds of a friend" (Proverbs 27:6). If true friends wound you, they wound you for a good reason. In fact, many times that is the only way you can tell a really good friend from a "fair-weather friend," one who is only along for the benefits you offer. A really good friend doesn't agree with you all the time. No matter how rough and tough you act or how mightily you roar or how forcefully you do your macho act, a real friend will look you in the face and say, "I hear you, *but you are still wrong.*"

You won't get any real help from so-called friends *until you find a true friend who loves you enough to stand up to you.*

God is saying, "I've come to stand up to you. I am going to confront you and make you uncomfortable. I've come to move you away from mediocrity!"

Most of us are so "normal" that it is sickening. We're not earning F's or A's; we're just getting by with C's in the class of life. We're just mediocre. Boredom leads to sin. When there is no excitement, we "go hunting."

It is dangerous for you, as a "mighty man" of God, to spend too many days in mediocrity. If you do, you will find yourself creating your own challenge. Look at masculine entertainment. Man was meant to hunt.

When God created Adam, one of His commands was to be fruitful and multiply, to replenish the earth, and to subdue and exercise dominion. To *subdue* means to conquer, and *to exercise dominion* means to maintain control over what has been conquered. Embedded deeply within your masculine nature is a need to subdue. *There is a hunter in you.*

Oh yes, there is a hunter in you, whether you're stalking a contract, a deer, or a woman. You've got to hunt something.

It doesn't matter whether it's a business deal, a broker, a CD, or an annuity—all men love to hunt. We have to capture something. We have to chase and apprehend it, even if we don't really want it.

Many times fishermen catch a fish and just throw it back in the water. They're more interested in catching the fish than in eating it. God says, "I've come to challenge you before you catch the wrong thing. I've come to contend with you before you spend all your strength, your youth, and your talent asserting yourself in the wrong direction. I've come to wrestle with you before you waste your moments on frivolous living."

God knows that if we are not stopped, if we are not saved from ourselves, we will come to the end of our lives and regret what we have done. All our possessions and conquests will be meaningless. We will become jealous of other men who avoided our foolishness, and we will wish we had lived our lives differently. Men become cynical when they see other people who took advantage of opportunities and succeeded while they failed.

Don't Waste Your Life

God has given you a marvelous gift. He has given you life. What are you going to do with it? Life, energy, force, power, thought, and creativity are surging through your body right now. Adam was just a clay pot until God *breathed* on him! God has breathed on you and given you life. Yes, you've been through a lot of trouble, but God breathed on you, and you're alive.

God is out to confront you before you lose your greatest commodity—life. God gave you an opportunity. Now whether you notice it or not, that gift, your opportunity, is seeping away like a slow leak in a punctured tire. Sure, you're still rolling, but you're losing pressure all the time. You're losing hair, you're losing teeth, you're losing eyesight, and . . . I won't list *everything* you're losing, but you're losing a lot of things.

God wrestled with Jacob, a man whose name actually means "supplanter"[1] or trickster. Every time people called Jacob's name, they were calling him a con man. "Hey Schemer, dinner is ready. Hey Trickster, come and eat! Hey Con man, hey Crook, come on in the kitchen and chow down!" Every time they called Jacob, they were calling him according to his *characteristics*. Jacob lived up to his first name until God met him on the wrestling mat!

Lord, I thank You for not giving up on me!

God will wrestle with you to show you that you are wasting your life. He will wrestle with you to make you appreciate the wife He gave you. Be thankful for the wrestling times, for if God doesn't wrestle with you, you will give up the greatest for the least.

Sometimes God has to wrestle with you to make you understand how blessed you are. He will wrestle with you to give you the ability to stick to a job, even when it feels like it is going nowhere. He will confront you and say, "Son, you quit your last three jobs. When are you going to stand? When are you going to let Me plant you so you can bloom? You have been in ten churches; when are you going to be steadfast? You opened up five churches and left all five of them! When are you going to stick it out and fight?"

God's way is to tell it like it is. He doesn't put a bandage on your infected wound—He demands that the problem be dealt with, not merely tucked out of sight. He tells you, "You are unstable and are making excuses. You look like you are here, and there, and everywhere. You need to be planted."

God is waiting to wrestle with you because He knows that time is running out.

---

[1]James Strong, *Strong's Exhaustive Concordance of the Bible* (Nashville: Abingdon, 1890), "Hebrew and Chaldee Dictionary," p. 51, entry # 3290.

Running Out of Time

And Jacob was left alone; and there wrestled a man with him until the breaking of the day.
GENESIS 32:24

A lot of people will confront you, but after a while they will give up. The Bible says that God wrestled with Jacob "until the breaking of the day." God had set His watch; He wanted to get Jacob to his reserved seat. He wanted to salvage Jacob's destiny before he ran out of time.

God is not going to let you get by with all the little things He used to overlook; you are running out of time. He used to let you make excuses for the little things in the early hours of the fight. Now He is saying, "Excuses don't work anymore; you're running out of time. I must do a quick work to get you to your reserved seat. The enemy is chasing you; you are on the hit list of hell, but I am determined to get you first."

Satan has assigned assassins to ensure your demise, but God is saying, "I'm out to get you before you lose everything I gave you. I'm out to get you before you lose your life, before you lose your wife, before you lose your name, before you lose your dignity, before you lose your son, before you lose your seed, and before you lose your future."

We don't have time to play games or fool around and act like little boys. We're too old for that foolishness. "When I was a child, I thought like a child, I spoke as a child, I understood as a child. When I became a man. . . ." We have to commit our way unto the Lord because we don't have time to play games. We don't have time to be "Pentecostal pimps" or "church playboys" who ransack churches and cruise choirs for attractive women. We don't have time for an extramarital affair. We don't have time for sin—we have to make it to our reserved seat on time! We have to say goodbye to distractions. We have to grow up and learn how to pray for ourselves.

Smoke crack? I don't have time. Run around with another woman? I don't have time; I'm going somewhere. I'm running somewhere. I'm hunting God. I have to work while it's day. I don't have time.

"And there wrestled a man with him until the breaking of the day" (Genesis 32:24). God wrestled with Jacob until the breaking of day. When God sees that the day is breaking and the man in His grasp is running out of time, *He escalates the fight.* He says, "I will do a quick work in this man—he is running out of time."

Now God doesn't run out of time or get old or lose strength—but we do. If you or I were Jacob wrestling with the Lord in the middle of the night, we might be saying something like this: "No, I'm not going to pray. No, I'm not ready to give it up. No, I'm not ready to surrender. I want to steal some stuff. I want to cheat—I live pretty well by my wits. After all, my friends call me Trickster. No, I don't want to treat my wife better. No, I don't want to spend time with my kids. I'm strong enough to do it on my own. I'm holding my own with You, aren't I?"

When the Lord saw that the day was breaking and the party was over, He struck Jacob in his hip joint with a precision possessed only by the Master Physician. If that had happened to us as Jacob, the tireless wrestler, the sly con man, suddenly we would be saying, "O Lord, I can't fight You anymore. I've been hurt so bad that I need Your help just to get up from the ground! Can I lean on You? Would You hold me up? I'm hurting; I'm in trouble. If You don't help me, I'm afraid I'm going to lose everything! I've been fighting the only One Who can hold me up. I've been fighting the only One Who can help me!"

Wrestle Till You Know

And when he saw that he prevailed not against him, he touched the hollow of his thigh; and the hollow of Jacob's thigh was out of joint, as he wrestled with him. And he said, Let me go, for the day breaketh. And he said, I will not let thee go, except thou bless me. And he said unto him, What is thy name? And he said, Jacob. And he said, Thy name shall be called no more Jacob, but Israel: for as a prince hast thou power with God and with men, and hast prevailed. And Jacob asked him, and said, Tell me, I pray thee, thy name. And he said, Wherefore is it that thou dost ask after my name? And he blessed him there. And Jacob called the name of the place Peniel: for I have seen God face to face, and my life is preserved.

GENESIS 32:25–30

When you are brought to the place of "aloneness," you may find yourself fighting the only One Who can heal and preserve you. When Jacob's strength was broken by the power of God, he changed from a confident, cocky wrestler to a wounded, clinging man who wanted God's blessing more than anything else in the world! Now this Jacob, this trickster, was clinging to the Lord, saying, "I'm going to keep calling on You *till you bless me.*"

When the angel asked him what his name was, he said it was Jacob, the "trickster," but the angel gave him a new name, a new identity, and a new purpose.

That's what you and I need. We need to be asking the Lord: "Why didn't I die in the car wreck? Why didn't I get shot in the club? Why didn't I go crazy? Why have You always blessed me? Why have You always kept me? Even when I wasn't thinking about You, You let me survive. Why? Bless my soul and tell me who I am. Tell me what You want me to do. Tell me what I will be. Tell me why You love me and why You have blessed me? Why have I survived?"

Haven't you ever wondered who you are, why you are still here? Why did you make it through everything you made it through? Do you really think it's because you were that slick, or that gifted, or that smart, or that cool? You could have been dead. You could have been a statistic in a book. You could have had a nervous breakdown. You could have died of a dread disease. Somebody could have been shot. You owe it to yourself to wrestle until you find out who you are!

What's Your Name?

And he said unto him, What is thy name? And he said, Jacob. And he said, Thy name shall be called no more Jacob, but Israel: for as a prince hast thou power with God and with men, and hast prevailed.

GENESIS 32:27–28

Don't be surprised if God asks you the same question He asked Jacob. Whenever God asks a question, He is teaching, for He is too omniscient to need to know anything. Like the old-fashioned teachers, He asks us questions to see if we are learning anything. He said, "After all that fighting and struggling, and that last test I took you through, I want to see if you wised up any. *What is your name?"*

That is the real test that every man must face: "Who am I?"

Who Are You?

Examine your life. Look at all you've been through. *You are still here.* God brought you here and put this book in your hands to ask you a question: "What is your name?" God started a thought process in Jacob's mind. He made him stop long enough to assess his identity. He wrestled Jacob into a revelation. (There is nothing like pain to bring forth a revelation.)

What about you? God isn't asking you about your pastor; He wants to know if you know your name. He isn't asking you about your wife or your parents, He is asking about you: "What is *your* name? Who are *you?* Aside from other people, aside from your image, aside from your clothes, aside from your car, your house, and everything else that you possess, who are you? What is your name when nobody is around, when you're all alone?"

When God asked Jacob who he was, his answer was pitiful. He said, "I'm Jacob." It's sad, for he was saying, "I am *who people say I am.* I guess I'm just Jacob—at least that's what everybody always calls me. Aren't I who they say I am?"

All his life, Jacob had defined himself according to what *somebody else* called him. He never thought to argue with their opinion. He said, "I am Jacob. I am a cheat, a liar, a thief, a con man: I can't be trusted. I'm a trickster."

God has commanded me to tell you that *you are not who others say you are!* Get it into your spirit. *You are not who others say you are.* You are more than other people's opinions. Why should others name you, determine who you are, and set the limits of your success? Why should others be allowed to forever limit your potential? Why have you allowed other people to tell you who you are?

What is your name?

You are not who others say you are. I want that fact to sink into your spirit: *You are not who others say you are.*

You may be one of the thousands of good men who just can't talk or open up to others. You can't explain the pain you feel, and you're ashamed to reveal it or to be naked with your emotions. I know what it feels like to think you have to be a "tough guy" and hold up an image. But I want to tell you something. If you can hear me somehow behind your mask and the protective shell you've built around yourself, then I want you to know this: You are more than your childhood. You are more than your past. You are more than your bank account. You are more than your circumstances. You are more than your finances.

You are not who others say you are!   .

A Prince of God

God says your name is Israel. In Hebrew *Israel* means "he will rule as God"[2] and is derived from another Hebrew word meaning "have power (as a prince)."[3] You are a prince, and you don't even know it! You are part of a royal priesthood and a holy nation. (See 1 Peter 2:9.) You are an overcomer. (See 1 John 2:13–14.) You are the head and not the tail; you are to live above and not beneath. (See Deuteronomy 28:13, 14.) You are a prince, and the devil knows it. That's why he has been trying to assassinate you.

You are a prince, and all hell is afraid of you. The enemy knows what you can be, and he wants to destroy you before you become what God said you will be. You are a child of the King, and your Daddy is King of kings and Lord of lords.

What are you doing in that mess? Your Father is the King. He is King over poverty, disease, and affliction. Do you know who you are? You're a prince! You've been through a whole lot of stuff; the devil tried to kill you, but you're still here! Get ready. God is going to raise you up and set you in a high place.

Start declaring, "I don't know about anybody else, but I'm coming out of this. I'm a prince of God, and I'm fighting mad. Give me my children. Give me back my marriage!" If you confront every weakness, God will deliver you. If you face your past because you want your future, God will open up the windows of heaven and pour you out a blessing!

It is difficult to handle the pressure and stress of being everyone's hero all the time, to act like a man when you feel like a little boy inside. It is perplexing to comfort other people when you wish there were someone who would comfort you. God knows that once you've been "smitten at the hip

[2]Strong, p. 53, entry # 3478.
[3]Strong, p. 121, entry # 8280.

joint," it's hard to keep going. You try to keep up the facade. "I'm hurting, but I can't stop. I'm limping, but I have to go ahead. I'm going to drag my pain with me. Everybody is counting on me. I'm a man, I can't get tired, and I'm not supposed to get my feelings hurt."

Underneath the Disguise

There has to be some place we can go where there is no need to impress anyone, a place where we aren't expected to be "Superman." I'm talking about a "Clark Kent" kind of place where no supermen are allowed. This has to be a place for plain, ordinary men.

I'm serious about this. For many men, things can hardly get worse! Some of us have lost a marriage. Some have lost a ministry. Some have lost a child, and some have lost their dignity. Some have lost their self-esteem, and others have lost their masculinity. Millions of us are halt, blind, and lame, and we don't dare tell anyone that the light has gone out in our eyes!

The spring has gone out of our steps, and we're tired of our Superman suits. We're sick of the boots, we're sick of the cape, and we're especially sick of all the impressive theatrics it takes to *disguise our true identity* (and it's not Superman). We are just men. We are not God's angels; we're timid and tired of hiding behind a cape. We are just men who have felt the stroke of God. The wound of our Best Friend has pierced our souls. We're about to discover who we really are under all the trappings of the trickster.

Some of us have been abused, some have been molested, and others have been molesters. We've been wounded and mistreated; a few of us have served prison time, and many of us are adulterers. We're depressed and discouraged because our ministries are wrecked and our marriages are dying. Some of us reflect on our lives with unbearable sadness: "Once we were lovers who couldn't bear to be apart—now we're just roommates splitting the space. We share the same house and the same meals. Where has the flame gone? Will we ever live again?"

I wonder what would happen if we would pray? What would happen if black men and white men, and Baptist men and Methodist men joined with Pentecostal men and Presbyterian men in prayer? If rich men and poor men, educated men and illiterate men, if all would come together and pray? I wonder if the nation would be changed more by the church house than the White House?

What would happen if we decided to help our brothers get their dignity back? It is time for men to pray. We've left the job to women for too long. It is time for us to go to war as men, as princes of God. There are hands holding this book right now that will not be here next year if someone doesn't pray for them. If we don't pray, then some of the respectable men reading this book who have served as pastors for twenty-five years will find themselves tied up in illicit affairs. Some of the young men reading this book, men whose blood is clean today, will die of AIDS if we don't pray.

I wrote this book to be used of God, to call out the mighty army of princes to wage war on the enemy. It is our job to batter him down with the weapons of our warfare until we get our dignity out of his clutches. We need to pound him through prayer until we pry our homes out of his fingers, until we get our minds, our emotions, our appetites, and our sexuality out of his grasp.

Brother, there is a demon on assignment that has come against you. He has been tailor-made for your destruction. He has assessed your childhood and your past, and he knows where you limp. He knows where to hit you to bring you down. He's after you. If you, and those who *really* know you, don't pray for you and strengthen you in your weak place, you won't be able to stand against the wiles of the devil. He already knows where you have been wounded, and he is coming after you.

It is time for God's princes to be real with Him and with one another. It is time to seize every opportunity to pray for the men the devil wants to kill. It is time to pray for our brothers and sisters, for our homes and families, for our emotions, for our sexuality. It is time to pray about the "crooked places" in our lives, the places that always want to turn in the wrong way. We need to pray until we make the crooked paths straight.

Right now you are wrestling. You wrestle to know yourself. You wrestle to know your place. You wrestle to know the power of God. The Spirit of God is waiting for you. God has a warrant for your arrest. The Spirit of God wants you. Only the wound of your Friend can deliver from sin.

Tonight, you wrestle until the break of day. . . .

CHAPTER FOUR

WHEN I BECAME A MAN

When I was a child, I spake as a child, I understood as a child,
I thought as a child: but when I became a man,
I put away childish things.

— 1 CORINTHIANS 13:11 —

When the Apostle Paul used the phrase, *When I became a man*, he seemed to consider it an event (because it was). The "when" suggests he was remembering his own *bar mitzvah*, the Jewish ceremony marking his public recognition as an adult "son of the Law." We too must make a mark in our lives that declares our "rite of passage" into manhood and the purposes of God.

Making the Crossover

Jesus told His disciples, "Let us pass over unto the other side" (Mark 4:35). It is when we attempt to cross that the storms arise. The turbulence of change can be overpowering because the one thing the enemy doesn't want us to do is change. No, he doesn't care if we come to church. He doesn't even care if we slip into a robe and sing in the choir. He just doesn't want us to change.

Many of us are held captive in our miserable habits or lifestyle because we no longer make a "beeline for the hive" in times of change. We can't seem to find a place to cross over, so we wander aimlessly, wasting our time and energy. We need to experience an unmistakable rite of passage. We need a permanent marker of our manhood burned into our memories. In other words, we need to declare: "I am crossing over right here."

If you do this, then expect a storm right in the middle of the passage! It is when you attempt to change that the enemy decides to rain on your parade. Just count on adversities arising to keep you in your old place outside of grace. Don't act surprised when the storm winds blow and the rains dampen your zeal. Just face the storm and watch God give you peace in the process. This kind of peace can only come through prayer. If you are going to have peace in the process of change and the stress of the storm, you must guard your heart and mind with prayer.

Be careful for nothing; but in every thing by prayer and supplication with thanksgiving let your requests be made known unto God. And the peace of God, which passeth all understanding, shall keep your hearts and minds through Christ Jesus.
PHILIPPIANS 4:6–7

Change isn't cheap. It will cost you a "death to the old" in order to experience a "birth to the new."

We have not put the child in us to death. Just as Abraham offered up his young son, so we must offer up our own immaturity. Why? Like Abraham, we must do it because God has required it. We must bring our childish things to the altar and raise a knife to slay them if we are ever to pass over to the other side of a real experience with God.

Realize this: No one can do it for you! Neither a preaching pastor nor a begging wife can bring you to the altar and make you offer up your childish things. You alone can make this painful sacrifice before God. It is your personal offering, and without it, you can't cross over.

Unfortunately, many of us are stuck in the middle of the lake because a storm arose, and we failed to offer up some "childish things" when we were supposed to. We could not—or would not—give up our childish immaturity, and now we are rocking in the boat of mediocrity when we could have crossed over into inner and outer abundance. Inner abundance refers to wholeness within, and its contentment and tranquillity should be ours. However, because we fail to put away "childish things," our lives are as tempestuous as boiling water in a steaming tea kettle.

Celebrate Masculinity

Despite the turmoil caused by our halfhearted attempts to pass into true manhood, our actions and appearances seem to prove that we don't enjoy being men. In fact, we give manhood a bad name by making it look boring.

We have never celebrated our own masculinity. Instead, we dress boring and act boring. We are so drab and emotionless (except during sports events or temper tantrums) that nobody even wants to put money into our clothes. Frankly, we look like we are having a terrible time being men. In fact, manhood looks so bad that some of our young men are leaving it and turning gay! We have made being a man a terrible "go-to-work, come-home, go-to-work" task that is uncreative and unappealing. If appearances count for anything, then we are miserable. We need to celebrate masculinity. Somehow, we need to overhaul the whole thing.

Have you ever asked yourself why women seem to have so much fun being female? Their path isn't any easier than ours. They have to deal with unbelievable social pressures, menstrual cycles, childbirth and child rearing, and they face menopause at the end of their childbearing years—yet women *celebrate femininity!* They like being female, and they do a wonderful job of making us like their femininity also! They have cosmetic parties where they practice applying the latest makeup products with exact precision and care. They shop in packs or alone, hunting the perfect clothing and accessories at just the right price. Then they excitedly share the news of their latest find with friends (and get upset if that "find" shows up in the same room on another lady).

Women, for the most part, enjoy being women. They surround themselves with beautiful things—flowers and lacy, delicate things that help frame and enhance the beauty of their femininity.

Men are different. We fail to celebrate our masculinity. We come home to nothing because somewhere inside us, we think our needs are unimportant. Some of us excel at such "manly arts" as belching, beer guzzling, and female chasing, but no one is impressed. Dumb animals can do that—real manhood calls for much more than a big supply of hormones, alcohol, and bad manners.

At one point, I bought all the men in our organization a subscription to *GQ* magazine. I know some Christians might take that act as a sign that I have "lost my salvation," but I bought those men a man's magazine for an important reason. We don't spend time finding out anything about being men, and we act like we don't enjoy our masculinity. Just as we don't really know anything about women's bodies, so we don't really know anything about our own! When our bodies start changing with age, we are shocked! "Why is this happening to me! Who put that spare tire there?" We don't know why because we're ashamed of our "failure." We have no idea of what should be happening to us when we're thirty or fifty because we have not been educated about being men.

Years ago, on the day a girl first experienced her menstrual cycle, she would be shocked to find herself bleeding unless her mother had prepared and educated her. She would rush into her mother's arms in tears and bring the terrible news that she might die because she was bleeding. Then her mother would gently wipe away the tears and explain to her daughter that she had just entered womanhood.

Men are just as ignorant and uninformed about their bodies and physical cycles. We know almost nothing about the ways our bodies react to aging. We don't realize that our physical and sexual performance, our emotional peaks, and our whole mentality change at certain stages in life. We know nothing about it, so we are completely unprepared for it. When it hits us, we feel like we've been run over by a freight train.

Young boys don't have a dramatic right of passage like menstruation to mark their entrance into physical maturity. Their transformation may not be as traumatic, but on the other hand, it doesn't turn the focus on the responsibilities of the gender either. When a young woman experiences her first monthly cycle, her whole being becomes focused on the fact that she is uniquely equipped and designed to bring life into the world through her body. A young man just keeps hoping his voice will finally change so his peers will stop making fun of him. The appearance of secondary sexual characteristics like body hair and the voice change come in a scattered, almost haphazard way. Unfortunately, this is the way most of us enter manhood and discover our sexuality.

Later in life, we're in for equally difficult passages. While a woman must face the difficulties of menopause, we have to face something that has been called a "mid-life crisis." I'm talking about the man in his forties who can break down a computer and put it back together again, but who doesn't know enough about his own sexuality to understand why his world seems to be falling apart. I am talking about the management genius who can run a corporate office, but can't deal with the loss of an erection. In our ignorance and isolation, we cry, "Shame, oh shame, oh woe is me."

We need to celebrate our manhood from our first entrance into adulthood to the end of our "grandfather phase." We need to learn about our bodies and receive instruction about our God-given responsibilities as men. We need to celebrate who we are in God's plan.

The Jews celebrate a young man's entrance into manhood after his thirteenth birthday with careful instruction and preparation for the ceremony of *bar mitzvah*. This event marks a young man's entrance into adulthood and is considered to be a spiritual passage as well as a physical change. The Jews require candidates for *bar mitzvah* to learn and commit themselves to the biblical duties of manhood before they are recognized as adults. Many men and fathers in America seem to think all it takes to become a man is to acquire a copy of *Playboy* magazine and a six-pack of beer.

In the Promised Land

Between the wanderings of the wilderness of "childish things" and the settled place of manhood, all men should aspire to become planted in the promised land.

For men, the promised land is the place of steadfastness. This is the place where the wanderings cease and the building begins. It was there that Israel began to build houses and throw away tents, and it is there that unstable things in us become solidified. It is the place where the irresponsible become committed. While in the desert, the Israelites owned nothing, conquered nothing, and acquired nothing! But in the promised land, the men of Israel rose up to confront enemies, subdue entire territories, and attain property by conquest.

The promised land is the place where we keep our promises to ourselves, to our wives, and to our children. It is the place where our words can be trusted. It is the place where we cease to wander in our marital commitment—whether we wandered in the secrecy of our own mind, or wandered literally, creeping stealthily home in the late hours of the night. The promised land allows us to keep our promises, while God keeps His!

We need to celebrate male adulthood by learning what it means and what it takes to be real men. We need to "continue our education" through all the rites and experiences of courtship, marriage, child rearing, and even grandparenting!

Every major stage of our lives brings *change,* and most of the time, we're unprepared for it! Many of us in our forties have families, yet we have never celebrated our manhood! If we celebrate manhood with all our strength and heart, and honor God as men who appreciate their masculinity, we will discover that the women in our lives will celebrate too! God made us to be men. It is time to take the challenge and live up to the manly destiny God has given us!

The Jordan River is the place where Israel crossed over from the wilderness into the promised land. It was cold and it was high, but God helped them to cross over. That same God helps us today to cross over our limitations and obtain our promised land. Remember, the Jordan River empties into the Dead Sea. We must count the "childish things" as dead. We must never attempt to get to the promised land without going through the Jordan River.

Your "Jordan River" may be a time of crisis that causes you to reprioritize your life. It may be a trial that leaves you in a place so low that "you have to look up to see the bottom." It may involve having your hidden childish secrets discovered and exposed, so that embarrassed and ashamed, you are forced into the cold Jordan River. Your Jordan may simply be a matter of receiving the ministry of the Holy Spirit, whether through preaching or through reading this material. Wherever the motivation, the Jordan River is the place where you align yourself with God's purpose. It puts to death every diversion that keeps you from the place God has designated as your dwelling place!

The Second "When"

> *When I was a child, I spake as a child, I understood as a child, I thought as a child: but when I became a man, I put away childish things.*
>
> 1 Corinthians 13:11

You will notice there are two "whens" in this text. The first one addresses the "when" of childhood. The second addresses the "when" of manhood. To the tormented man who fights his feelings and wrestles with his urges, the pressing question is, "Lord, when can I get to the second 'when'?" His wife is probably asking the same question! "Lord, when?" There is no magical date on the calendar.

You may have missed the age at which you believe others crossed over, but that is nothing to be ashamed of. Many men live with tremendous remorse and regret because they feel "it's too late." They fear that they are doomed to be less than a man because they missed their chance to change. That simply is not true!

There may be a lot of people who don't want to give you a chance, but God is not like people. Every morning that you open your eyes and fill your lungs with air, God gives you another chance to change. The whole message of Christianity is permeated with the possibilities of change! In the midst of this unforgiving society we have created, it is nice to know that God has given us the gift and the grace to change!

You can't change "what" has already happened any more than you can change "how" it happened. But the rite of passage into true manhood is not a matter of changing the "whats" and the "hows" of life. This is a change of the "who" in life—*and the "who" is you!* You are the most important issue to God. When you can't change what happened, remember that *God wants you to change!*

Most of us understand who is to change, but we wonder when the change can be accomplished! The process begins within, when we look at the face of God and are transformed.

A Man After God's Own Heart

David celebrated masculinity. He is a very good picture of what a man should be. God called him "a man after mine own heart" (Acts 13:22), and I can see why. David's heart was so attuned to God and so free of the opinions of men that he was the Bible's premier *worshiper* of God! He worshiped and danced with such force and freedom that he danced right out of his clothes! He laughed, he cried, and he even wrote some of the most exalted prose in human history. Yet when necessary, David was incredibly violent! He was one of the few military leaders in history who *never lost a battle!* And David celebrated his manhood better than anyone else I know of.

I will praise thee; for I am fearfully and wonderfully made: marvellous are thy works; and that my soul knoweth right well.

PSALM 139:14

David openly admired his body and enjoyed the deep male passions God gave him. He gave God thanks for what he had been given, and he did the most he could with what he had to work with. We need to do the same.

"Yeah, but that was King David. He had it made. Just look at my problems!"

Not true. David was the baby brother who was always left out of things. He wasn't as big as his brothers, and he didn't have any say in family matters because he was the "runt," the last one in the litter. Despite his handicaps, David rose to the top. How? He somehow learned about responsibility in those fields while he was alone with God.

What would you do if you were a young teenager miles from help, and a bear or lion came for lunch? You are armed with a guitar, a sandwich, and your favorite slingshot. I don't know about you, but I'd be thinking, "Mr. Lion, maybe you'd like some lamb chops today? You can have the sandwich too!" Not David.

And David said unto Saul, Thy servant kept his father's sheep, and there came a lion, and a bear, and took a lamb out of the flock: and I went out after him, and smote him, and delivered it out of his mouth: and when he arose against me, I caught him by his beard, and smote him, and slew him.

1 SAMUEL 17:34–35

God was preparing a boy in the fields to shepherd His flock as a man in the palace. When a bear and a lion each took a lamb from David's flock, he didn't sit down in tears and make up excuses to tell his father. He didn't even think about what to do. He yielded to the Spirit of God rising up in him. Like the Great Shepherd Who would come years later, this young shepherd left the "ninety and nine" to recover the lamb that had been snatched away.

No predator has a right to steal one of our sheep!

David ruthlessly hunted down those predators with such speed that he caught them on the run, while the lambs were still alive between their teeth. He didn't stop to think about the danger or to make elaborate battle plans— he had a job to do, he had a lamb to save, and these beasts had gone too far! With the livid anger of a righteous shepherd, young David hit the bear and the lion in the face so hard that the lambs they'd stolen dropped out of their mouths! He didn't stop there though.

Those flesh-eaters had underestimated the manhood and the authority of the secret prince who stood between them and their prey. They pounced on David, assuming he would fall like any other animal would fall. It was the last mistake either beast ever made! David didn't shoot the lion with a high-powered rifle from the safety of a Land Rover. He didn't go after the bear from a safe distance with a Winchester and a scope. The Bible says he "caught them by the beard." In other words, he grabbed the lion and the bear by the tufts of fur under their jaws and hit them right between the eyes. David didn't stop in his righteous anger until he had killed his enemies and forever ended their ability to ravage his flock. That is manhood, God's style.

Our Source of Strength

David didn't take karate classes or go through basic training in the army. His strength and training came from *knowing who God is*. What are you drawing your strength from? Even the most skilled soldiers of David's day discovered that their training couldn't help them with Goliath; he was a problem who was bigger than they were.

We are in the same situation—we're facing challenges that are a lot bigger than we are! We know we're not up to the job, and we're far from perfect. So what do we do? We do what David did. While the entire army of Israel cowered under Goliath's massive shadow, King Saul, in his royal tent, was asking a young shepherd from the country how he expected to defeat the giant.

And Saul said to David, Thou art not able to go against this Philistine to fight with him: for thou art but a youth, and he a man of war from his youth. And David said unto Saul, Thy servant kept his father's

sheep. . . . Thy servant slew both the lion and the bear: and this uncir-
cumcised Philistine shall be as one of them, seeing he hath defied the
armies of the living God. David said moreover, The Lord that delivered
me out of the paw of the lion, and out of the paw of the bear, he will
deliver me out of the hand of this Philistine.

1 SAMUEL 17:33–34, 36–37

David didn't rely on his own strength, ability, or skill. He didn't claim to be a mighty warrior or a great tactician. He just claimed to serve a mighty God Who was mighty mad! David's brothers thought he was crazy, and they were embarrassed at their baby brother's outrageous claims. They thought David had only been with the flock. They thought this little shepherd only had eyes for the sheep, but his eyes were on the Maker of the sheep, and he had been transformed into a man of war.

And Saul armed David with his armour, and he put an helmet of brass
upon his head; also he armed him with a coat of mail. And David
girded his sword upon his armour, and he assayed to go; for he had not
proved it. And David said unto Saul, I cannot go with these; for I have
not proved them. And David put them off him. And he took his staff in
his hand, and chose him five smooth stones out of the brook, and put
them in a shepherd's bag which he had, even in a scrip; and his sling
was in his hand.

1 SAMUEL 17:38–40

David didn't rely on another man's stuff—God had planted treasure in David's heart, and that is what he leaned on. He trusted the things he had worked out in his own heart and life with God. He used the gifts God had given him: the materials and tools of a shepherd.

Jesus delivered our entire race with the tools of a shepherd, not the tools of a soldier. A true shepherd in the hands of a mighty God can deliver any nation, church, or family. God made man to subdue and have dominion, so every true man of God is a shepherd on the inside. There is something in a man that compels him to lay down his life for the sheep God has given him—whether those "sheep" are his wife and children, his congregation, or the circle of friends God has given him to influence for the kingdom.

David didn't know it, but he actually began to shepherd and inspire a nation the day he faced the giant. He preached his first "sermon" as a teenager under the high anointing of God:

> Then said David to the Philistine, Thou comest to me with a sword, and
> with a spear, and with a shield: but I come to thee in the name of the
> Lord of hosts, the God of the armies of Israel, whom thou hast
> defied. . . . And all this assembly shall know that the Lord saveth not
> with sword and spear: for the battle is the Lord's, and he will give you
> into our hands.
>
> 1 SAMUEL 17:45, 47

Did your spirit leap as you read this? That's the *man in you* responding to the God in David! Real men applaud when someone dares to stand up for what is right in God's sight! David's bravery was contagious. When he threw down God's enemy, the fearful army of Israel was transformed into an unstoppable military machine that destroyed the best army Philistia had to offer. The Israelites not only "bloodied their noses," they chased the Philistines all the way home to the gate of their city and knocked them down again!

David tapped into the true source of manhood. His strength didn't come from male hormones, macho movies, or his male-dominant culture. If male hormones were the key, then David wouldn't have lasted a minute with Goliath. He was outclassed in the hormone department: Goliath was a seasoned fighting machine who stood between nine and ten feet tall! His armor alone weighed about 150 pounds. Fortunately, true manhood doesn't flow from the natural, it flows from a supernatural source. Like David, the only way you can be a real man is to be "a man after God's own heart."

David didn't come into manhood from a perfect childhood. He had disadvantages too. David's father, Jesse, actually forgot about his youngest son when Samuel the prophet came to anoint Israel's future king—but God knew where David was. Little brother was stuck on the backside of nowhere with the sheep while his brothers were sent off on a great military campaign. But none of that happened by accident—David had a divine appointment with God in those deserted fields. God separated David so He could operate on him! By the time this young shepherd finally emerged from the hills, he was a proven warrior and a king-in-waiting. This prince unawares was destined for greatness because he had discovered where God lives.

David, the Man

After David won his battles against the bear, the lion, and the giant, he never lost a military encounter. There were times he avoided battle, and there were times he failed off the battlefield, but he was a real man who knew how to protect his own. He was strong, deadly, and tough, but his manhood went deeper than that. He was so secure in his masculinity that he was also sensitive, tender-hearted, and affectionate. He was both a poet and a warrior. David had a harp in one hand and a sword in the other. He lived a man's life in all its fullness.

David was a lover of women. In fact, he was such a lover that in the sunset of his life, his servants put a young girl in his bed as a final test to see if he was near death. When he wasn't aroused, they knew he was gone! They must have said, "Uh oh, we need a new king. Now we *know* the king is near death." (See 1 Kings 1.)

David was also a lover of men. He showed us the right way to love true friends. He openly loved Jonathan, without any taint of homosexuality. We're so uptight that we can't even touch one another, except for a slap on the rear after a great play on the football field or the basketball court.

David loved Jonathan, and he showed it. He was comfortable with his own sexuality. He celebrated masculinity. We make being a man look so bad that our sons think, "It doesn't look like Dad is having a good time. Who wants to grow up to be like that?" When we go off to work in the morning, we aren't energetic and enthusiastic. When we drag home from work in the evening, we look sad and dejected. So when we tell Junior it's time for him to be a man, he says, "Oh, no way. I'm gonna stay a kid for life. I'd rather die a kid having fun than live like a dull adult having none." We need to model masculinity before our sons and help them celebrate their developing manhood. In this area, we can learn some things from David.

David learned how to be a man by communing with God in the hills, and then he inspired manhood everywhere he went. Every male who came under his influence seemed to become more manly. The first glimpse of this influence comes with the transformation of the Israelite army that took place when David defeated Goliath. It became even clearer when David was on the run from Saul.

David therefore departed thence, and escaped to the cave Adullam: and when his brethren and all his father's house heard it, they went down thither to him. And every one that was in distress, and every one that was in debt, and every one that was discontented, gathered themselves unto him; and he became a captain over them: and there were with him about four hundred men.

1 SAMUEL 22:1–2

A miracle happened in the cave of Adullam. David's anointing transformed that ragtag band of rejected men into an elite army of fearless warriors. The "mighty men" of David described in 2 Samuel originally belonged to this group of "down and outers" who gathered together in the cave. A true man inspires manhood in others. David inspired manhood in an entire nation, and he continues to inspire us today through the Scriptures!

David had failures in his life too. Despite his manliness and his heart toward God, David failed to confront his secret sins and weaknesses. He didn't control his sexual passion for Bathsheba, and he failed to properly discipline his sons. If he had confided in and leaned on other godly men, these weaknesses could have been turned into strengths. Instead, David's secret weaknesses led to his greatest failures with Bathsheba and Absalom, and they contaminated the future of his family and his nation.

We all know about David's sin with Bathsheba, but he was also too lenient and partial to Absalom, his son. Absalom's disrespect and rebellion toward his father gave birth to outright rebellion and eventually brought death in his family. All of David's sons knew how to wage war, and they were smart and well-educated, but somehow he didn't pass along to them his personal intimacy with God. Perhaps he was too busy with the "ministry" to attend to his boys. Whatever the reason for his failure, we can learn from David's personal defeats as well as from his military victories.

Manhood isn't merely some chronological age you are trying to attain, it is a stage in your development. It doesn't necessarily have to occur at a particular *age*; it needs to occur at a particular *stage*.

When you realize that you have outgrown your old thoughts and previous understandings, prepare for change. When what was once wisdom to you now sounds like foolishness, change is in the wind. When you admit that the old toys are not as enjoyable as they once were, then it is time to go through the rites of passage.

This is a celebration that requires sanctification. Paul says, "When I became a man, I *put away* childish things." Part of the celebration requires a conscious decision to put away childish things. Paul didn't say that there was no pleasure in these things anymore, he merely said he "put them away."

The Lion and the Lamb

Our richest model of manhood is Jesus Christ. More than any other man, Jesus demonstrated perfect balance in what I call "the duplex nature of a man," the perfect pattern of holistic masculinity.

One absolute prerequisite to the celebration of manhood is that there must be a *lion and a lamb* in every man. David was both poet and warrior, shepherd and general, priest and king. Jesus Christ was both God and man, lion and lamb. The art is to have both and to know when to be which.

There are some things that Christ did as a lion that He could not do as a lamb. There are also some things that He did as a lamb that He could not do as a lion. If Jesus had roared on the cross as the Lion of Judah, He would have been weak. His strength in that situation was rooted in His identity as the sacrificial Lamb of God Who was to take away the sins of the world by giving Himself up to death—the Innocent taking the blame for the guilty.

Yet, when Jesus comes again, if He whimpers as a meek Lamb, He won't fulfill His destiny as the supreme King of kings and Lord of lords, Whose name is above every name! The sacrificial Lamb of God will return as the triumphant Lion of Judah!

Similarly, there must be a tightrope within every man, a dichotomy of two completely different natures. One is so lamb-like, vulnerable, fragile, and meek that we are willing to lie down so others can nail us to a cross. At the same time, there is another part of us that roars like a lion, that comes alive in a fight, that is mighty in battle. True men can't be ashamed of either side of their nature. We just have to hold them in tension. The true definition of meekness is strength under control. We can only celebrate masculinity after we recognize and walk in that duplex nature within us.

Man of God, you must walk a tightrope between being a lion and a lamb, and only the Holy Ghost can give you true balance in that walk.

I have begun to understand why women get so angry with men. Sometimes we roar when we need to whimper, and we whimper at times we should be roaring! Our wives get frustrated when we insist on roaring and "swinging from trees and vines" in a hormonal rush when they need us to be loving lambs who provide them with tenderness and affection. There are also times when our children come to the lion of their lives and ask for masculine guidance and protection, but instead of roaring as protectors or correctors, we sniff in selfishness or whimper in weakness, "Ask your mama."

David was a "man after God's own heart," even though he had disadvantages just as you and I do. The difference is that he learned how to be a man in the presence of God, and he turned his nation around. Your nation, your home, your wife, and your children are crying out for *a real man in the house.* It is time for you to celebrate your *bar mitzvah* and rise up as a prince and a man of war in the house of God!

CHAPTER FIVE

THE PARTY IS IN PROGRESS

Celebration is in order! Any time a man comes into his own, there needs to be a celebration. There is a time to sow, and a time to water; there also is a time to wait, but now is the time to celebrate! God has called us out from under our childish shadows and into the brilliant sunlight of manhood!

Past mistakes and pitiful failures have no place in the light of our divine summons. The King is calling His sons. It is time for us to "come to ourselves," repent, and return to our rightful place with our heavenly Father. Like the prodigal son who returned home to his father, we too must hurry home to receive our robes, our rings, and our manhood.

And he said, A certain man had two sons: and the younger of them said to his father, Father, give me the portion of goods that falleth to me. And he divided unto them his living. And not many days after the younger son gathered all together, and took his journey into a far country, and there wasted his substance with riotous living. And when he had spent all, there arose a mighty famine in that land; and he began to be in want. And he went and joined himself to a citizen of that country; and he sent him into his fields to feed swine.

LUKE 15:11–15

This young man broke allegiance with his father and "joined himself" to a citizen from a far country. "Far-out friends" are dangerous; they inevitably lead us to the hogpens of life. They have different values, and they will undermine what God has purposed in our lives. In fact, most of the time they will have us doing the very things we hate and despise the most!

Jesus told this story of the prodigal son to a Jewish audience that had been raised to carefully observe the dietary laws in the books of Leviticus and Deuteronomy. Swine were absolutely unclean and were not to be touched for any reason—so in the eyes of a devout Jew, being forced to live in a pigpen was a fate worse than death!

Have you ever been manipulated into being something that "wasn't you"? Have you ever found yourself in a relationship that made you feel ashamed, used, or outcast? Have you ever betrayed or belittled someone else—even while you felt his pain? All of us have spent a little time at the hogpen in one way or another.

It is time to celebrate, but you may be tangled up by the crippling memories of your failures and excesses. Have you shared parts of your life with someone you shouldn't have? Have you shared intimate thoughts or actions with someone with whom you have no covenant? Women are always concerned about men being seduced into having affairs, but affairs don't start in the flesh—they start in the mind. Like a brushfire in a windstorm, thoughts gradually engulf the passions and alter the judgments of their victims.

And he would fain have filled his belly with the husks that the swine did eat: and no man gave unto him. And when he came to himself, he said, How many hired servants of my father's have bread enough and to spare, and I perish with hunger! . . . And he arose, and came to his father. But when he was yet a great way off, his father saw him, and had compassion, and ran, and fell on his neck, and kissed him. And the son said unto him, Father, I have sinned against heaven, and in thy sight, and am no more worthy to be called thy son. But the father said to his servants, Bring forth the best robe, and put it on him; and put a ring on his hand, and shoes on his feet: and bring hither the fatted calf, and kill it; and let us eat, and be merry: for this my son was dead, and is alive again; he was lost, and is found. And they began to be merry.

LUKE 15:16–17, 20–24

Influence is a powerful thing. Be careful whom you allow to influence you. The prodigal son was influenced by a citizen of a far county. We are told in Psalm 1:1, "Blessed is the man that walked not in the counsel of the ungodly"! If you want to be blessed, be careful whom you allow to influence you. Many men allow themselves to be manipulated by godless men or by men of God operating with ungodly motives.

One of the greatest liberties you can have is the freedom of choice. You choose. God doesn't even save you against your will. The Almighty God of the universe spoke through Joshua, "Choose you this day whom ye will serve" (Joshua 24:15). Wrong influences can dilute or pollute what God is doing in your life. You are not immune; you are human.

Samson was destroyed because he allowed Delilah to influence him! At first he resisted, but gradually this ungodly woman polluted his wisdom. She seduced him by playing up to his secret, unaddressed weaknesses until, against his better judgment, he shared more with her than he should have. Immediately his doom was sealed. The last thing this man of God saw with his mortal eyes was the sight of the woman he loved receiving money from his tormentors for his betrayal! (See Judges 16:16–21.)

A Parting in Every Party

The praise of God is strong in the mouth of any man who has recognized his own hogpen. The Spirit of God has restored us to our senses. Now we can see how narrowly we escaped. Thanks to our loving Father, the prodigal becomes powerful. It is time to feast at the Father's table and revel in our newfound manhood and Godward masculinity. At the same time, it is important to understand the wiles of the devil. He makes sure there is a parting in every party. He plants an exception in every reception. He dilutes every salute!

Lest Satan should get an advantage of us: for we are not ignorant of his devices.

2 Corinthians 2:11

The celebration has started, but there are dark clouds hovering near our pavilion of joy. This is not a new revelation; it is an ancient device of the enemy to discourage and dismay God's men from God's way. If any man had a right to rejoice in God's delivering power and sovereign purposes, it was King David. Yet Satan raised up a root of bitterness in the middle of David's harvest of joy.

And David danced before the Lord with all his might; and David was girded with a linen ephod. So David and all the house of Israel brought up the ark of the Lord with shouting, and with the sound of the trumpet. And as the ark of the Lord came into the city of David, Michal Saul's daughter looked through a window, and saw king David leaping and dancing before the Lord; and she despised him in her heart. . . .

Then David returned to bless his household. And Michal the daughter of Saul came out to meet David, and said, How glorious was the king of Israel to day, who uncovered himself to day in the eyes of the handmaids of his servants, as one of the vain fellows shamelessly uncovereth himself!

2 SAMUEL 6:14–16, 20

David grew up hearing all the stories of the "good old days" when the Ark of the Covenant was still in place in the tent, or the tabernacle. His battle with Goliath was a natural extension of the age-old tension between Israel and Philistia, the invaders who had killed Eli's sons and taken the Ark to Ashdod. (See 1 Samuel 4; 5:1.) Now the Ark was in the care of the Obededom (see 2 Samuel 6) and David knew it was time for a celebration. It was time to reap a harvest of joy and return the *shekinah* glory of the Lord to Jerusalem. For a man whose life was rooted in the presence of the Lord and unprecedented worship to the Most High, there could be no greater event than this!

David's unrestrained worship and praise to God before the people is still a model of true worship for us today! Never has there been such free and uninhibited worship to the Lord as there was that day. Yet in the midst of this pure worship without restraint, there arose a slanderous complaint!

When David returned home in triumph to share the joy of seeing the Ark of the Covenant returned to the city of David, his own wife met him with a biting accusation of lewd conduct. Even worse, her words were seasoned with the withering heat of feminine scorn for his manhood. It was a slap in the face that could level the self-esteem of even the most secure man among us—but David had already begun his celebration. He had just returned from basking in the presence of the living God. He had crossed the Jordan, and there was no turning back. He returned home to bring his wives and family into the blessings of God as well, but still they each had to make a choice.

Michal had once withstood the power and anger of her own father, the king of Israel, to save the love of her life, David. While he was a fugitive from the king, Michal had hidden her husband and lied to save his life. In return, her father had removed her from David's house and given her to another man as his wife.

By the time David returned the Ark of the Covenant to Jerusalem, Michal had been forcibly returned to David's house. She had been under the influence of another man and another house, and it showed. Back home again, she had to share David with other women who had become his wives too, according to the custom of the day. Michal also faced a crossing, but she chose to sit "in the seat of the scornful" described in Psalm 1:1. Of all the people in David's household, Michal held the greatest power to inflict pain and sorrow on him. She was his first love, the bride of his youth. But on David's greatest day of joy, she chose to become bitter and aloof.

Not Everyone Enjoys the Party

Have you ever felt the dejection of rejection from your oldest loves and closest companions? Have you felt the piercing pain of betrayal by your most trusted confidantes and dearest family members? Not everyone will rejoice with you when you kill the fatted calf or rejoice at your crossing into the promised land. The prodigal son also experienced the bittersweet emotions of elated acceptance and belated rejection on the day he returned to his father's house.

Now his elder son was in the field: and as he came and drew nigh to the house, he heard music and dancing. And he called one of the servants, and asked what these things meant. And he said unto him, Thy brother is come; and thy father hath killed the fatted calf, because he hath received him safe and sound. And he was angry, and would not go in: therefore came his father out, and entreated him. And he answering said to his father, Lo, these many years do I serve thee, neither trans-gressed I at any time thy commandment: and yet thou never gavest me a kid, that I might make merry with my friends: but as soon as this thy son was come, which hath devoured thy living with harlots, thou hast killed for him the fatted calf. And he said unto him, Son, thou art ever with me, and all that I have is thine. It was meet that we should make merry, and be glad: for this thy brother was dead, and is alive again; and was lost, and is found.

LUKE 15:25–32

While the younger son faced his sin, repented of his wrong, and threw himself into the loving arms of his father, the elder brother stood stubbornly on his own "rights and self-righteousness." He refused to obey his father's loving request and join in the celebration; he chose to remain in the pain of isolation. Once his choice was made, he didn't even hear his father's solemn assurance that "all I have is yours."

The elder brother clung desperately to his jealousy, choosing to whine and complain about the wrongs and the pain. All the while, a party of res-toration was sweeping through the house that was but part of his rightful inheritance! Faced with his father's genuine manhood, the elder son clung to the now selfish fruits of his childhood, and failed to cross his Jordan.

As you begin to celebrate your *bar mitzvah* and mark your entrance into true manhood, don't be dismayed if some of those you love and trust don't rejoice with you. There are no guarantees that everybody around you will be glad for you. As long as men and women dwell in houses of flesh, jeal-ousy will be waiting in the wings to stifle every cause for joy or triumph. Yet, part of the crossing into manhood is the determination to follow God's lead no matter what it costs. Manhood requires leadership, and leadership requires the commitment to lead though some may never follow.

When you experience liberation and restoration by the Father's hand, what is important is to celebrate—even if no one else joins you! The prodi-gal son entered into his father's joy and never looked back. The father left the celebration to entreat his eldest son, but I'm positive he quickly returned to the celebration and the fun. Jesus endured the scorn of an entire planet and a necessary separation from the Father He loved "for the joy that was set before him" (Hebrews 12:2).

David, the ultimate human model of flawed holiness through the grace of God, responded to Michal's scorn with an incredible boldness and declaration that rings with the power of inspired manhood:

> *Then David returned to bless his household. And Michal the daughter of Saul came out to meet David, and said, How glorious was the king of Israel to day, who uncovered himself to day in the eyes of the handmaids of his servants, as one of the vain fellows shamelessly uncovereth himself! And David said unto Michal, It was before the Lord, which chose me before thy father, and before all his house, to appoint me ruler over the people of the Lord, over Israel: therefore will I play before the Lord. And I will yet be more vile than thus, and will be base in mine own sight: and of the maidservants which thou hast spoken of, of them shall I be had in honour. Therefore Michal the daughter of Saul had no child unto the day of her death.*
>
> 2 SAMUEL 6:20–23

Michal's choice to yield to wrong influence, to cling to past disappointments and present bitterness, had terrible consequences for her and her father's house. Her scornful disdain of God's anointed yielded a barren womb, a loveless marriage, and countless sorrows for the rest of her days. Even the five nephews she raised for her brother-in-law were killed by the ancient enemies of her father's house. (See 2 Samuel 21:8–9.)

Stand Fast

Many times those closest to us are unprepared for the dramatic changes that accompany our passage into the promised land. They are not ready for the passion it brings. They can't perceive the invisible hand that has taken firm control of the reins of our hearts. All they see is the "little brother" they have relegated to the benign "hills of mediocrity." They still see the man who liked to play with a boy's toys, the image of impotent potential who passed the hours away in the back room of their lives.

Manhood means change.

You may be one of the countless thousands of men who left the house to play one day and encountered the living God on a lonely hill. When you returned as a man with a plan to wage war, your first adversary arose in the eyes of your spouse! Perhaps you came home rejoicing over the return of God's presence to your life and dreams, only to be greeted with scorn and mocking glances.

Take heart, O man of God! Stand fast in your decision to possess the land, and your household will yet yield to the gentle persuasion of the Holy Spirit! Turn neither to the right nor to the left—and appropriate the ancient promise God gave another man who was destined to lead his own across the Jordan from the desert to the promise:

Have not I commanded thee? Be strong and of a good courage; be not afraid, neither be thou dismayed: for the Lord thy God is with thee whithersoever thou goest.

JOSHUA 1:9

You may be facing the cutting edge of the same unwavering jealousy faced by such men as the prodigal son, Abel, Isaac, Israel (Jacob), Joseph, Moses, Aaron, David, Solomon, Jesus Christ, and the Apostle Paul. Each of these men faced hostile emotions and sometimes fatal attacks from their own brothers, family members, wives, countrymen, or co-workers. Yet they didn't waver from their destiny of manhood in the purposes of God. Their faithfulness brought eternal life and joy to you today. Who is waiting in the generations to come to taste the fruit of your manly obedience and determination today?

Don't be dismayed by the brothers outside the door who jealously complain about your late return to the River Jordan and the Father's house. It is time to celebrate your manhood! Let nothing hold you back. Your manhood will bring new health and blessing to your life, to your home, to your marriage, and to the generations who follow after you.

The church and the children of tomorrow cry out for men to arise and wage war on their behalf. God has called His sons together for a victory celebration. It is time to celebrate; it is time to mark our crossing. This is the day we put away our childish things. This is the day we enter into manly praise without fear or thought of the criticism or disapproval of others. We are only concerned with the opinions of the One Who has called us, the One Who has reserved the ring of sonship and the robes of the priesthood for us.

It is time for every man of God to arise in his manhood and dance before the King with all his might! A world is waiting to be possessed and blessed by the sons of God, children made men and delivered from sin.

Man of God, be of good courage! The *bar mitzvah* party is in progress—and you are the honored guest!

CHAPTER SIX

WHEN THE YOKE ISN'T EASY

There are times when men find themselves struggling to maintain a dying relationship, one in which the flame of intensity has gone out and the thrill has left. The naked truth is that it becomes difficult to rekindle the old flame if you are at the point where you would rather "hunt in the yard than in the house."

Like many men, you may become easily discouraged when you sense rejection or apathy in your mate. You may resent having to creatively and aggressively pursue your wife's affections. The hunter and conqueror in you likely jumps at the chance to explore any aspiration you haven't yet conquered. However, your enthusiasm probably dissipates when attention and effort are required to maintain something you feel you have already captured or achieved.

You may want to believe that once you have ignited the flame of your wife's love, you can sit by that fire for years to come—but that just isn't true. The cold winds of life often asphyxiate the flames that once danced in her eyes, leaving behind only smoldering embers that scarcely resemble the exciting relationship you once shared. God knows your nature. He wants you to continually woo and win your wife's heart, just as He continually woos His Bride. It is the continual chase for the prize that fans the flames of marital love.

Our challenge as men is to overcome our reputation for being unable or unwilling to recognize problems in our relationships. Then we have to over-power our propensity to procrastinate once we know a problem exists. It is especially painful to both persons in a marriage when a husband actually makes positive changes, but makes them too late.

Beneath our bulging biceps and bloated bellies lies a sensitivity that most women don't realize is there and very few of us men will admit exists. The simple truth is that most men get their feelings hurt when they feel they have changed, but the change is not accepted by the woman in their life. I realize many women have good reasons for being skeptical, but once a woman is leery of her husband's actions or motives, it takes a supernatural move of God's Spirit to get her to change her mind.

The Chasm of Time

When David sent for Michal in 2 Samuel 3:13, he still viewed her as the wife of his youth, his first love. Although more than seven years had passed, David still saw Michal framed in the rose-tinted memories of his late teens. He didn't perceive the pain she had endured when he fled from her life to avoid Saul's soldiers. He didn't know there were scars hidden beneath her smile, ugly reminders of the deep wounds she had suffered when her venge-ful father the king totally rejected her and "gave her" to another man.

The first year Michal spent as an unwilling wife in a strange man's house, she probably hoped in secret that David would appear at the door with his sword in hand to deliver her and reclaim her as his own. But he didn't come. Michal couldn't know the desperation he faced as he fled for his life from Saul's armies, living in a wilderness cavern with a band of misfits, bitter rejects, and all their kin, hiding out in a hostile Philistine city. The Michal he received was different from the Michal he had left—she had changed, and so had he.

David was now at the apex of his career, and he was gaining ground. He was fully operating under the anointing of God and had finally overcome his enemies. The nurturing words that had affirmed him in the dark years, and the loving arms that had encircled him in that cave were not Michal's. The once devoted newlyweds had not taken the time to reconnect and build bridges across the chasm of nearly a decade spent apart.

The boy/man that Michal had known and had once loved had died in a cave years before. A thousand brushes with death; hundreds of prayer watches through lonely, tension-filled nights; and the deaths of thousands of enemies in bloody battles had transformed the young lover in her memory into a scarred but anointed visionary who commanded an army a quarter of a million strong!

David was now the husband of six other women besides Michal, beautiful women who each had accomplished something Michal had never done—they had borne David sons! The stage was set for confrontation between David and Michal. The crucible of change was about to illuminate and reveal the contents of their inner hearts, and the things they had sowed in secret over their years of pain were about to yield a bitter harvest.

Dancing Alone

And as the ark of the Lord came into the city of David, Michal Saul's daughter looked through a window, and saw king David leaping and dancing before the Lord; and she despised him in her heart. . . .

Then David returned to bless his household. And Michal the daughter of Saul came out to meet David, and said, How glorious was the king of Israel to day, who uncovered himself to day in the eyes of the handmaids of his servants, as one of the vain fellows shamelessly uncovereth himself!

2 SAMUEL 6:16, 20

When King David danced into Michal's view, he danced alone. The joyful, devoted companion of his youth was now cynical, critical, and cold.

Have you ever felt like you were dancing alone? Many of us return to our homes each day, filled with excitement and exultation about a major victory or success in our careers, only to find that our wives—like Michal—are unimpressed and uninterested. Their stinging disdain of our newfound joy can rob us of every month and year of labor we invested in our victory. The flames of our joy and happiness can be instantly neutralized and consumed by a soul-quenching outpouring of bitter scorn. The greatest triumph in any man's life can be reduced to a mere monument of the bitter rejection received through a withering remark or icy glance from a jealous wife!

Many times our relationships arrive at their demise because we fail to discern problems before they escalate to emergencies. If your wife begins to feel that your career or ministry has stolen your attention, your affection, or your time away from her, she will react like a woman rejected and a wife betrayed.

Heav'n has no rage, like love to hatred turn'd,
Nor Hell a fury, like a woman scorn'd.[1]

Do you honestly expect your wife to sit alone in an ivory tower and be happy while you roam the countryside in quest of private adventure? Granted, she may not enjoy tramping through the woods in search of the perfect buck, or battling the corporate whiz from Company X for client of the century. Her heart may not leap at the thought of preaching the gospel on the corner of Sixth and Vine, but you should at least try to keep her involved in the most important things you do away from her. She will appreciate the leadership and anointing you display elsewhere—if you exhibit leadership and love for her at home!

You must realize that your adventure may not be her idea of success. That is why it is important for you to *find out* what success means to her. Her idea of success may be having you slow down enough to sit by the fire and listen to soft music while she shares the trials and joys of *her life* with you.

Brother, unless both of you develop some interest in compromise so you can harmonize, you may find yourself dancing alone. Your willingness to compromise and revise your behavior and perceptions provides a rich barometer of your personal value system and a precise yardstick of how highly you esteem your spouse. (Of course, there are some things that simply cannot be compromised, such as your personal devotion and obedience to the Lord.)

If you and your wife fail to tie together the fields of your toil and joy with love and common care, then you will be like a dancer in a spotlight doing the tango alone. You will look ridiculous because your partner's cheek is gone, your solitary chin is starkly lit against the empty darkness, and your muscular arm encircles only emptiness.

Separation and dislocation not only happen when you take your wife through sudden change, you also will be doomed to dance alone if you fail to grow together. If your wife is motivated by one thing and you are moti-

---

[1]William Congreve, *"The Mourning Bride"*

vated by something else—it is time to build a bridge on the foundation of another common joy or shared interest. Without this bridge, your separate interests may drive you apart rather than together!

Be aware that your needs are different and constantly changing. What was important to you at twenty may not be important anymore at fifty! It is normal to expect your priorities and needs to change with time and maturity, but if you fail to keep your wife abreast of the changes within you, don't be surprised or upset if she continues to give you what you used to need and wonders why it isn't working anymore. It is at this point that the two of you may seem to find pleasure in opposite places. It is at this point that the heart of a man grows heavy!

This is the heaviness that causes disenchantment with the way things are. It can give birth to the alienation and depression that can doom a marriage relationship. From this dismal dance comes a deathly cold silence, and in its grip, somewhere in the marriage, when no one is listening, the music stops.

When the music stops between two individuals who were once joined at the heart, there is a feeling of unnatural distance. A disjointed sense of loss and detachment assumes the control of their emotions and will. They find themselves staring blankly and silently across a room at someone *they are not sure they like anymore.*

In Bitterness . . .

Michal Saul's daughter looked through a window, and saw king David leaping and dancing before the Lord; and she despised him in her heart. . . .

And Michal the daughter of Saul came out to meet David, and said, How glorious was the king of Israel to day, who uncovered himself to day in the eyes of the handmaids of his servants, as one of the vain fellows shamelessly uncovereth himself!

2 SAMUEL 6:16, 20

The original Hebrew implies that Michal went out to aggressively encounter and confront David. Her words seem to prove the point. Michal chose to get bitter instead of better, and she was out to "put her husband in his place." Unfortunately, she didn't realize that her husband was in the place *God intended for him to be.*

In her bitterness, Michal embraced three deadly attitudes and sins with very unpleasant results.

First, she chose to watch her husband's triumphant return standing alone and apart in *apathy.* She watched the return of Israel's greatest symbol of God's leadership to her nation from the darkness of her room, peering out at the jubilant crowds in aloof isolation. She was a joyless spectator, not a passionate participator. (Men are actually guilty of this sin more often than women!)

Michal also gave herself to a consuming and self-centered *jealousy* that had its roots in nearly every part of her personality and memory! She belittled David for his uninhibited praise of God in public. That means in order for him to have "pleased her," he would have had to rob God of the praise and worship due Him. She wanted to possess her husband—even if it meant stealing his heart from God and robbing Jehovah of His praises! Her father, King Saul, did the same thing years before when he chose to covet the praises of men rather than the approval of God. He wanted to please men first and apologize to God later. Because she dared to covet what belonged to God alone, Michal's empty womb was doomed to remain barren for the rest of her days!

Third, Michal was filled with *scorn.* She sat "in the seat of the scornful" described in Psalm 1:1 and ridiculed her husband publicly for three reasons.

First, she scorned him because he didn't look and act like a king, which meant that David didn't conduct himself like Michal's father, Saul. David was a commoner who had worked his way to the "top" through obedience and devotion to God. The fact is that if God had wanted another king like Saul, He would have installed such a king. He didn't because He had carefully chosen David, a man after His own heart. It didn't make it easier that David had just replaced Michal's brother on the throne of Israel, fulfilling God's promise to remove Saul and his descendants from the throne in favor of David. Michal's last blood link to the "royal life" was gone. Her only grasp on her special status was through the man she had married and now despised.

Second, Michal was especially scornful because she felt her husband had shamed himself (and her) in front of his bondservants' female slaves. David was worshiping God under the anointing of the Holy Spirit, and all inhibitions had been removed from him. He was fulfilling the great commandment when he worshiped the Lord with all his might and all his strength. (Somehow I don't think David would be content to sit in a pew, sing lifeless hymns, and fold his hands during a dry sermon!) Michal should have known better. Her own father had become a legend throughout Israel as well, for when the Spirit of God had fallen on him, he prophesied before Samuel, stripped off all his clothing, and lay naked before God for a full day and night! (See 1 Samuel 19:24.)

Finally, Michal compared King David to a vain and worthless fellow because he dared to worship God freely! He was worshiping, leaping, and dancing only to please God, but Michal drew from the bitter wells of her own heart and accused him of lewdly exposing himself to win the hearts and inflame the lusts of female slaves! Michal was calling good evil and evil good. She implied that to quench the Spirit of God, to restrain the joy of the Lord, to hold back the flood of praises at the triumphal return of the *shekinah* or visible glory of God to Israel would be "good." David's uninhibited worship and intimate relationship with God was the driving force behind everything that Michal despised.

Get to the Heart

Beneath the angry placing of blame and the desperate press of tearful excuses, the underlying issue is simple. It defies intellectual treatment because it is a matter of the heart. David had changed, but his driving motivation was still the same as it was the day he faced Goliath. He loved God and wanted to honor Him.

Michal had changed also, but her change involved the deepest motivations and drives of her heart. Both spouses had been hurt, but while David chose to defy the circumstances and get better, Michal had yielded to circumstances and gotten bitter. The same woman who had saved David in his distress mocked him in his triumph!

The issue is this: "I played my music and you missed your cue." The unspoken epilogue is, "What happened to you?"

Tragedy comes to our marriages when we fail to *discuss* our discouragement rather than argue about guilt. Most of the time, we come to this point with so much emotionally charged baggage and heartache that we launch into heated argumentation, not discussion and mediation. There is a difference between discussion and argument. A discussion *airs the issues,* but an argument *alleges charges and appoints blame.*

Blame is difficult for us to deal with if there are underlying reasons for our wives' resistance that we have failed to heed. For instance, your wife may be saying, "I missed my cue because *you changed songs* in the middle of the dance. You changed from a slow-paced romantic melody to a grotesque marching song and left me alone on the floor while you pranced around me in circles—oblivious to my embarrassed abandonment! You changed objectives and directives. When we began, our plan was to go here, but now you're going there! Why did you leave me out? You changed without warning or communication. You failed to give me a signal, and your abrupt turn left me alone and apart!"

A visionary has to be able to communicate, but most of the time, men are the most noncommunicative species on this planet! God has always intended for us to go beyond the grunts and gestures some say we inherited from apes! We graduated from that stage around the age of two, but we seem to reenter our infancy on the day we marry! I don't know where we got this guttural, almost non verbal communication system. I must confess that I too have often thought of directives and ideas that *should have been spoken,* then wondered why there was no response from the bride of my youth. The answer was simple. She couldn't "hear" my mind!

CHAPTER SEVEN

MARRIAGE: MISSIONARIES OR MEN?

M any times the fear of rejection has closed down the hearts of men because they are traumatized and paralyzed by its pain. Massive men we may be, but our bulging biceps, strong backs, and bass voices are only outward decorations adorning (and concealing) our fragile hearts and the trembling boys locked away beneath the sacred walls of our masculine shells! We surround ourselves with images of success to hide our secret fears.

Distrusting the luxurious and the fashionable, we insulate ourselves behind our facades and hide beneath the fig leaves of our elaborate efforts to impress. The simple truth is that most men have insecurities. "If I give myself to you, will you give also? If I let down my defense, will you let down yours? If I fail, will you laugh? If I miss, will you walk away?" These questions haunt the halls of the hearts of men who have been taught all their lives to perform.

From football fields and corporate offices to the church pew and the bedroom, men wrestle with the demand for *performance*. Quite frankly, the stage theatrics are wearing us out. As the banks of our personhood steadily erode under the growing pressure of the swirling flood, we become more and more like actors portraying a part. The tragedy is that beneath the props, the masks, and the stressful stage lights, we are just men. If we were stripped of all decorum and pretense, the little boy in each of us would be left trembling beside our elaborate costume, now heaped on the floor. That little boy within wonders quietly, "Am I enough?"

Marital Missionaries

Fear spawns defense mechanisms, and most of our defense mechanisms are more dangerous and bizarre than the insecurities we avoid. The greatest problems arise in our marriages when we decide to become "marital missionaries." A marital missionary is a man who thinks he is called to change his wife rather than to understand her! The secretly insecure man thinks of himself as some great missionary with a message, while he views his wife as a simple-minded native in need of nurture and direction!

We are so convinced that "our way is right" we fail to realize that in the marriage relationship between two individual adults, there is often neither a right way nor a wrong way—just differing perspectives.

Have you ever thought about the consequence of your confidence in "your way"? What kind of mess would you have on your hands if you actually succeeded in "evangelizing" and converting your wife to your way of doing things? What if she started thinking and acting just like you? Believe me, whatever you do, *stay out of the missionary position!*

God doesn't like it when you start changing His creations around. Besides, you are displaying plain egotistical arrogance if you always attempt to alter others without checking yourself for "childish things" that could be put away! The truth is that the little boy in you is trying to stack the blocks around you to create a "safe place" in the middle of your fears.

Playful boys and fearful men seek to control their environments. Secure men don't force those around them to conform to some artificial standard. They are strong enough to share their world with others who are different. If God had wanted bland uniformity, then He certainly wouldn't have divided the human race into the male and female genders!

Furthermore, your wife's feminine philosophy and womanly sensitivity was at one time a feature and asset rather than a blemish or liability! If she had been "just like you" when you were scouting for a companion, you probably would have quickly locked horns or become uninterested!

In short, the unique female you married was never meant or designed to be a "product" that you could arrogantly "change into your image." There is only one image worthy enough for all of us to conform to, and that is the image of Christ Jesus.

If you haven't noticed it lately, then wake up: your wife is a woman! (That fact alone should be enough warning to you.) She isn't supposed to be just like you! If you can't accept that truth, then I hope you are prepared to be miserable and encumbered with care the rest of your days. Just remember that people who insist on banging their heads against a wall have no right to complain of chronic headaches!

Sometimes we wrestle with failure because we have a distorted definition of "success." Anytime you enter into life with a partner whom you feel you need to personally change and alter to conform to your own "superior" standards, you are guaranteed to experience failure and frustration (and you probably deserve it). Your wife is virtually guaranteed to become a frustrated woman because even if she makes the changes you request, you are almost certain to *change your requirements* with the passage of time!

Is it any wonder our spouses feel resentful? We have trapped them in a "no win" situation. It is hard to be intimate with someone who makes you feel like you should be wearing a grass skirt and a bone in your nose!

The citizens of every nation on earth deeply resent any foreign missionary who is foolish enough to disregard or disdain the local culture and ethnicity. Yet we blindly persist in our efforts to "reform and remake" our wives into our own image, even though we know they will resent it!

Brother, you cannot predicate the success in your life upon your success in making your mate over again. The sad reality is that if her nature is so important to you, then you should have done her a favor and married a person who already had the basic personality you "needed." Since you didn't, then it is up to you to learn to appreciate the difference. You may be in for a surprise when God reveals the fact that He planted some things in your wife to which you desperately need to conform!

Sometimes we try to rearrange others as a way of hiding our own deep discontentment. The spirit of blame takes over, and we begin to say and believe, "You are the reason I am not happy!" Some men are miserable because they are not finding fulfillment in their relationships. Many of the men who seek multiple relationships are still unhappy; their infidelity is just masking their emptiness and fear of loneliness with the illusion of excitement. However, when the thin veneer of excitement dissipates, the emptiness remains.

Ox or Ass?

Thou shalt not plow with an ox and an ass together.
DEUTERONOMY 22:10

It is important for us to exercise maturity in the choices we make, especially in our choice of a mate. We cannot afford to be driven by lust or to choose a companion merely on the basis of some external attribute. (You would be surprised at how quickly external attributes change.)

Once the honeymoon is over, and once you have peeled away the outer wrapping, you will have to live with the human being inside. It is sad that many men are so distracted by the hormonal rush triggered by a woman's outward attractions during courtship that they never really examine the woman within. In short, they were so impressed with the package that they never noticed the contents! The tragedy is that we actually marry the contents, not the containers.

Deuteronomy 22:10 warns us that it is counterproductive to yoke an ox with an ass. Be sure that you team up with the same "species." Opposites do attract and effectively interact, but when it comes to the deepest heart motivations and drives, there must be compatibility. The Apostle Paul warned, "Be ye not unequally yoked together with unbelievers: for what fellowship hath righteousness with unrighteousness? and what communion hath light with darkness?" (2 Corinthians 6:14).

Don't yoke with an "ass" and try to remake her into an "ox."

Choice is a great freedom that men don't seem to fully appreciate. Christian men seem especially prone toward hasty decisions, and I believe a great deal of it is due to the fact that many of them are trying to overcome lust with fornication. They quickly commit and then often regret their decision because they failed to be controlled by their brain!

I am always amazed at the men who bounce blindly from one broken relationship into another doomed commitment. Brother Hormone is crushed through a divorce, yet ten months after crying his eyes out and losing half of his income in child support, here he comes again with Sister Maybelle Feelgood on his arm! He says, "Pastor, I am ready to be married!" It makes me want to commit him for psychological evaluation! I would have been running from that pain like the roadrunner in a cartoon! But here

Brother Hormone stands, ready to enter the marriage relationship again without making a rational, conscious decision.

Many men fall into this dangerous pattern because they are struggling with loneliness or lust. Some men have never lived a moment in their lives without someone else to share it with and they are terrified of being alone. The questions Brother Hormone should ask himself are: "Am I in love with Maybelle Feelgood, or am I in love with the idea of being married? Do I just think I can live with her, or is it true that I can't conceive of living the rest of my life without her?"

If you foolishly allow yourself to be yoked with an ass, and you feel in your heart you are an ox, the two of you will pull one against the other the rest of your lives. You see, the ass wants to play and have fun while the ox wants to work and make progress. There is absolutely nothing worse in this world than pulling your own load, and then having to turn around and pull both your spouse's load and your spouse! No wonder so many good men are succumbing at early ages. Good men aren't dying from heart attacks— they are dying from bad choices!

If you are single or divorced, please pray about these issues, and be honest with your heart and your intended. Never step into the yoke with someone just for the sake of the yoke, the sex, the image, the partnership, the business, the ministry, or the money! You will be miserable! God knows the yoke will not be easy, even if you choose the right mate! Why? God uses the yoke of the marriage covenant to work things in us that probably cannot be done any other way. It is hard work to live in love, intimacy, honesty, and harmony with another human being for half a century! Frankly, marriage is perhaps God's richest planting bed for miracles in the human heart.

By this time, I know I have left some young man feeling depressed and distraught because he feels that he has inadvertently married the wrong person! If that is the way you feel, don't worry, you aren't the only one. Most of us experience such doubts at one time or another in our married life.

What can the ox do if he feels he has married out of his species? *He can pray!* Yes, I know that may not be the solution you would prefer, but have you ever really begun to pray for your marriage? Oh, I don't mean one of those "Lord, straighten her out" prayers. I'm talking about those soul-searching, openhearted prayers that say, "God, perhaps You have allowed me to get in this situation to help me become more like You. What must I do to love my wife correctly? I confess I have not done a good job of loving her; I haven't loved her unconditionally as You have loved me. Lord, You already know that I really didn't have any role models in my own childhood to guide me into wholeness of marriage. But, Lord, if You will teach me, I will learn!"

Love Like Jesus

Husbands, love your wives, even as Christ also loved the church, and gave Himself for it.
EPHESIANS 5:25

What a challenging command for a man! God commands us to imitate His Son, the ultimate Lover. We are to build our love according to His pattern, the pattern of self-sacrifice and utter submission to the will of God.

How many of us can say that we have loved our wives as Christ has loved the church and given Himself for it? Not many, if any.

I can almost hear you say, "You just don't know how bad my wife is! I am miserable. That woman fights me and belittles everything I try to do. I am an ox married to an ass! I'm sorry, but I don't want to love her—I want to leave her!"

I hear your protest and I understand your frustration, but you need a good dose of the truth: *You will be leaving your greatest opportunity to turn a test into a testimony.* Besides, O man of God, how can you leave your wife when you haven't read the "troubleshooting" instructions in the manual (the Bible)? Or have you already read them, but unlike Jesus, you have simply failed to obey them? In either case, you are still inexcusable.

The most challenging part of Ephesians 5:25 for most men is not just the loving, it is the giving. Men are masters at giving things. We give advice, we give provision, and we give sex. But we have big problems when we're asked to give *ourselves!* Christ gave Himself. He gave us His attention, His affection, and His assurance. These gifts are often missing from under the tree every Christmas. You may be a master at giving things, but the real truth is that your wife doesn't need more things—she needs *you!*

Women often wonder what thoughts are locked behind the weary eyes of their men when their conversations lapse into silence. They have wondered silently and among themselves, "Where do men go when they lapse into silence and become distant?" Silence wraps itself around a man like a blanket, insulating him from the cold insults of rejection. Silence does for the quiet man within what jokes do for the comedian. It shields him from the risk of rejection and gives him a glass to stand behind and peer through while perched in a safe place of introspection.

Rumbling beneath the silence, the joking, the jesting, or whatever the camouflage, boils the tempestuous kettle of friction and frustration. If we emerge from the shell and sacrifice our protection, we feel we will be either applauded or booed from the stage. So we plot a safer course and stick our hands out like turtles in a shell and give *what we can afford to lose*. We give what we can risk having dropped—we give things!

I know we do our best to bluster and pretend that we really are the macho men within that we pretend to be on the outside. But I believe most men find it hard to give themselves because they are often afraid of themselves. We are afraid of being exposed for what we really are, and we are afraid to acknowledge that we are vulnerable. God is out to strip us down to our core. No matter how valid their basis or how traumatic their appearance or how desperately we want to avoid them, we must confront our fears. If we don't fix them, let us at least face them! Our investment in marriage must go beyond "things." It must move across the Jordan; it must move up the hill to the cross where, like Jesus, we offer *ourselves*.

Brother, it is wonderful to give objects. God gave us the sun, the moon, and the stars. He gave us day and night and the incredible seasons of the year. He even gave us cascading waterfalls and sun-drenched beaches. However, none of these *things* saved our relationship with Him! Finally, He wearied of giving us laws, ordinances, and rituals. He got tired of giving us prophets, priests, and kings. He decided to give Himself, and when He did, He saved a dying world!

No matter how much you have given to your wife and family in other areas, you must give *yourself*. Yes, you can make a difference. Just you! Your personal attention, your loving affection, and your gentle assurance can ignite the redemption of a destitute relationship! If you haven't given your wife these things, then look at your marriage from her perspective. You may be shocked to realize that from her point of view, she is the ox and you are the ass!

Not Easy, But Possible

I want to confess that it is not easy to cover all the things God has put in my heart for you. But if you believe in the sovereignty of God as I do, then you know that God can make a bad decision turn out good. He can make a miracle out of a mistake.

I also know that the yoke of marriage is not easy—or perfect. Marriage is simply the uniting of two imperfect people who are trying to build a perfect life in Christ. We are guaranteed to find ourselves stumbling and falling along the way. Yet the miracle of marriage isn't found in the stumbling; we can manage that all by ourselves. The miracle appears in the rising, in the rebirth of love, in the rekindling of the flame, in an ability to forgive that stretches from the cross of Calvary to the creased sheets of the marriage bed!

Realize that I am as human as you are. I am neither perfect nor a pattern; I am just a brother raised up in the body of Christ to help fight the plague of pain. That plague may have dulled your eyes and attacked your heart, but by God's grace and mercy, I am here to pray for you. I am praying for your fears and inhibitions. I am praying for your frustrations and limitations. I want your house to be a home. I want your wife to be your friend. When you lie down at night and wrap your weary body in the soft sheets of your marriage relationship, I want you to be at rest.

My prayer is for your pain to diminish and your confidence to increase. May God give you the grace to leave your troubles at the office at the end of the day and bring *yourself* home at night. When your head hits the pillow and your arms reach out for love and understanding, may they be as open to give as they are to receive. God has given you life, and you are alive. Share that life with the one He has given you—to love.

You don't have to be a missionary to your wife. You don't have to be a perfect performer. You don't even have to be a "ten." You just have to be a man. Your bride doesn't have to be a "convert" to your image, and she doesn't have to be a perfect performer or a "ten" either. She just has to be a woman, a genuine woman of God. Strong and weak. Wise and foolish. Right and wrong. Through it all, you are both still surviving . . . rest in peace!

CHAPTER EIGHT

MIGHTY MEN STILL NEED REST

We live almost as if we were on the losing side in a war zone! The young men are tired and the old men are weary. What happened to our joy and our strength—our zeal for life itself? We're too exhausted to struggle against injustice, and we're too worn out to overcome our fatigue.

What happened between our mothers' arms and life's clutches? What has produced our angry tantrums? We are part of a generation of weary men whose fatigue is exemplified in raging tempers and savage domestic violence! In our day men are desperately seeking a place—any place—of refreshing. We seek an oasis from the parched responsibilities that endlessly consume the remaining hours of our lives. We seek some place of intermission, some refuge of healing repose. The continual denial of our need for rest is driving us over the edge! We need a vacation from the stress and duress of day-to-day activity.

Lead Me to the Rock

> . . . when my heart is overwhelmed: lead me to the rock that is higher
> than I. For thou hast been a shelter for me, and a strong tower from the
> enemy.
>
> PSALM 61:2–3

David's heart was overwhelmed when he wrote Psalm 61. Like David, our stress and strain make us cry out in pain, and we are haunted by failures and plagued by temptations. Our mistakes rob us of the very comforts life has afforded us. Regret makes us thirsty for second chances. "If I could only do it again, I would spend more time with my son . . . I would spend more time with my wife . . . how can I recapture what I have lost?"

We can never rekindle the motherly warmth of the womb that incubated our masculinity, nor recall and relive the days when our father shaped us and helped to train us. The sweet taste of childhood, once savored, dissipates forever, and we are left to be stable and responsible.

Every boy who stands up to the test and attempts to be a man quickly realizes that *the need is greater than the supply.* It is to him that we must deliver this urgent message! There is nothing wrong with weariness. Even Christ Himself grew weary.

Yet we feel like the whole world has lodged on our shoulders! Our knees are buckling beneath the unbearable weight of the expectations of those around us. What is wrong with us! The problem isn't simply that we need a break. We need to identify and define *who we really are by where we turn for relief.*

Brother, you must go beyond being a believer. Allow yourself to be trained so you will know where to safely find rest. It isn't safe to rest just anywhere with just anybody! Somewhere, this very moment, some weary man is trying to rest on the jagged rocks of a sinful relationship. He is flirting with danger and playing with death!

Samson's Fatal Fatigue

Like Samson in the Bible, most of us can withstand attack, peril, distress, and criticism. We can survive failed marriages and aged parents. We can even survive moral weakness, decadence, and conflict. It is *fatigue* that threatens to undermine us!

Do you realize that Delilah didn't kill Samson? It's true. *Samson died of weariness!* He could have handled Delilah if he hadn't been so tired. Samson's sin was not in "being tired," though. He fell into sin because he went to the wrong place for rest.

My friend, *keep your head out of Delilah's lap!*

Woe to the "Samson of the twenty-first century"! He has strength and might, power and potential. His career, his talent, his ministry, or his "whatever" has a taunting potential that he finds rewarding. He can move immovable gates and endure unbearable circumstances to make a profit or win confrontations. The modern Samson has incredible strength and ability to survive under pressure. If you toss him naked into the desert, in a year you will see him walk out of the sand dunes wearing a new suit and a pair of alligator shoes!

Blessed with success while cursed with ambition, the Samsons of our age are never defeated, but often deflated. These are the men who dare to build an empire with a nickel and a nail! We need them desperately, but they are almost extinct. They are a dying breed partly because they have a tendency to self-destruct, and partly because they fail to mentor their precious gifts into the next generation. Either their gentleness has been destroyed by their cancerous drives, or they are so busy being successful they don't realize that "success is not successful without a successor"!

Pass It On!

How are the mighty fallen, and the weapons of war perished!
2 SAMUEL 1:27

How can you die without sons? Manpower is in crisis! This country's history is a revolving account of abused and hurting people who rose to power, only to raise sons who perpetuated their fathers' sorrows on others!

In our trauma, we attempted to build a nation with God at the helm, but we forgot to tell our sons about it. We rooted our dream in the freedom of religion, in the free exercise of our faith in God—a God Who is now scoffed at by the children of the very forefathers who died to win that freedom!

The nation brought forth by the pioneer families who sat down at banquet tables to give thanks at the first Thanksgiving meal is now watching families disintegrate in divorce, murder, and abortion clinics. We need to return to God, but it will take a resurgence of fighting fathers whose Samson-like courage has not been destroyed by fatigue and moral failure!

Trapped in Delilah's Lap!

Delilah the temptress is reserved for the mighty man; she is the assassin of the successful. Her tools are not her hips, lips, or fingertips. Her tools are his tiredness, numbness, and inner void. She doesn't have to do much because she knows that once Samson's head is nestled on her knees, he will begin to share his heart with her.

If he is not careful, the harlot becomes the businessman's wife. The woman he lives with becomes his roommate. But he does not come to her so much to ravish and caress as to find a place to rest and refresh! In the house of the harlot, the mighty man becomes the helpless man.

The Bible's description of Samson and Delilah in Judges 16 says almost nothing about twisted sheets and panting breaths. We see a lonely, empty man who is so vulnerable to affection that a hostile government hires a harlot to seduce him! Burdened with fatigue and loneliness, Samson didn't want to swing from vines and play Tarzan. He wanted to cuddle in the warmth of feminine arms that reminded him of his mother's warm embrace. Samson *sought rest* in Delilah's bed. Then the mighty man fell asleep as the harlot stroked him and murmured softly in his ear.

Delilah realized that he had finally told her the truth, so she sent for the five Philistine leaders. "Come just this once more," she said, "for this time he has told me everything." So they brought the money with them. She lulled him to sleep with his head in her lap, and they brought in a barber and cut off his hair. Delilah began to hit him, but she could not see that his strength was leaving him.

JUDGES 16:18–19 TLB

Isn't it odd! Samson *knew* Delilah was trying to kill him, yet he compromised his safety for the "rest" she provided!

Delilah had created a haven for Samson. This man had a successful career but a failed marriage. He had everything to share and no one to share it with. He had been driven, and suddenly in the middle of his life, the mighty man realized that he was tired! The man was looking for a vacation. He was looking for rest. He was looking for some place to lay his head.

And Jesus said unto him, Foxes have holes, and birds of the air have

nests; but the Son of man hath not where to lay his head.
LUKE 9:58

Run From the Harlot's Flame

A tired man is a vulnerable man. When you are tired, you do the "Samson thing." You lie down too long and you talk too much. Samson knew Delilah was working for his enemy. She had tried to kill him several times! He foolishly thought, *I can handle it!* I think Delilah was the most terrifying opponent in Samson's entire life because *she used his own thirst against him!* He was so desperate for solitude and solace that, like a moth attracted to the flame, he flew into what he should have run away from!

Brother, are you weary? Do you feel empty and alone right now? Don't run to what you should be running away from! Many mighty men have fallen prey to something they knew the enemy had sent because they were too proud to acknowledge their peril. Never expose yourself to the enemy's assassin!

Your "Delilah" can be *anything that comes into your life to deplete your strength!* It can be your career, a relationship, or a habit. Delilah's arms may be the forbidden place you go when you have had enough. "She" will provide a haven, an escape, or the vacation of your dreams, but don't be fooled. The harlot doesn't want to delight you—she just wants to destroy you! Get up while you can! Sometimes a good run is better than a bad stand!

> *Father, I pray for every Samson, for every mighty man whose force and fight have left him weary and vulnerable. I pray, dear God, that this man's strength will be renewed by Your presence. I pray that Delilah's plan will be aborted and that he will not fly into the blistering heat of the fire because he is distracted by the illustrious beauty of the flame! In Jesus' name, amen!*

The Silent Cancer

Busy men don't "schedule" tiredness, but it slips up on them when they least expect it. Fatigue is the silent cancer of our judgment and emotions. It robs us of creativity and secretly steals our potency and discernment. When we are tired, we tend to be more vulnerable and less careful. Our nerves stand on edge, our tempers flare, and even our simple problems seem insurmountable!

Many men make permanent decisions based on the stress of temporary circumstances when fatigue robs them of their better judgment. Creative men feel guilty because they are tired, and they run from the fear that their gifts will one day dry up and they will no longer be able to *achieve*. Often, tremendously successful men are hard to work for and hard to love. These men are not led, they are driven . . . to total exhaustion!

A normal night's sleep can no more cure a Samson's exhaustion than a Band-Aid can cure invasive cancer! Modern-day Samsons are walking zombies who feed on their pain like a junkie feeds on his drugs. Success is their addiction and affliction, but beneath it all, they desperately need rest. Even good things are dangerous if they get "out of balance." More importantly, what good is the blessing without the Blesser? What good is the provision if you lose the Provider? What good is the woman if you lose the wife? These are valid questions that deserve an honest answer!

There is a time and a season for all things. (See Ecclesiastes 3:1.) Even the soil becomes depleted if it tries to produce year after year without a rest. The winter chill arrests growth, but it allows time for recycling as well. We need time to renew and reassess—we need balance. Most of us who drive hard and play little are *men who have seen the wolf* of failure, of hard times, and of poverty. Some of us run from our terror of failure, forgetting that fear is the opposite of faith! Fear may feel like the fuel of faith, but its acidic nourishment only gives ulcers to the body and anger to the heart!

You and I may press wildly into the battle because of some inner need to establish our worth. The tragedy of our compulsion is that our critics will seldom change.

Never run to win the favor of critics or to silence their endless criticism. The false standards of scoffers are fueled by unlimited and effortless cynicism. It doesn't take effort, preparation, intelligence, or skill to criticize. That's why it is the favorite pastime of untrained children and unaccomplished adults.

The worst part of being "driven" is that the disease is contagious; our unspoken desperation threatens to leave behind anyone who will not keep up the pace. We seem determined to run our loved ones as well as ourselves. Will we never realize that God sends different types of people into our lives to *balance* us?

Rest in God's Arms

There remaineth therefore a rest to the people of God.
HEBREWS 4:9

I want you to understand that *rest does exist.* It is more than sleep—it is peace and calmness. It is the calm breathing of an unthreatened baby, safe in the arms of the one who gave it birth.

In your natural birth, you were born of your mother. In your spiritual birth, you were born of the Spirit. You need to climb back into the arms of the Spirit Who gave you birth and find rest in His presence and peace in His arms!

God's river of refreshment is designed for the stumbling, not for the starchy. The stable are sustained for a time by their own agility, but the stumbling man is desperate for His refreshment.

He gives strength to the weary, and to him who lacks might He increases power. Though youths grow weary and tired, and vigorous young men stumble badly, yet those who wait for the Lord will gain new strength; they will mount up with wings like eagles, they will run and not get tired, they will walk and not become weary.
ISAIAH 40:29–31 NASB

We will always fail if we do not return to God and look only to Him for support! In the words of the hymnist, we "dare not trust the sweetest frame, but wholly lean on Jesus' name"!

Every man needs rest. If you deny that need, it will eventually cause you to collapse into the arms of Delilah! You need rest, and the only place you can safely rest your head is *in the will of God.* No matter how rough His will may seem to be, there is a certain comfort that comes from understanding and fulfilling your purpose!

All of us tremble at the cold reality of Delilah's lap looking so inviting when we are tired. Her arms always seem to be conveniently opened wide as she calls out, "Come to me." The good news is that our vulnerability can ignite great prayer and give birth to the first frail gropings of an honest heart seeking rest in the right place and not the wrong place. Neither alcohol nor greed, neither lust nor anything else can soothe the savage beast in our souls like one good moment in God's presence!

Oh God, don't let us become so religious that we fail to bring men into Your healing presence!

We need the kind of anointing on our worship and church services that brings mortal men (and weary Samsons) into the very presence of God. Nothing less will do. Whether we admit it to our wives, our friends, or anyone else, we know that without the continual guidance of God, any one of us could find ourselves resting in the wrong place—no matter how anointed we may be.

Samson was anointed, but he failed to take his troubles to the Lord. *Take time out to come away and refresh yourself in the presence of the Lord!* Yours are wounds that only He can heal! Any other kind of rest will only camouflage another attack. Only God can grant you a safe place to lay your head. Do it—we need you. Your wife needs you. Your sons and daughters need you! We must have another generation of mighty men. Birth your sons, reach your stars. But then, in the quiet of the evening, wrap yourself in the warmth of God's presence. When you do, with a soft hum, a peaceful heart, and an inner sanctum of solace, He will say, "Rest in peace."

And the peace of God, which passeth all understanding, shall keep your hearts and minds through Christ Jesus.
Philippians 4:7

CHAPTER NINE

YOU ARE STILL MY SON!

*And he shall . . . turn the hearts of the fathers to the children,
and the disobedient to the wisdom of the just.*

— LUKE 1:17 —

He is filled with my blood, and he stands on my bones. His eyes are moist with my dew, and he looks like me. He is my ticket into the next generation, my spaceship into the land of the young. He is my chance to give support, strength, and solidarity to a part of my destiny. He offers me my one opportunity to be all that I wanted someone else to be to me.

Healing him is the same as healing me. To love him is to love me. The process of saving him from making my mistakes somehow gives purpose to my deepest pain. I will endure whatever it takes to help him reach a star. He is like warm clay waiting to be shaped into a man. He is my self, my friend, my comrade. He is my son!

Chosen by my heart or fathered by my loins, he is all that I invest in him today for the challenges of tomorrow. God grant me grace for fatherhood and wisdom for parenting. Without the guidance of God helping and training me, I cannot parent my son as I should.

Dear Daddy

Fatherhood was exemplified in the thunderous voice of God as He broke through the clouds and spoke at the River Jordan. He publicly endorsed a Son Whom many saw as controversial. He said what every son longs to hear his father say: "This is My beloved Son, in Whom I am well pleased!"

It is paternal approval that makes the smallest Little Leaguer run harder than the rest. It makes timid little boys brave the strange night noises and biting bugs of Boy Scout overnight campouts just to hear their fathers say, "Well done, son." The smile of a pleased father is sweeter than candy and richer than diamonds to his son!

What has happened? Our heroes have changed from our fathers to an endless chain of drug-crazed actors and jaded, ungrateful athletes. When I was a child, I believed that my father was the strongest man in the world! But wholesomeness has slipped away. Times have changed, and the movies have changed. Fatherhood was pushed to the back shelf with the dusty reruns of the Brady Bunch. Has anyone noticed? The needs of our sons have *not* changed!

Grieving for Fatherhood

One of the greatest deceptions in our society is the notion that men are hurting over women. There are exceptions, but you will find that we are not grieving over our mothers or our wives. No, we miss our fathers. It is from them that we most often draw our strength, our weakness, our pleasure, and our unbearable pain. Somebody has stolen our heroes.

Absentee fathers and deadbeat dads have littered this nation with confused sons and angry husbands. Millions of bitter and abandoned young males are growing into men without mentors. How can we expect them to touch hurts and needs in others like real men when their own deep hurts have never been healed? This void of longing and brokenness in the men of this generation has spawned a raging flood of conflict, promiscuity, perversion, and domestic violence. Broken and hurting sons are asking their fathers for a deposit of true manhood, but their fathers are bankrupt—no one has made a real deposit in them!

It is painful to admire someone who isn't there. A one-sided love affair is never fulfilling. Empty arms do not offer a heartwarming, reassuring hug. Empty arms only reflect the emptiness of a son who took the risk to open himself up, only to be rejected and discarded on the abandoned porch of a broken home.

Our young men have grown weary of playing sports before empty bleachers. As toddlers, they carefully colored pictures and proudly brought them home, but Dad wasn't there to admire their work and reward them with a father's priceless praise. Now, at the end of their hope and childhood, they have thrown away their coloring books. They have angrily punctured their footballs and bought guns. They have grown tired of dancing to the haunting melody of manhood alone.

Fill in the Blanks

Our young men are dying in anger and pain, wondering, "What did I do to drive away my daddy?" A father is an image of a young man's destiny, a living testimony of what time may bring to pass. Dad is our first definition of masculinity. His absence leaves us desperately looking for someone else to "fill in the blank." If the church doesn't do it, the gay community will. If the church doesn't do it, the gangs and drug lords will. If the church doesn't do it, the pornographers will. Empty sons will always look for someone to fill in the blank left by the father who isn't there.

Well-tailored dark suits and vibrant silk ties cannot drape the gaping void of the empty blanks in the broken hearts of men. Even the most voluptuous of fast-paced and lace-clad women cannot console the anguish of masculine tears blocked and cries muffled. Broken men try to mask their hurts behind empty emblems of success, but hidden behind those frail facades are screaming hearts bound in a forced silence. They all share a common thread of desperate need, a familiar hollowness that traces their broken places and the jagged edges of nearly emasculated men!

A crimson river drips unchecked from the wounded hearts and hidden places of modern men. We hide behind our masquerades and attempt acts of chivalry, then like little boys, we brag about sex, though we have never known true love. We long for a tender touch, but are afraid of tenderness. We want to be strong enough to be leaned on, yet tender enough to relate to the pain of others. Can the wounded heal the hurting?

Weeping and Raising

Jesus wept. Then said the Jews, Behold how he loved him! . . . Then they took away the stone from the place where the dead was laid. And Jesus lifted up his eyes, and said, Father, I thank thee that thou hast heard me. . . . And when he thus had spoken, he cried with a loud voice, Lazarus, come forth.

John 11:35–36, 41, 43

My idea of a hero is a man who is soft enough to cry at his friend's funeral, but strong enough to call him from the grave! Jesus was tender enough to respect the vulnerabilities of the women He loved, but then He wiped away their tears and assumed the responsibility to change the circumstances that had created the pain!

I hope you haven't buried your trauma, thinking it could not be healed. Remember, your God raises the dead! If you really want to resurrect a dead situation, then stop crying. Stand up and command it to arise! Go find your son in a tomb of drugs! Raise your drunken father from the gutter of a city street! Perhaps you must approach anew the cold and impersonal pain of your father's indifferent glance. No matter what killed them or separated you, if you want your father or son back, you must raise him up!

Jesus wept! But when He finished weeping, He started raising. The tragedy with Mary was she thought it was too late. Do not make Mary's mistake. The evidence may look bad, and by now the situation may be stinking. But if you want him, raise him anyway—in spite of your disappointment. Reach beyond the breach and choose to love anyway. If you want your relationship healed with your son, your wife, your daughter, or your dad, then "roll the stone away" and get involved! (Even if it does stink, it will be worth it to see a resurrection!)

"Come to me," said the father to the prodigal son. If we are still alive, if we still have breath, then we will disappoint each other. It is part of being human. If our love cannot overcome disappointment, then we will die lonely, bitter, and stubborn.

Fathers who are angry and disappointed with the outcome of their sons often try to train or direct their grown sons as if they were children. That day is over. Your son will never be a toddler again, so take off the training wheels and put the long lectures in the closet. They are only driving him away. If Lazarus is ever to be raised, you must call him toward you, not drive him from you. Jesus said, "Lazarus, come forth."

Missing in Action

Angry son, *beware of your critical attitude!*

At the age of sixteen, I heard the slow creaking of the pulleys that eased my father's cold body into the red Mississippi clay, and I learned that dead men can't talk and can't listen. I stood there with a thousand unresolved issues on my heart. Burning tears streamed down my face as I wept for my father. I wept for the questions I could not ask him. I wept for the grandchildren he would never see. I wept for the twinkle I would never see in his aged eyes. I wept for my mother, who never married again.

In spite of my father's flaws, I wept for his attempts to provide, to love and protect us, and for his tragedies. But most of all, I wept for myself. Dad was gone like a gust of wind. He slipped through my fingers like sand. I clenched hard, but when I opened my hand, it was empty. He had slipped through the cracks, and I wondered, "How could he leave without saying good-bye?"

I suppose I am a bit envious of men my age whose fathers are still alive and able to stand by their side. I am always drawn toward father-and-son teams. I love those gray-haired men whose sweaters are too big and whose backs are starting to bend. You know the men I'm talking about—the elderly men whose teeth are a little too prominent and who are full of stories you have already heard. When I see them pull back their leathery jaws and smile until their eyes twinkle at their sons, I always try to tell those sons, "You are blessed." No matter how much your dad did or did not do, if his wrinkled ears can hear you and his glazed eyes can see you, then you can work it out!

The ultimate absentee father is the one who is dead. There are no arguments to be had and no issues to be resolved. He is gone—like a breeze that blows by your face. You feel it, you touch it, and then it is gone. No matter how badly your relationship with your father has deteriorated, if he is still alive, then find a way to reconcile! It has been twenty-two years since my father's death, and during all those years of living and loving and raising my own sons, I have never, ever seen him again. Yet I still long to see that familiar smile on his face and hear his reassuring voice.

I am grateful for the memories of my father's hand—the caressing hand that brushed my forehead and the playful hand that rubbed my belly when I was a child. I am thankful for the noises he made as he blew on my stomach until I giggled as a little boy. At least I have a memory and a moment with my father. I know there are many who have never felt their father's touch, wrestled on the floor, or been pushed in a swing. I still wonder what it would be like to sit on a porch today and listen to my father tell me some of those ridiculous stories about people I cannot even remember. I can only imagine the beaming smile that would light up his face if he could hold one of his squirmy little grandbabies in his arms today.

Most of all, I felt the pain of my father's absence as I performed on the football fields of life. I have made touchdown after touchdown, and I have heard the roaring of great crowds, but there was always one face missing from the stands. I longed to hear one special voice above the roar of the crowd . . . but he was missing in action!

Fill the Emptiness

Then Jonathan said to David, To morrow is the new moon: and thou shalt be missed, because thy seat will be empty.

1 SAMUEL 20:18

If you can fill the empty seat in your life with a body, then do it. If you have to sober up your father just to talk to him, then find him and touch him! In a flash, he will be gone. In a moment, he will fade. His wisdom may sound antiquated and his advice may be unsolicited, but just listen to his voice before it floats away.

If your father is alive, find him. If your father is deceased, then reach out to your children and be a father to them. If you cannot have one—be one. Overcome your loss or lack by becoming what you would like to have. Give your children what you lost! Overcome every obstacle to love and restore what is missing. Release the pain of your divorce, abuse, and fear to God, and open your arms to your son. Whether he is the president of a bank or dying with AIDS, he is still your son!

When the prodigal son pulled himself from the muddy troughs of the hogpen and headed for home, he was not greeted with scorn, or "I told you so," or even a warning. His old arthritic father squinted his eyes to gaze down the road as he had done every morning since his youngest son had gone. When he saw his mud-caked son coming down the road, neither cane nor walker was needed! That old man leaped off that porch and ran down that dusty road to meet his long-lost son. The prodigal had lost all he had; he was a miserable failure and a disgrace to everyone else—*but not to his father!* His father opened up his arms wide in unconditional love and acceptance.

It is time to open up your arms, man of God. Open your weary arms to your wife. Welcome your sons and your daughters, in spite of their failures or yours! If we are going to have families, we must let love carry us beyond the wounds that drive us apart. It is time to forgive and be forgiven.

Welcome Home!

I will arise and go to my father, and will say unto him, Father, I have sinned against heaven, and before thee. . . . But when he was yet a great way off, his father saw him, and had compassion, and ran, and fell on his neck, and kissed him. . . . But the father said to his servants, Bring forth the best robe, and put it on him; and put a ring on his hand, and shoes on his feet: and bring hither the fatted calf, and kill it; and let us eat, and be merry: for this my son was dead, and is alive again; he was lost, and is found.

LUKE 15:18, 20, 22–24

The runaway whose heart is full of fear has no trophies to line his mantle. He comes with no merit or accolades. He bears only the scars, wounds, and lacerations that mark his journey from folly to failure. Does it really matter whether you are the father or the son? We have raised a generation that has lost its way. Fathers are missing, and young men are asking, "May I come home?"

What did the father of the prodigal son know that made him avoid the "I told you so" speech? I know what it was. In spite of the boy's filthy hair and putrid smell, and in spite of his moral bankruptcy and rebellious mistakes from the past, his grateful father fell on his son's neck and kissed him because he knew that *when he touched his son, he had touched himself!*

Your son may be disabled in his morality or twisted in his sexuality. He may be irresponsible and unstable, and he may need hours of love and reassurance before he accepts the God of his father. His only glimpse of the God you serve may come at the moment he feels your fatherly arms around him. No matter how dark the night and no matter how hot the tears, embrace your prodigal son and declare, *"You are still my son!"*

If you are a son who is lost and you have no earthly father or place to call home, then I declare to you this moment: *"You are a chosen son, a precious one. Though you were lost, today you are found! Welcome home, my son, in whom I am well pleased!"*

CHAPTER TEN

SURROGATE FATHERS

How can we restore what never was? What number can we dial when there are no places to call? Where can we go when there are no addresses to find? For millions of men and women, the opportunity for a genuine father-child relationship was stolen at their conception by the secret affairs and one-night stands of children playing grown folks' games. They left behind babies doomed to a future filled with rejection and a destiny cursed with confusion!

Fatherless men wander our streets in unending pain, searching the tombs of their lost heritage, crying out, "Who is my father?" Some learn the truth only to wish they had never asked the question. It only increased the pain of their loneliness. Still others, like me, were cruelly snatched from the nurturing arms of their fathers by the icy fingers of sickness, disease, and death.

What shall be done with those of us who have been left behind and left alone? Like a puzzle whose pieces were lost, we can never create the full picture of our identity. There always seems to be a part of us missing. Is there no way to recapture the missing pieces?

Unmentionable Memories

Some of us have been abused, beaten, and battered. Some have even been brutally raped and molested, although the silence over male molestation is deafeningly quiet. (What man rushes to the front of a room and admits before his friends that he was molested?) How many of us evolved into dysfunctional manhood from memories as little boys trembling in a corner trying to protect mother from a man we called father? What confusion erupts when the alcohol-soaked protector and provider staggers home and beats his family?

How can a mere boy defend himself or stand against his father, whose hands have slapped his mother over and over again in the night? Countless black eyes, broken limbs, beaten backs, and bloody legs have left scars on the bodies and gashes on the minds of boys-become-men, men who remember much more than their mothers would ever allow to be discussed.

"Shhh, I heard a car door. Oh God, is that him?! Don't let him be drunk tonight . . . please, I have to go to school! I could kill him. Why does he always act like that? Doesn't he love us? What is wrong with us? No, what is wrong with me? What makes him hate me like he does? Why else would he ruin my life, slap my mother, and attack me? He is wonderful sometimes, and then I think I love him, except when he comes home like this. . . ." Once again, the door slams and the cursing begins.

These memories plague legions of men. No, these are not the gentle "Ozzie and Harriet" scenarios acted out on television. These dark dramas are filled with careening ambulances, bloody kitchen floors, and fearful lies—the standard props for an endless cycle of misery in many dysfunctional homes.

Tragedy occurs when the one you admire does something you hate. How would you feel about a man who loves your mother one minute and beats her senseless the next? One moment you are in the park, and the next moment you are in the emergency room. How many times can a little boy lie and say, "I fell down the steps" when his family's home doesn't have steps? All they really have is a house filled with pain.

While most men remember fishing poles and Little League games, others can only recall childhoods speckled with blood, tainted with rape, and sealed with silence. These are the secret afflictions behind their pain, the burning issues that make the drunk drink. These are the fires of torment that drive grown-up men to play perversely with innocent children. Somewhere deep within the tormented man there is a tormented child who feels doomed to torment others!

And, ye fathers, provoke not your children to wrath: but bring them up in the nurture and admonition of the Lord.

EPHESIANS 6:4

Rage has infected our manhood like a contagious disease. It has stolen our normal development because many men were never allowed to enjoy the innocence and freedom of boyhood first! Who triggered such rage in their souls and taught them to act out such anger? Who mentored them in such uncontrollable fury?

Loose the Man

I know you want answers, but the answers vary from house to house and from man to man. Behind every dysfunction you will find dishonor, disloyalty, or at least disorder. The love of Christ still draws broken men from their tombs of pain today just as it drew Lazarus centuries ago. They quickly respond to the call of hope, yet when they emerge, they are still bound, trapped, and wrapped in the odor of decay.

Will we dare to obey the command Jesus gave His shocked disciples at the grave of Lazarus? Will we risk contamination to "loose them, and let them go"? (See John 11:44.) Untying the knotty problems of real-life men will force us to get personally involved with foul-smelling issues we don't even like to discuss, let alone unravel with our carefully manicured hands! What happened to the simple hymn-singing and harmless pew-sitting that we've grown to love? The praise has given birth to a resurrection, and there is a captive to set free. The pews have been pushed aside; the Master calls us up front to help Him loose the man!

When we call these men out of their dungeons of despair (and they are coming by the thousands), who will be waiting outside the crypt to loose them and let them go? If these freshly resurrected men are to be untied, then mature men will have to do it! It is a laborious process, but *we need men who will loose men.* We need selfless men who will lay their own hands on the putrid bandages of their brothers and say, "Strip by strip we are going to unravel the nightmares. We are going to unravel your attitudes, anger, and temperament. We refuse to let you go back in the grave!"

And when He thus had spoken, He cried with a loud voice, Lazarus, come forth. And he that was dead came forth, bound hand and foot with graveclothes: and his face was bound about with a napkin. Jesus saith unto them, Loose him, and let him go.

JOHN 11:43–44

Many of us are bound and tied with the paralyzing issues of the past. We have moved into the light of the God Who calls us, but we can move no farther; we are bound hand and foot with the graveclothes of our pain.

When God's called ones remain tied up, they often become cynical, angry, and tempestuous. Can you imagine what it would be like to wake up and discover you were tightly bound in a sheet, with no hope of escape? Now do you understand why we are called to rob society's graves to reach decaying personalities like Lazarus who have been trapped, wrapped, and rolled into a tomb? We are also called to help men like the Apostle Paul, who openly confessed that his success was not complete. He was still in pursuit of perfection, but he at least had been disengaged from his past.

Brethren, I count not myself to have apprehended: but this one thing I do, forgetting those things which are behind, and reaching forth unto those things which are before, I press toward the mark for the prize of the high calling of God in Christ Jesus.

PHILIPPIANS 3:13–14

The fear of failure can paralyze the runner and immobilize his pursuit of wholeness. Some men are terrified that they will not be able to make it to the light or survive among the whole. They have dwelt in the confinement of their dungeons for so long that they are absolutely terrified! They complain about the church, the pastor, and about this and that and the other, but the real issue is that Lazarus doesn't believe he can make it.

Lazarus is right! He cannot make it unless someone is willing to come close enough to smell the decay and yet choose to stay to loose his soiled bandages. If we can find men who will unravel us, we are blessed. These men become like fathers to us. Their ties cannot be analyzed in microscopic tests because they are our fathers in spirit, not in blood. These surrogate fathers give back to us what life has taken.

Find a Spiritual Father

Once we escape from our tombs, we will discover that missing pieces are filled in and damaged places are repaired through our relationships with our spiritual fathers. If we want to touch men, then we must learn how to "adopt" one another. Some men desperately need to be adopted because they need to experience a relationship they never had in their childhood. They are searching for a father and mentor.

I believe this is what caused David to be so longsuffering with Saul. When David came to Saul's palace, he was "fresh out of fathers and brothers." When Samuel the prophet came, David's father and brothers "forgot" to mention him as a possible candidate for the throne. He was obviously not his father's preferred son. If Samuel hadn't persisted, then David would never have been called by his brothers or his father. Maybe you know how it feels to be excluded from the chosen number and branded a misfit. Take heart, for God loves to anoint misfits to fulfill His divine purpose and destiny!

David was honored when King Saul asked him to join his royal household. It sounded like a great opportunity, but Saul was the wrong man. Never choose a father who is jealous of your success, for he will only molest you. Figuratively speaking, he will only touch you for his own pleasure or gain. Many of us who have never been sexually molested know how it feels to be emotionally molested by people who only touched us for their own corrupt gain. In both cases, the result is the same: We are afraid to trust. We are locked up and locked out of a chance to heal deeper issues.

Don't allow Saul to win in your life. If you had a bad experience in your search for a godly mentor, then try again. God will supply you with a trustworthy surrogate father.

Elijah passed by him [Elisha], and cast his mantle upon him. And he left the oxen, and ran after Elijah, and said, Let me, I pray thee, kiss my father and my mother, and then I will follow thee.
1 KINGS 19:19–20

A bond was forged between Elisha and Elijah that day. It was born out of their mutual need for covenant relationship. The best relationships are secured by mutual need—the insurance that defies betrayal. The mutual need of the vine and branch creates a relationship that can be fruitful and productive. This is the bond that God sends into the lives of men who need a father to complete their training. Most men need the approval of a father, and for this reason, a surrogate father must be someone you respect, or his approval will mean nothing to you.

Don't Misuse—Mentor!

One of the wonderful things about the church is that it recreates a sense of family. This is especially true for men who never enjoyed the love and approval of a father in their lives. Pastors need to remember that just a touch or a smile from them will reassure even the most staunch of men. It gives men a sense of pride and affirmation rivaled only by the praise of a respected coach whose personal attention gives a football player a warm feeling of accomplishment.

As a pastor, I admit that it is easy to get busy and forget how important my personalized attention is to the performance level and well-being of those with whom I serve—particularly the men who are associated with me.

For though ye have ten thousand instructors in Christ, yet have ye not many fathers: for in Christ Jesus I have begotten you through the gospel.
1 CORINTHIANS 4:15

Many men entering the doors of the church are bleeding from deep wounds inflicted by natural fathers who beat and abused them throughout their childhood. God is outraged when His wounded sons then find a surrogate father in the church who unfairly wields his authority and goes off on a tangent of spiritual domination, inflicting fresh abuse on men already crushed!

We need fathers who are sensitive to the fact that they are mentoring and fathering men who have been through traumas and abuses that would stagger the mind. Too many leaders simply inflict more of the very same abuses their proteges already suffered in the natural! These leaders are dictatorial, abusive, and insensitive—all in the name of Christ Jesus. There is a big difference between being "strong and definitive" and being "dictatorial and abusive"!

Many men who fill our pulpits have just as many unresolved issues as their members. No one is perfect, but if these undershepherds do not allow God to reveal, confront, and heal their own problems, they will perpetuate a vicious cycle of generational curses. Thus the pain passes down from father to son. This pain must stop!

> *Today, right here and now, I rebuke the curse and the pain that has locked up the bowels of our compassion and made us cold and indifferent! Before this man ruins all who respect him, release him to love his wife and father his sons, both natural and spiritual. Release him from being cold, indifferent, and abusive. He is hurting and imprisoned by his own point of reference. In Jesus' name, I declare: "Let that man go!"*

The bond between Elijah and Elisha was so powerful that Elisha walked away from his natural parents and family position to follow Elijah! Elisha burned the twelfth yoke of oxen he was driving and forever left the fields because he had found a surrogate father and a spiritual mentor. This is proof that surrogate adoption doesn't always mean a man's natural father was abusive. Elisha's surrogate relationship had more to do with his inner need to fulfill and stir up the spiritual gift and calling inside him.

Pour Water on His Hands

If you want to climb from the mediocre into the supernatural, find someone who is doing what you want to do. People can never give you what they have not received. When you find such a person, don't allow selfishness and manipulation to dominate your life. Don't rob him or rape him with your greed or need. Pour water on his hands—that means *serve him!*

> *Give, and it shall be given unto you; good measure, pressed down, and shaken together, and running over, shall men give into your bosom. For with the same measure that ye mete withal it shall be measured to you again.*
>
> LUKE 6:38

The greatest investment you can make is an investment in people! That's what God did. He invested His Son in humanity, and He reaped the harvest of the church. Make an investment; pay your dues. Give, and learn the art of being blessed! Truly great men serve. Truly great men wash each other's feet. You will never be whole unless you learn to serve someone other than yourself!

If you show me a Lot who survived Sodom, then I will show you an Abraham who made an investment in Lot. If you show me an Elisha who did twice as many miracles as his predecessor, then I'll show you an Elijah who stayed up late at night, educating his successor. If you show me a Timothy who shook his generation and became a great leader, then I will show you an Apostle Paul who kept writing to his surrogate son, even while facing the sneering grin of death.

If you have achieved any level of success, then pour it into someone else! Success is not success without a successor! Paul shared his spiritual memoirs with Timothy as he stood on the banks of time and gazed through the window of death into the scenic sights of eternity. He had already taught him how to preach and how to pray. Now he was teaching Timothy how to die:

> *Stand steady, and don't be afraid of suffering for the Lord. Bring others*
> *to Christ. Leave nothing undone that you ought to do.*
> *I say this because I won't be around to help you very much longer.*
> 2 TIMOTHY 4:5–6 TLB

Catch the Mantle

Every now and then, among the press of the pompous pretenders and the prideful prestigious, someone comes along who has the ability to eternally influence your life. He enters your existence humbly, through a side door, and is only a guest for a few moments. Nevertheless, he has a unique ability to show you your own strengths. When he shines, you can better see your own abilities. With a simple smile, he can heal the scars of your childhood. With a word, he can rebuild the broken walls of your self-esteem. His fatherly attention dignifies your existence, and you blossom in his presence like roses in the sun and ripening wheat in a flourishing field.

I warn you, and I warn every member of this generation: the kind of men I am speaking of come in one door and exit through the other. They are strangers passing through the days of our lives. They are phantoms in the night, sent by God to the destitute. These men are like angels in disguise. Neither perfect nor flawless, they are nevertheless powerful and effective agents of God commissioned to leave with those they touch an imparted mantle of excellence and power.

If God grants you the opportunity to walk in the presence of a surrogate father, you will know it without asking another's opinion. When you hang up the phone, you will be renewed by his reassuring voice and wise words. When you leave the room with him, you will discover you are "pregnant" with expectation! Cherish the moment and savor the exchange, for in a flash he will be gone from your view.

> *And it came to pass, as they still went on, and talked, that, behold, there appeared a chariot of fire, and horses of fire, and parted them both asunder; and Elijah went up by a whirlwind into heaven.*
> *And Elisha saw it, and he cried, My father, my father, the chariot of Israel, and the horsemen thereof. And he saw him no more: and he took hold of his own clothes, and rent them in two pieces.*
> 2 KINGS 2:11–12

They are whisked away in a wind, taken from view in a cloud. Moved like a crutch from a healed leg, their sudden departure leaves us wobbling as we are forced to stand on our own. Whatever you would give to honor and cherish them at that moment—do it now. If they stepped in when the natural fathers stepped out, if they gave method to the madness and purpose to your pain, then speak quickly, love intensely, and thank them! Then "poof!" they are gone.

The greatest compliment you can give a father is to catch what he gave you and carry on! We cannot worship at the shrine of another man's success; we must catch what he gives and go quickly on. In a single whirlwind event, Elisha lost his crutch, his mentor, his teacher, and his friend. This stranger who was not his father had become his surrogate father. By the time Elijah took his exit, Elisha didn't merely long to have *what* his mentor had; he cried out in longing for the man himself—the father and the gift had become one! He realized in one gut-wrenching moment of exploding pain that God had given him a surrogate *father,* and he cried out in anguish, "My father, my father. . . !" In a flash, that father was gone.

If you feel you have outgrown your need of a father, then at least *be a father*! Somewhere there is a desperate young man whose natural ties are broken. He needs you to mend the breach and repair the jagged edges of his broken heart. Bind him and train him, teach him and pour into him all the things you want to say to the next generation! He is your spaceship to the future; board him quickly and stock him well. When the time of your departure is at hand, before you step from ship to shore, leave a mantle of blessing and anointing behind you. Leave something for us to catch!

I am glad that I am a father to young men, and I am glad I am a son to my precious older fathers. My sonship and my fatherhood are not always by blood, but are always by bond! We are wrapped, tied, and entangled together in the divine fulfillment of God-ordained needs. To my surrogate father, I am a filled heart and an open hand. My heart is filled with the many deposits made by others, and they have made me stand in the heat of the day. My hand is open and ready to grasp what is left behind by those who went before me. I stand ready to maintain their heritage of spiritual excellence. My hand is open and my fingers extended. I will grasp all that is dropped to me!

And he took the mantle of Elijah that fell from him, and smote the waters, and said, Where is the Lord God of Elijah? and when he also had smitten the waters, they parted hither and thither: and Elisha went over.

2 KINGS 2:14

To my sons, I say, "Walk behind me and watch me close. I am a train in motion. I am a word in flight. I will not stay. I will move like my fathers and lift from your view. Hear my fading voice and touch my weakening pulse, and know that I was here. I am a bubble bursting in a glass. Catch the moment, not the man—he cannot be held. Seize the day, my sons, and catch the wisdom of my heart and the benefit of my pain. When my chariot comes and you feel the wind, catch what I leave behind for you; and for God's sake . . . go on!"

CHAPTER ELEVEN

A MAN'S BEST FRIEND

*These things said he: and after that he saith unto them, Our friend
Lazarus sleepeth; but I go, that I may awake him out of sleep.*

— JOHN 11:11 —

L azarus was beyond sleep; he was dead! Jesus called him "friend" anyway. Some people only call you "friend" as long as they can use you or
benefit from your existence. Jesus considered Lazarus His friend even
though he seemed to be at a point of no return. Their relationship was
stronger than the predicament that threatened to divide them.

Our Savior keeps His commitment to men who have been discarded and
buried by others. He has always befriended the sick, the decomposing, and
the rotten. Jesus is the Friend of sinners. He comes when others have walked
away, and His brilliance shines brightest when life seems darkest. He shouts
a grave-shaking word of deliverance into the dismal, dank crypts of our
lives. He is a God of relationship, and His creation can never escape its need
for intimacy with its Creator. It is God Whom we must have. Nothing less
will do.

*Which was the son of Enos, which was the son of Seth, which was the
son of Adam, which was the son of God.*
    LUKE 3:38

There was nothing in Adam that God hadn't touched, for he was formed by the hand of God. God didn't speak him into existence from a distance. He personally touched, caressed, and molded Adam's shape to perfection.

God's divine fingerprints are etched into every fiber of our beings, as they were with Adam. God knows us in ways more intimate than sex and more probing than surgery. He knows our inward parts. We are graphically naked and totally exposed before His eyes. Nothing is hidden from His view.

> *But we all, with open face beholding as in a glass the glory of the Lord, are changed into the same image from glory to glory, even as by the Spirit of the Lord.*
>
> 2 CORINTHIANS 3:18

We have an "open face" relationship with God. He sees our deepest yearnings and knows our darkest cravings. Our all-wise Creator has every right to find our weaknesses obnoxious, but instead He has chosen to love us beyond our failures and lift us beyond despair! We cannot impress Him into loving us—we are already accepted. He has already made up His mind about us, and the blood of Jesus has purchased a righteousness we could not afford.

Runaway Man

Insecurity keeps us from knowing God. We try to impress Him with our performance, but without Him it is basically a facade. It is knowing God that transforms our wretchedness into righteousness, but we cannot know Him when we are running or hiding from Him!

It began when Adam tasted the forbidden fruit of disobedience and brought death into the world. In the beginning, Adam's obedience held death at bay and locked it out of the earthly realm. Adam's sin opened the lock and allowed death to walk right in through the door of his failure, bringing with it the generational curse of sin on his offspring.

The curse murdered Abel outside the Garden of Eden; mercilessly drowned men, women, and children in the flood; raped Dinah; and plucked out Samson's eyes. It left Lot drunk and his daughters molested. It emasculated the men of Sodom and Gomorrah, and burned little babies as sacrifices in the hungry arms of the demonic deities of Molech, Astarte, and Baal.

That consuming fire of sin and death burned out of control all the way to the foot of the cross of Jesus. There the flames of hell encountered One Who couldn't be consumed! He broke the curse and forever destroyed the power that disobedience had unleashed. Jesus Christ broke the curse on the splinters of the cross!

Having cancelled out the certificate of debt consisting of decrees against us, which was hostile to us; and He has taken it out of the way, having nailed it to the cross. When He had disarmed the rulers and authorities, He made a public display of them, having triumphed over them through Him.

COLOSSIANS 2:14–15 NASB

The "first Adam" was so humiliated by the atrocity of his sin that he did what most of us tend to do when we are ashamed: he hid. The great tragedy is that we have been hiding ever since!

Men are great "hiders." We hide our weaknesses, and we hide our proclivities and curiosities. We hide our love, and we often hide our fears. Our hiding habit is destroying our homes, robbing our wives of intimacy, alienating our children, and frustrating our relationship with God. Our "trench coat mentality" has left us with collars up and hats down, draped in pretended secrecy and cringing in false obscurity before the eyes of God.

And he said, I heard thy voice in the garden, and I was afraid, because I was naked; and I hid myself.

GENESIS 3:10

Adam's words echo fearfully in the hearts of most of us who wrestle with our failures, foibles, and the demands of our families.

Most men avoid open confrontation. The same confident men who are so tough and brash and brawny elsewhere—these master negotiators of the workplace—find themselves nervous and anxious about facing the 110-pound woman who waits for them at home! Men are intimidated by the voice or rebuke of those they love or respect. Even abusers have anxieties about confrontation, and they sometimes overreact in their unreasoning efforts to camouflage their own inadequacies and insufficiencies.

Adam expressed this fear when he said, "I heard thy voice in the garden, and *I was afraid*" (Genesis 3:10). As you go through stress and strains, can you still hear His voice beneath the struggles?

I Was Naked

When the chief executive officer of the Garden of Eden fell off his throne and exposed himself through sin, *he was naked.* God's man of faith and power was *vulnerable.* That's right, I said the male curse word: Adam was *vulnerable.* Men avoid it, but women are forced to live with this feeling perpetually. They are vulnerable in the bedroom, in the boardroom, and in the labor room!

Some incidents and accidents can cause the palms of our hands to sweat because they strip us of our feeling of safety! We seek the safety of disguise and hide in the shadows to avoid vulnerability in any form—physical, emotional, or financial.

We men are uncomfortable with worship because true worship requires us to become vulnerable by expressing our need for God. We are great at saying "I want you," but the prospect of saying "I need you" drives us into the land of vulnerability. It puts us on a street called "Suppose." Have you ever been there? "Suppose others don't respond?" "Suppose I am rejected?" "Suppose someone laughs?" Many of us will avoid any route that might take us down Suppose Street.

The real danger is that some of us are so vulnerable when we are stripped that we are paralyzed with fear! We claim we are not emotional, yet we are so sensitive that a vicious word from a cruel woman can leave the most manly of us impotent! A cutting statement can undermine the strength, vigor, and vitality of even the strongest of men. Most women greatly underestimate the power of their words to magnify or crush their husbands' strength.

The angry words a mother hurls around her son can greatly damage his self-esteem and leave him wilted and insecure—even if they were aimed at his father! At the risk of shattering myths and losing our "me Tarzan, you Jane" reputation, we must teach our sons and daughters to guard the femininity of their sisters and the masculinity of their brothers. They are bleeding because they have been stabbed with loose words and angry tongues. These tools of cruelty are crucifying those who will be missed when they are gone.

Adam stood naked before God because he failed to properly handle his relationship with his wife. He failed Eve by joining her in her failure instead of acting to save her. We men are still committing that sin, and women continue to hope we will do better. We have merely *reacted* long enough, we need to *act*. God wants strong men who lead instead of weak men who only follow. This may sound chauvinistic, but it is God's plan, not mine. (See 1 Timothy 5:8.)

Have you ever looked back at your past and said, "If only I had . . ."? Those words reveal a deep level of nakedness and the absence of excuse or alibi. It is the recognition of your own responsibility in your dilemma. It is frightening to stand naked before God, but He can never heal what you are afraid to reveal.* It is time to deal with fear.

Fear creates extramarital affairs when men are afraid to confront unresolved issues with their spouses. It causes them to carry weapons when, down on the inside, they are wrestling with the fear that someone will see the frightened little boy hiding behind the big gun. The man who beats his wife is also beating himself, for deep within his soul he knows his life is out of control. His wife is wrongly receiving the blows that he is really aiming at himself. Beneath all his screaming and swearing, he is a terrified little boy having a temper tantrum.

Now that we have exposed the naked truth, what do we do with it?

I Was Afraid

Adam confessed to God that he had heard His voice. Adam's sin had left him vulnerable for the first time in his brief existence, and he realized that his imperfection was exposed and naked. Then he had to admit the truth: "I was afraid."

Many men are wrestling with inner fear. Most of us are afraid of intimacy and feelings. Masculine emotions have become the twenty-first-century version of "Pandora's box." We don't know all that is in there, but we have the

---

*This important principle of wholeness is presented in more detail in another book I have written titled *Naked and Not Ashamed*.

feeling we had better not let it out! We avoid the unknown within and cling to the false disguises of the outer man.

We have fallen in love with the empty symbols of masculinity—the faint suggestions of manhood provided by our jobs, our cars, our guns, and our women. We use them to validate and vindicate our bruised and fragile egos. We are offended and dismayed because the times have changed *without us!* When did we lose so much control? When did it go? How do we regain it? Whose fault is it? Like Adam, we want to point a finger and say, "She made me do it" or "The devil made me do it."

Let's be honest: We are afraid of losing our jobs. We are afraid of aggressive women who are pushing us out of line for a promotion or opportunity. We mourn our dying sense of aggression and fear our growing sense of passivity. We are afraid of age and change and time, and many of us are wrestling desperately with mid-life crises. The lion of masculinity has lost much of his roar. He is angry, and he is violent. Masculinity is being redefined without our permission—and we have become like pussy cats who are afraid to face their fears in a dark room.

Most threatening of all, like our ancestor Adam before us, we are afraid of our God! Our sin is uncovered, and our guilt has driven us into the bushes to hide!

We are dangerously out of touch with our children. We have told them, "I don't know, ask your mother!" so many times that they have given us a bill of divorcement from the "parenting game." We have acted as though we don't want to play, so our children have taken their marbles and gone to find more willing mentors. Our own actions have removed us from the decision making process in our own homes!

Lazarus, wake up! The enemy is stealing your home. Are you just "the guy who comes home at night and goes out in the morning"? How important are you to your family?

"But I'm tired. I work hard."

Listen, the enemy wants you to be so tired that you become an absentee father in your own house! Well, just say, "No, devil!" Lazarus is coming out of his sleep. His wife is tired, and his children are lonely. In the name of Jesus Christ, "Loose the man, and let him go!"

Like weary Jacob, who spent his wedding night with Leah and didn't realize until morning that she wasn't his beloved Rachel, we have failed to really know the women we hold through the night.

Have you touched your wife and fondled her, have you toyed with her and played with her, while failing to know her? How long has it been since you looked her in the face? In the beginning she was more than warmth in the bed and food on the stove; she was more than just another paycheck—she was the melody in your song and the aroma in your rose! Whatever happened to that marvelous woman who was the comforting blanket that shielded you from the cold winds of discontent? Are you feeling cold again?

Man of God, *you have been robbed!* The enemy has stolen the warm, giddy feeling of excitement out of your heart! He has snatched the twinkle out of your eye! How could you let him steal the chase, the pursuit, and the trophy of your loving, nurturing—and yes—your mutually vulnerable relationship with your lover and bride?

Do you want it back? *Fight for it!* Roll up your sleeves and reclaim your creativity. Recall the soft songs, light those fragrant candles, take those long walks of longing, and once again murmur passionate words in your mate's ear. Take back what the enemy is trying to steal from you. Don't be afraid; his devices won't work. Don't believe his lies—it isn't too late. Lazarus, come forth!

God commands us to stand, and He calls us to chase down the blessings and make the miracles happen! God came out to personally confront Adam; now He is out to confront *you!* God has been calling you *through* the things you have been experiencing! Your problems are calling cards for a confrontation with the living God you fear!

Are you afraid you won't be accepted if you respond to His call? Many of us act like Adam: we have prejudged God by assuming that open confrontation with Him will be negative. The truth is that without Him we are left trembling and afraid in our lonely weakness. Our attempts at anger are just a thin camouflage for the gnawing uncertainty and fear that are consuming us.

It is tragic that most men assume God doesn't love fallen and fearful men as much as men who "have it all under control." Look a little closer at Adam! He seemed to have everything under control. He personally named all the animals, subdued every creature, and exercised dominion over the Garden of God. Why was he hiding behind his bushes in Genesis 3 like a naked gardener in the backyard? Adam did not realize that God loves the fallen man as much as He loves the forceful man. If we allow Him to touch us, His love will turn the fallen into the forceful. Unfortunately, the enemy knows that will never happen if we keep hiding in what we used to control. God is calling us out of the bushes and into the light.

I Hid Myself

Adam was afraid to reveal himself, so he hid himself. Men who are afraid to reveal themselves like to give "things" like money, gifts, houses, or even sex instead. All these things are easier to give than *ourselves.*

Adam didn't hide his work; he hid himself behind his work. Have you hidden who you really are from those around you? Have you hidden how you are changing or aging from those around you? Have you hidden your needs and then become angry because they were not being met?

"I hid myself." You can't have genuine friendships if you hide your true self. If you hide, then your friends will love *what you do and not who you are!*

Suppose that for some reason you can no longer "do what you do." Does anyone love you just because you are you? Have you revealed the "real you" to anyone else? True friendship and intimacy are achieved when you feel so comfortable around others that you can be yourself. Stop hiding yourself. If you don't, you may lose your true self and become the lie you pretend to be!

Your loving God is seeking the man He has made who is hurting. God is your only hope, your last chance, and your only solution. Yet, instead of running to the embrace of God, you insist on hiding behind the ridiculously small, dying fig leaves of human achievement! Adam's little apron was falling apart even as he made it, and he didn't have the good sense to come out of hiding! You don't have any excuse either.

Are you facing situations that are falling apart? You may be tired and worried, but there is a God in the Garden Who longs to heal the hurting hearts of broken men. Have you heard His voice? He is searching through the dying twigs and crumbling leaves of your makeshift disguise because He wants to uncover the real you. No performance is necessary. You don't have to impress Him, and you can't anyway. He already knows every pain you are hiding, so step away from the bushes. Whether you are right or wrong, weak or strong, your Father is calling you.

Most of your jobs and relationships were built on your personal performance and achievement, but God's call is not like that. All He wants is you—complete with your embarrassment, failures, fear, and scraped knees.

He is your best Friend, and He longs to wipe away your secret tears, strengthen your heart, salvage your home, and change your life! You can relax with Him because He loves you, whether you are weak or strong, tall or short, thin or fat, right or wrong.

> *Greater love hath no man than this, that a man lay down his life for his friends.*
>
> JOHN 15:13

Jesus is the only One Who was willing to die to be your Friend! His love is secure; He already knows about your hidden fears and secret sorrows. He may not agree with everything you think or do, but He is committed to help you become what you are destined to be—spotless in His love.

Loneliness is impossible once you understand that God is committed to you.

Men struggle with commitment. When I met my wife, I knew in my heart that she was the one for me. Yet the hardest thing in the world for me was trying to get my lips to part and force my tongue to cooperate in forming the words, "Let's get m-a . . . m-a-r- . . . m-a-r-r-i-e-d!" Little boys seldom talk about "what kind of woman" they want to marry. Commitment comes hard for us males because we fear regret! We are afraid to think, "Perhaps I am making a mistake." I have never regretted my decision to marry Serita, but it was hard to make my mouth line up with my heart and say those unmentionable words, "I do!"

Many of us struggle with commitment because we seldom see it in others. We should look at God instead of men. He has committed Himself to love us, though we are a "walking crisis" at times. He is passionately faithful to a race of "living messes."

Face it: God dares to be your Friend. If He can stand to love you, surely you can learn to love the imperfections in your wife and other people (without using their imperfections as an excuse for promiscuity!).

God teaches us to love by example.

The need for performance and achievement is gone. Once you step away from the bushes and drop your ridiculous apron of dying fig leaves, you will discover how refreshing it is to be forgiven and accepted for who you really are. When you come to God in your nakedness, He tells you to relax: "It's just Papa." One of the most masculine warriors in antiquity unveiled the secret of God's rest. Read every word slowly and out loud to yourself. Let these words bring healing to your weary heart:

The Lord is my shepherd; I shall not want. He maketh me to lie down in green pastures: he leadeth me beside the still waters. He restoreth my soul: he leadeth me in the paths of righteousness for his name's sake. Yea, though I walk through the valley of the shadow of death, I will fear no evil: for thou art with me; thy rod and thy staff they comfort me. Thou preparest a table before me in the presence of mine enemies: thou anointest my head with oil; my cup runneth over. Surely goodness and mercy shall follow me all the days of my life: and I will dwell in the house of the Lord for ever.

PSALM 23:1–6

David is saying, "Relax, my friend. God's blessing is not achieved by your efforts, but by His goodness. He has done you a favor by blessing you because He is your Friend."

As men, you and I are reflections of God. We were created in His image and His likeness. Yes, you and I were created to reflect His deity and represent His wholeness to a fallen world. Isn't it ironic that we must be naked before Him in order to do it?

Calm yourself by remembering that God is with you. You may face struggles in your marriage and delays in your career. You may still feel driven to validate your self-worth by desperately groping for things, women, or some other unacceptable sacrifice. Whatever you face, take it to God— even the issues that you feel no one would understand. He knows you. He can heal the pain you hide behind your stern looks and rugged stance. Don't build your success on an ulcer. If you don't learn how to step away from the bush and communicate openly with God, then you will suffocate behind the stifling mask of false manhood and collapse on the stage of opportunity. You will reach the peak of success only to collapse on the mountain you spent our energy to climb!

Jesus told His disciples, "Our friend Lazarus is asleep; we must go and wake him up." He is trying to wake you too. Slow down and live. God is calling.

"Hey! Wake up before you begin to deteriorate in the cold mausoleum of machismo. Neither pride nor ego is worth the destruction of your potency as a father, a husband, and a man. Wake up and take My hand!"

Look for His Hand

Peter tried to walk with God in a storm and in a palace. In one situation he was nearly buried beneath the turbulent waves of an angry sea and in the other by his betrayal of God's trust. In each failure, just before he was completely swallowed up, *he saw a holy hand reaching out to him!* It was the warm hand of God Who was saying to him, "In spite of your failure, you are too valuable to Me to lose!"

God is extending His loving hand to every recovering man. This hand can usher a man right through the tangled maze of his boyhood pain and into the brightness of godly maturity and stability. Admit it or not, you need His hand! Times and circumstances are changing. If you don't swallow your pride, admit your sin, and accept God's outstretched hand, then you will perish! God didn't bring you this far to see you drown. Just keep your head up in the storm and look for His hand.

It is there for every dark night, for every tainted secret, and for every wounded marriage. The hand of God is warm and tender, yet firm and strong. He wipes away the hidden tears we never allowed to fall. He can raise and cleanse the dead things in us, and strengthen the weak areas we have tried to hide. His hand touches the turmoil and corrects the wrongs in us.

No matter what you lack, there is one thing you have! No matter how deep the pain, no matter how scarred your trauma leaves you, you are still blessed. The hand of God has lifted you from the storm and into His presence! He has lifted you from emasculated failure to sure manhood and sonship.

Your blessing transcends commerce and merchandise. It excels all trophies and temporary human accolades. You are blessed beyond the trivial pursuits of self-aggrandizement. You have ascended to another level. You have embraced the stars and held hands with the Maker of the universe. You will attain no greater success than that which you will experience when—through gross despair and trembling peril—you stagger into the arms of God. In Jesus, you have found a Friend closer than a brother!

CHAPTER TWELVE

THE SAUL SYNDROME

And the women answered one another as they played, and said,
Saul hath slain his thousands, and David his ten thousands.
And Saul was very wroth, and the saying displeased him; and
he said, They have ascribed unto David ten thousands, and to me
they have ascribed but thousands: and what can he have more
but the kingdom? And Saul eyed David from that day and forward.

— 1 Samuel 18:7–9 —

K ing Saul was the star of his day, the premier potentate of his hour, the most respected man in the kingdom. He was chosen of God and was a blessing to Israel. David admired him so much that even when Saul's sin undermined his purpose, David continued to respect him for what he had once been. Saul was the king, and young David had killed the giant for him. However, no matter how much David admired and respected Saul, nothing could alter the greater purpose of God.

Saul was not all bad; he simply could not accept change. His great tragedy is shared by millions of men in our day: It is the inability to say farewell to parting strength! Don't allow pride to rob you of life and strength. Enjoy each stage of your life, and when God says, "Release it!" then give it all to Him!

Graying beards, balding heads, and sagging triceps denote certain realities that cannot safely be ignored. They don't always signal a significant decline; sometimes they are messengers confirming our arrival at a stage where God wants to reassign us. (He has reassigned me many times throughout my life.) One warning rings true for us all: We become vulnerable to the "Saul syndrome" whenever we lose elasticity and become possessive and afraid of change.

I call myself a "fairly young middle-aged man," but I have to accept the reality of certain changes in my stamina, intensity, and endurance. (Yes, I am being kind to myself.) These changes are driven home daily by my five children, whose rapid growth is a public billboard that constantly announces my chronological "progress."

I am a reluctant but sharp contrast to my sixteen-year-old twin sons whose masculinity is awakening like a sleeping giant. Their youthful dawn is fresh and vibrant, and their reflexes are quite keen. They wake up in the morning as if they have just worked out in the gym and had a massage! When I awake in the morning, my bones sound like a breakfast cereal I used to eat as a child—the one that goes "snap, crackle, pop." I am somewhat consoled by the knowledge that after a series of stretches, scratches, and whatever else we all have to do but don't need to discuss, I can generally crank my "mature" body into gear.

When my older sons challenged me to get up from the dinner table and do a series of somersaults, I smiled and wisely said, "I can do anything I have ever done. It's just that at this stage, I need a better reason to do it than I did at your age!"

Seriously, I would be silly to compete with my exuberant young children. I am not called to *compete* with them; I am called to *cultivate* them. I can only be comfortable with that situation if I have learned to appreciate the various stages of life. I understand that this stage has different advantages and disadvantages from other stages in my life.

Few things are more pathetic than the sight of an old man shuffling his walker out of his garage to get into a new Corvette. The car is too fast for the hand that controls it. That's how ridiculous we look when we fail to appreciate where we are and what we ought to do in that particular stage of life!

Physical and mental abilities vary from person to person, but never be afraid to redefine your priorities. Learn to appreciate the various stages of life rather than fear them. It is not a sin to want a Corvette in your old age, but it may not be the wisest desire to pursue. The greater part of wisdom says it might be wiser to go for a *ride* in a sports car rather than to *drive* one at the age of ninety!

Ages and Stages

How old is old? At what age are we aged? I cannot tell you, and when I am old, I probably will not know it. My grandmother, who is quickly approaching her one-hundredth birthday, once told me, "As long as you can get out of a chair without having to plan it thirty minutes in advance, you are not old!" The chief concern in her mind is the issue of being inoperative.

Some people simply age without becoming old. They resist the temptation to become antiquated without being ridiculous. They dress and act appropriately for their age and physical stage, but they refuse to dry up! These are not the men who chase young women only to catch them and fall asleep with the smell of deep-heating rub in the room. These are men who have found richness at every stage of their lives and have developed an appreciation for each stage they have entered.

I can do some things as a man that my sons cannot do. I enjoy independence and the ability to make my own decisions. I am too old to be a child, but I am still too young to be an old man. This intermediate stage of life allows me to sit by the fire with the elders, gleaning from their wisdom and perspectives, and then enjoy the option of playing ball with the youth, feeling the fire of their enthusiasm.

My children are enjoying their ages as well. They have provision without having to provide. For them life is a pearl, still nestled in its protective oyster. They have the excitement of the unexplored, and they are intoxicated with the erroneous feeling of being immortal! They are also drunk with plans and excited by the promises of people I am suspicious of and not interested in believing. Their idea of a good day is the one in which they somehow get their hands on my car keys. My idea of a good day is the one in which they send me the car title and say it is paid in full!

Older men enjoy certain things that I cannot enjoy now. They can dismiss the daily duties and concerns of child rearing in their home (although parental love never allows us to be completely free of parental entanglements). If they have been wise, they can afford long vacations or retirement. They have entered into a stage of maintenance completely apart from the struggle to attain.

It is foolish to get to that senior stage and attack life rather than simply enjoy it. The men who are seasoned survivors and victors become a tribute and testimony to younger men and to the older men who will soon enter that senior stage themselves. We are not opponents; we are simply men running the same race at different stages and in different lanes. Let's stay in our lane and run on!

The bodies of the men who have gone before us have changed, but their past accomplishments and fruitfulness make them living monuments of excellence and masculine wholeness. They are time's prime collection of trophies. They stand in wisdom and look at us through wrinkled eyes with smiles that reflect pride and quiet strength. They are old lions calmly surveying the world from a secluded corner, or walking through life with wisdom won through decades of right and wrong decisions. *We need them!*

Each stage of life has its own challenges and potential. Somewhere ahead of me in yet another stage is the smile of contentment that I will display if I have handled this stage correctly. It is the smile that comes from knowing I had my day and I lived it to the fullest. I have been up to bat, and I hit hard and ran fast. It is the smile that is birthed in the contentment of fulfillment.

We can't stop time. Everything is moving. The movie stars of yesterday no longer entertain us to the degree they once did. Public opinion is fickle, and as many famous and fallen have discovered to their dismay, people will change their mind about you in a flash! One moment they throng you, and the next day they rush past you to enthrone someone else. Do you want some good advice? Don't take the opinions of people too seriously.

Saul struggled with the changing whims of the people. He was addicted to their praises, but the crowd that once roared for him now cheered for another. The enemy will often use our ego against us as we pass through the portal from one stage to another. Unlike Saul, you and I need to prepare for tomorrow financially, spiritually, and emotionally. Life insurance policies, wills, retirement plans, and investment portfolios are the tools of a visionary who understands that seasons don't last. We need to be good stewards of our strength and use our "hay day" to prepare for the rainy day.

Many great men have failed to prepare for the rainy day; they have thought they would always be as they were in their prime. This is obviously not true. The dominant Christian philosophy has been to disregard plans for the future and just "wait on the Lord's return." If you have that conviction, I challenge you to live holy as if He will come in the morning, but prepare and build as if He will not.

Children are not responsible to save up for their parents, but parents for their children.

2 CORINTHIANS 12:14 NASB

We need to leave a heritage behind us for the next generation. Many of us had it hard because nothing was left for us to build upon! If each man only provides enough for his day and no more, then he sends his son all the way back to the first grade to start all over again! God wants His people to build their wealth and pass along their wisdom from generation to generation.

Father, prepare for your son. Pastor, prepare for your successor. If you dare to become involved with the next generation, then you will always be a *part* of their success rather than *intimidated* by it!

It is a tragic waste for a man to leave nothing to his credit except consumption. Be careful lest you become a better consumer than an investor. That is the mark of a self-centered man!

Many gifted people bless everyone else with their gift, and then die poor because they assumed they would always be able to build back what they had spent. Their overspending caught up to them because they failed to realize they wouldn't always have the same rate of production! Their children are angry because they were deprived of their parents' presence in life because they were "so busy." Now, after their death, the children are also denied their inheritance!

God wants you to be wiser than that. Leave your children a spiritual and natural heritage. Whoever comes after you—whether it is your child or your successor—he or she should have it easier than you did because blessed people always leave a blessing!

I have news for you: As you age, your money-making potential decreases drastically! What are you doing with the daylight you have left? My dear brother, when night comes, no man—no matter how gifted he is—can work! I know this doesn't sound spiritual, but it is true. God has given us space to prepare, but He cannot delay His purposes just because we have failed to plan. I challenge you to prepare a plan for your future! It is God's will that you not only be blessed, but that you become a blessing as a man of God. He told Abraham that all families of the earth were to be blessed because of him! (See Genesis 18:18.)

Teach your children wisdom. Show them how to make a dollar and how to invest it for maximum return. Teach them how to handle money without worshipping it!

Do you have a plan for your life, or are you asking your wife and family to follow you as you wander through the "carnival of life" choosing rides at random. You need a realistic plan that allows for the changing ages and stages of manhood. Since you know you will not always be at the stage you are in now, you need to know how you are going to capitalize on this brief moment in your history. God's grace is giving you a chance to prepare for the next stage.

Build a foundation in the prime of your strength and productivity for your senior years to rest upon, otherwise need and bitterness may produce jealousy, anger, and frustration. If you are a young man looking for a surrogate father, be careful to choose a man who has included in his plans a provision for his maturing years. If not, he may later become jealous of you and you may both suffer in the bitter bondage of the "Saul syndrome."

The kingdom needs safe fathers, spiritual fathers who will not financially, spiritually, or emotionally "molest" their sons. The only way to achieve lasting security is to make provision for your future needs during the time of your greatest strength. Create a plan that will allow you to be led by God and not driven by need.

Many fathers who were full of wisdom in other areas failed to prepare for the later stage in their lives. Nothing is more disturbing than to see a man in old age struggling just to maintain a subsistence income. He should be able to spend time in prayer and nurture his grandchildren. There has to be a better way!

Let's Be Men in Business!

It is time for you and me to grow up and move our concerns from games and girls! It is time for us to make our strength count in the summer so we can be warm and comfortable in the winter! Saul resisted the inevitable, and he wasted his last years trying to murder the young man he admired the most because he was jealous that God had chosen David to replace him as king.

If you feel pain every time you hear the crowd chanting for someone else, then you are not prepared for the change it signals. If you haven't learned to be proud to contribute your strength to someone else's success like a good coach does, then you are suffering from the "Saul syndrome"! In the end, Saul lost everything because he wouldn't move when God said it was time. It is a tragedy to ruin early successes by failing to understand whose turn it is on the stage!

Confess this with me: "I will transform, but I refuse to transgress the rights of others. I am strong at all ages. I am vibrant at all stages. I am a loosed man, not a man on the loose. I am neither out of control nor out of conquest."

My acceptance of change doesn't mean I am going to the farm to die; it just allows me to pursue the interest that each stage of life affords. I don't want to eat food that is too rich, drive cars that are too fast, or attack giants that are too big!

Everything Must Change

And Ishbibenob, which was of the sons of the giant, the weight of whose spear weighed three hundred shekels of brass in weight, he being girded with a new sword, thought to have slain David. But Abishai the son of Zeruiah succoured him, and smote the Philistine, and killed him. Then the men of David sware unto him, saying, Thou shalt go no more out with us to battle, that thou quench not the light of Israel.

2 SAMUEL 21:16–17

David's youthful strength terrified and intimidated his enemies in the early years, but time changes things. Even David discovered that his original strength and calling had changed. He was no longer needed or equipped to fight as a warrior. He was *still needed*, but now he was to lead as a king. His weapons were wisdom and God's anointing, not a sword and shield.

Who wants to hire someone who lacks flexibility? Who needs an employee who will not retrain or adjust to changing times and needs? Who would expect a brittle-boned general to carry heavy ammunition crates in the heat of battle when he could accomplish so much more in a command post, skillfully directing the young and the strong with his white-headed wisdom?

You must be careful to love your Assigner more than your assignment. You must love God more than whatever He has asked you to do! Ultimately, the day will come when He will not ask you to serve Him in that way anymore. Don't allow your job, your marriage, or your ministry to rob you of your walk with God—because all else is subject to change.

Learn from David's mistakes. In the heat of battle, he tried to kill a giant just as he had always done in the past. He was shocked to realize that he too was beginning to suffer from the "Saul syndrome." His character and his morality were intact, but he had failed to recognize the different stage in his life, and it was almost fatal. Only the quick intervention of a younger warrior saved him.

David realized that he no longer needed to kill giants—he had been given young men who could kill them for him. *Excellent leadership always works itself out of a job!* We should always be training and teaching until one day we step from labor into reward.

Stagnancy is the enemy of progression. Keep moving. When you learn the art of release, you will begin to expect greater things. People only hold onto something when they believe nothing else will come.

And he shall be like a tree planted by the rivers of water, that bringeth forth his fruit in his season; his leaf also shall not wither; and whatsoever he doeth shall prosper.

PSALM 1:3

Don't allow your leaf to wither just because your season is ending! Fruit-bearing and leaf-withering are two entirely different things. Saul let his leaf wither when he knew his fruitful season was over. His season had ended and David's was beginning, but Saul could have prolonged his season by obeying God's Word. (See 1 Samuel 15:22.)

When the fruit-bearing season is over, you still can keep the leaves! Withered leaves signify the presence of disease, or the impending death of the tree. Do not allow the disease of bitterness to wither your leaf and change your attitude. If you are wise you will be able to live on the harvests and prosperity of the past. Beneath your branches you should see new saplings coming up as a result of your presence. They may be new trees, but they are still your fruit. Continue to prosper and produce through the lives of your offspring.

Men may soon forget the work that you have done, but that is their loss. Any culture that fails to honor its parents will not last long, but I assure you that God has kept a record. He will pay you for every sacrifice you made and all the work you have done. The pay isn't limited to eternity after death—you can expect rewards even now. There will be blessings to wake you up in the morning and mercies to rock you to sleep at night!

Walk tall and stand firm. We need your presence! You are the light of Israel, and a bright point of revelation in our nation. You are too important to have to do what you used to do. Sit at the fire of our counsels like a wise chief. If you plan the strategy, then we will fight the war armed with both the wisdom of the aged and the zealous strength of the young! Your wisdom is sharper and more effective than the arrow notched on your battle-scarred bow, and your calm encouragement is the fuel that charges us to war. A simple smile from a godly elder will exorcise the demons of our youth and stabilize the fleeting fear of failure in our hearts.

We all get to play on the stage and stand in the limelight, but ultimately we will hear the applause offered to someone else. As the crowd thins and the cheering fades, we must understand that the moving of the crowd doesn't signify the moving of God! Roles change and costumes are altered because the stage is on wheels. The world continues to turn, and focus changes from act to act, but some things always remain the same: the weaknesses of men, the power of God, and the continual changing of the stage.

CHAPTER THIRTEEN

WHEN THE CLOTHES THEY MAKE DON'T FIT!

L azarus could not loose himself from his bondages. There are areas in your life where you too will have to wait and rely on others to loose you. Although your struggle to survive is over, theirs has just begun. They may face a struggle just to trust you again. Their struggle may be to understand the darkest and most corrupt part of you and love you anyway. When they first see you come forth out of your pit, they may be tempted to leave you the way they found you!

> *And he that was dead came forth, bound hand and foot with grave-clothes: and his face was bound about with a napkin. Jesus saith unto them, Loose him, and let him go.*
>
> JOHN 11:44

Lazarus was raised from the dead, but he was only halfway home to freedom. Now he had to wait for his shocked loved ones to hear the Master's call. He was at the mercy of his mourners. If you are raised from a grave of failure or weakness, you will still be tangled up with soiled bandages, tender scars, jangled emotions, and unsavory affairs that must be loosed *by other people.*

You and I would like to think that once Jesus calls a person out of a tomb by the power of His Word, it is all over. It isn't. Jesus has one more command, and it isn't directed to the grave or to the one who was in it. His words are for the people who loved and worked with the man in the rags of his death: *"Loose him, and let him go!"*

If you have been through a radical change or moral recovery, then be patient. The very people who encouraged you are probably leery of you. They were victims too. When children have had to condition themselves to distrust a father they desperately wanted to trust, it is not easy for them to suddenly turn around and draw close to him again. They are afraid. They have been caught in the clutches of grown-people problems. Problems that confuse adults devastate children. Be fair with them. You need to communicate as never before. Your only hope for healing is honest communication filled with compassion.

If you have just come through major struggles or failures, then you face other battles with the after-effects or fall-out from your crisis. Your struggles probably challenged everyone in your family, and it may have made victims of your wife and children! Sin, compulsions, weaknesses, and pride can inflict so much pain on those who depend on you that even after you have changed, they just can't seem to trust you as they once did. Once trust has been damaged, the drive to survive makes it hard for people to again trust anyone who hurt them.

Wives who have ridden an emotional roller coaster to survive a husband's adulterous affair or an addiction to cocaine, alcohol, or gambling, are usually in a state of emotional shock. They have fought the devil and won, and now they have their husbands back, but unfortunately, the struggle can leave them devastated and wary. To heal fully, these wives need time and prayer.

This interval amounts to a "probation period" that can be viewed as an insult to a man who has used all his strength to come back home to a reception that is less than what he thought it would be! He doesn't realize he is dealing with someone whose hopes have been dashed against the rocks so many times that her defense mechanism now mechanically guards her heart against any possible source of pain—especially from him. He is offended by her raw survival instinct because he feels that he deserves a little more positive support. Inevitably tempers flare, nerves get on edge, and the already strained family ties begin to fray.

Men often expect to be given understanding and patience, but don't know how to give them! If you have been through an affair and your marriage is being recycled, go slowly! A lot of damage is on the inside, like a hemorrhage. Your companion may be suffering from a blow to her self-esteem, and your children may be wrestling with the pain of embarrassment. You lasted this long; surely you can survive a while longer. Just don't look for shortcuts. This healing calls for patience and wisdom.

This "after-the-fact" tragedy is amplified because it is unexpected. You have made the hard choices and the changes to overcome a problem for the sake of your family and yourself. Surely you'll be greeted with a massive celebration when you get home! Instead, you come home to tension, and your exciting news of deliverance wins only a suspicious noncommittal response that leaves you confused.

Your original "problem" is no longer the primary one. You have come through that challenge somehow and have returned to take your place once again as a responsible male. Now you face the side effects of your original problem—can the situation possibly be worse? Take heart. The same God Who gave you the grace to survive and revive will also help you work through these residual problems. Life is filled with entanglements, complexities, problems, tests, challenges, and rewards. You are a survivor. You are destined to triumph.

Years ago, it was fashionable to teach the church about modest dress as an outward sign of sanctification. We carefully taught our young people what they could and could not wear, but we never dealt with the desires behind the actions. We limited our emphasis to outward appearance. As long as the "patient" sat up in the bed, smiled, and maintained a positive confession, then we were satisfied. We basically weren't interested in the fact that beneath the sheets, the patient was hemorrhaging and dying before our eyes!

The church and the world are full of "patients" who are "all dressed up but bleeding inside." Yes, they are driving nice cars and buying elaborate homes, but they are still bent over in pain and repressed rage.

Men fresh from the grave of failure are often rejected by those from whom they sought acceptance. Like disenchanted and disillusioned Vietnam veterans, they survived the jungles and caught the last copter out of Saigon, only to come back home to homelessness. They kissed the earth only to find there was no place for them to stay. Where could they go once the parade was over and the lone bugle ceased its plaintive call? The drum roll stopped, the majorette packed away her baton, and the veterans of conflagration became the victims of rejection.

Silent rage crept up in the hearts of young men who left home while still little boys with footballs in their rooms, and came back too old and cold to be who they were and unable to become who they would have been. They were trapped in a vacuum, just as much casualties of war as their buddies who died in the rice paddies. It was painful for all of us. Any time men survive an incident but are never treated for the residual struggles, we all end up in pain!

Many good men have not resolved bad issues that traumatized them early in life. They have buried their pain deep inside and consider it a weakness. We watch them drink too much, get angry too quickly, or withdraw in silent bitterness, and we are quick to scold them for the *symptoms* of their secret pain. We need to heal the *cause* of the pain. A symptom announces to the body that something is wrong. The symptoms of residual sins clinging to the lives of our sons are signs that "Lazarus may be raised, but he is definitely not loosed."

Some physicians will not give painkillers when treating certain injuries because they do not want to camouflage the symptoms that help them more accurately diagnose the source of the pain. Religion has been a painkiller ingested by the church. It only numbs the pain while hiding the cause of the sickness! There is a distinct difference between religion and deliverance. The church has been satisfied to camouflage problems by depressing the symptoms. Caution: This was the problem with the law; it only treated the symptoms and let the terminal affliction persist.

For what the law could not do, in that it was weak through the flesh,
God sending his own Son in the likeness of sinful flesh, and for sin, con-
demned sin in the flesh.

ROMANS 8:3

The real problem can only be treated if the symptoms are admitted. The church seems too embarrassed by the symptoms to deal with the problem. At first, only the parishioners wrestled with divorce and remarriage. Now the problem has swept from the pews to the pulpit. The church has failed because it has tried to legislate morality through legalism. The acts of sin are merely symptoms of a damaged or sometimes unregenerate heart!

Unfortunately, *we are not comfortable with other men's sins, just our own.* We seem to overlook the sins of the dead. We forgive men like David, but we gather like vultures to victimize such men as fallen televangelists. We have a double standard: "It's not what was done that matters—it's who did it! If it was my son, I will quote one scripture, but if it was your son, then I will quote another, less forgiving text." My brethren, these things ought not to be!

How can we condemn abortion and then shun women with illegitimate children? How can we condemn divorce and fail to teach and practice restoration for damaged marriages? How can we minister to drug addicts, homosexuals, alcoholics, and other addictive/compulsive behaviors, and fail to prepare to invest the weeks, months, or years it may take to untangle the grave clothes that are holding up the divine recycling process? What good is it to get the former criminal out of jail if we won't give him a job when he returns to society?

Let's face it, our men are tied up and entangled in some pretty stinky stuff. When Jesus wanted to raise Lazarus, his sister protested and promptly warned Jesus, "By this time he stinketh" (John 11:39). It is simple: Anyone who gets involved with a "riser" will experience some discomfort. His problem is not fragrant; it stinks. Even after conversion, such men are often still entangled in bondages and weaknesses that challenge the local church, the family, and even the man himself. He has awakened from a situation of death only to find that he is still tied and tangled. To whom can he turn? Very often the man's wife is afraid, his children are insecure, and his employer feels burned and uninterested. We need to untangle Lazarus, and let him go!

If you find yourself in Lazarus' position, you will have to know one thing for yourself: God would not have awakened you from your sleep if He didn't have a plan for your life! He is the Author and Finisher of your faith. (See Hebrews 12:2.) What He starts He finishes. He is not an incomplete God. He is Alpha and Omega, First and Last, Beginning and End. (See Revelation 1:8.) He will complete what He started in you. (Philippians 1:6.) Many areas of your life will need God's touch and care. Remember that the greater your injury, the more lengthy your recovery will be. It may take awhile, but it can be done. Jesus says, "Loose that man, and let him go!"

If you are the wife of a man who has been through a highly addictive situation that traumatized you both, then I understand your pain, your fear, and your reluctance to trust again. If you really want to see the glory of God raise him up completely, then you must be courageous enough to release him. The greatest gift you can give him as well as *yourself* is the gift of forgiveness. Take the handcuffs off him and allow God to heal—or unforgiveness will imprison both of you. If you can't trust him, then trust God. Mature trust says, "God, I believe nothing will challenge me that You and I cannot handle." That's devil-chasing faith, and if you believe it, hell is in trouble!

If you really want to loose your man, then it may mean you will have to allow him back into the part of your heart you keep under lock and key! It may mean you will have to trust him in an area that once caused you great pain. It will not be easy, but it is important for you to experience healing and forgiveness on a deeper level.

Many women have hidden so much of their heart because of pain that they have lost themselves to the problem!

The man is out of the grave, but are you? If you cannot open up what you locked up, you are still in bondage to the past. You must not only have faith for his recovery—you must also have faith in your ability to survive and God's ability to protect you and all you have established in Him!

Brother, if your mate has trusted in your deliverance enough to loose you, you have a responsibility to guard her trust with all your heart! Nothing holds people accountable like trust. Many continue in weaknesses because they feel they have been "licensed" by someone who refuses to believe they can change. Some men think unbelief gives them permission to continue as they were. Sometimes we feed on one another's weaknesses. Some wives need to feel needed, so they nag and fuss, thinking they are showing concern and care. Other wives nag because of "the mother syndrome," and scold the man as if he were a child. It all feeds into a confusion that perpetuates itself in a cause-and-effect syndrome that isn't healthy for either party.

Trapped Behind the Bandages

"Where are our men?" children and wives are asking. Single ladies are asking the same thing. Even God Himself wants to know, "Adam, where art thou?"

Here is the answer: They are trapped behind the pain of unresolved issues, bitter divorces, and court decisions that no longer allow them to see their own children. They are trapped behind the "macho myth" and the empty symbols of worldly success. They are trapped behind drugs, in prison within and without. They are trapped in dungeons of unforgiveness because someone will not release them, and they are powerless to release themselves. These are the next pastors, poets, artists, and presidential candidates. But we will never hear their message, listen to their song, or benefit from their leadership because we don't have the courage to loose them and let them go!

If we are going to hear the new ballads or admire the latest painting, we must loose them. If we are going to feel their arms around our children and hear their tenor in the choir, we had better get the scissors and cut them loose! Satan trembles at the growing sound I hear in my ears—the sound of tearing bandages. Like caterpillars loosed from their cocoons, men are coming forth all over the nation! Some are delivered from drugs, some from pain. There is a riot, a revolution; men are coming forth from Wall Street in New York to Watts in Los Angeles! They are black and white, rich and poor, educated and illiterate, for each man has his own brand of bondage to escape. These are the "Houdinis" of our generation; their magic is in their survival. They were left for dead, but they have survived. They have come forth, and they refuse to live in cocoons.

This is the day of the *hue man*, the man of many colors. I am a rainbow man—a sign and a promise from God! I am black, I am white, I am red, I am brown. I am black enough to join your clubs, live in your neighborhoods, and die with a deed in my hands. I am red enough to ride my horse off the reservation and onto the college campus. And I am brown enough to turn a "green card" into a credit card, teaching my sons to buy the orchards and not just work them. I am all men made of clay, for one clay made me and one blood fills me. One hell taunts me, and one God saved me. I am not strange or weird, peculiar or different; I am the same clay—just a different shade. I am a man just like you; I am just another hue.

Neither do men light a candle, and put it under a bushel, but on a candlestick; and it giveth light unto all that are in the house.
MATTHEW 5:15

Satan hates us *hue men* because we are created in the image and the likeness of God, and our spirits are "the candle of the Lord." We light up the dark places. Where there is impassable water, we build bridges. Where there is war, we sign treaties. Where there is tragedy, we send medicine. How can men work alone to cure ills, stop plagues, and subdue nations . . . and then die behind the walls of their own bandages? It cannot be done. It must not be done. Jesus said we were not made to be hid, but to be seen. It is time to loose the man and let him go!

Every time I see a prisoner's painting or read a poem written in a jail cell, every time I see a junkie paint a house or build a room for the homeless—I know I am seeing what could have been and what should have been. Even in the eyes of the most hardened racist, I have caught a glimpse of deep regret. What has happened to us? Why do we allow the bandage to survive but leave the man behind it to die? We need to wake up shouting in the morning! It is time for us men to awake out of our sleep. We are not dead—we are alive!

We may be bleeding, but we are alive. We may have to reach our children with long arms to bridge the distance between us; we may have to wipe our own tears or sing to ourselves in the morning light. No matter what it takes, let the record show that *this Lazarus is not dead.* He has problems and pains with even more struggles and tests ahead, but he is definitely not dead!

Sisters, you've been praying for us and we thank you, but we are back. We have been in hell, and we smell like smoke. We are strong but weak, right but wrong, masculine but feminine. We are dominant yet passive. We are Clark Kent and Superman; we are a touch of all things. We are many hues.

We have no image left to protect. We have already disappointed ourselves, our friends, and our families, but we are no longer ashamed. We are too grateful to be embarrassed. We were supposed to be dead, but like Lazarus, our life has been returned as a favor, a gift from God. Again, He has given the gift of life to men who were dead. We can never be who we were then! We are being transformed constantly, and we will change colors before your eyes. Many-splendored and multicolored, there is a new man in your old man. There is a divine education in the illiterate and a holy ignorance in the intelligent, for we are many hues.

I speak to my fathers, my brothers, and my friends. I speak to the *hue man* whose many hues have decorated the dark places and added variety to the mundane. There is nothing that can hold you! There is no bondage so tight, no tragedy so overwhelming, that you cannot unravel yourself and go on!

Leap Out!

I have always imagined Lazarus *leaping* out of the tomb. When he heard the Lord's call, he was too bound up to walk and too tenacious to stay! He made up his mind to come out, no matter what it took.

I challenge the men across this nation to make the same commitment as we start a new millennium: Our roles are changing, and we are constantly being challenged economically, emotionally, socially, and even maritally. If we are going to survive, we must be able to hear God when He calls, and leap when we hear. Leaping is what men do who are too incapacitated to walk but too determined to stay in the tomb!

God is looking for radical men who will move suddenly when their freedom is in danger. Society cannot hold down a leaping man. Divorce, drugs, or financial crises cannot hold a leaper. Leapers just keep leaping. These men will not allow their incapacitation to restrict their response to God.

If you are not dead, then don't play dead. The enemy wants you to lie down for life and play dead. But I command you in the name of Jesus, Who splits graves open, Who causes earth tremors, and Who shall return with a shout: *"Leap out!"*

This is not the day for the sniveling, weeping, weak, limp-wristed, emasculated man. This is the day for the leaping, jumping, rejoicing, resourceful man! Leap out! God has a plan for you. *You can't meander into the move of God. When you hear Him calling you, do what Lazarus did!* "Ready or not, stinking or not, dressed or not, here I come!"

Tombs are designed for men who won't be back, and Lazarus' tomb represents an area of your life in which you have been buried by those around you who gave up on your recovery. Sometimes they place you in these tombs when they are convinced you will not be back, or when they can't stand the roller coaster ride to your recovery. If you want to make a comeback, you must come out from the dead and the dead places. All who love you ride with you, whether they want to or not. The difference is that their decisions didn't create the ride, but they must ride nevertheless!

The tomb promises relief to others because it removes the pain of failed expectations and the disappointment of betrayal that comes along with failed promises. You and I can understand their pain, but it is important for you to believe in yourself. If you are going to be raised from death in your life, then your feet must do the leaping! Lazarus knew that if he was going to rise, then it had to be right then. Even though his sisters felt that their brother would never come back, he had to believe for himself before he could act decisively.

Release Granted! Support Denied!

Do you realize that we don't heal at the same rate? Every person in a crisis must go through his own unique recovery process. You may be healed, but that doesn't mean your wife, your children, your employer, or your parents have been healed as well. It may be time for you to show the same patience they once showed you. As much as you want the support of others, remember that the most important thing you can do in this practical part of the process is to support and encourage yourself!

Marriages often collapse at the end of a major trial, even though the stress is over and the partners have survived the crisis. Just when things begin to look up, one of them says, "I quit!" Why? It is difficult and depleting to "hold on for someone in crisis." These "other victims" simply may not have the stamina left to enjoy the spoils!

The story of David and Bathsheba reads like a diabolical soap opera. Their relationship emerged from lust and murder. Their passion led to the murder of Bathsheba's husband Uriah, and spawned an illegitimate pregnancy through the torrid throes of their lustful encounters. When sexual excitement was over and reality set in, David remembered his God and began the painful process of repentance to overcome the disgrace and shame of living too close to the edge.

David lay before God in sackcloth and ashes for seven days, desperately seeking cleansing for his sins and healing for the baby who had suddenly grown ill. When the child died in spite of David's prayers, he was devastated, but he accepted it as all men eventually do; it was something he could not change. He washed his face, anointed himself, and went into the house of the Lord. David overcame the tragedy well.

Bathsheba also mourned the loss of her child, but her recovery wasn't as instantaneous. David had to comfort her. If you find that others are not as resilient as you toward the sudden changes in life, remember to comfort rather than criticize. This is a subtle way to acknowledge their right to hurt and, most of the time, this is all hurting and wounded people need.

> . . . David said unto his servants, Is the child dead? And they said, He is dead. Then David arose from the earth, and washed, and anointed himself, and changed his apparel, and came into the house of the Lord, and worshipped: then he came to his own house; and when he required, they set bread before him, and he did eat. Then said his servants unto him, What thing is this that thou hast done? thou didst fast and weep for the child, while it was alive; but when the child was dead, thou didst rise and eat bread. And he said, While the child was yet alive, I fasted and wept: for I said, Who can tell whether God will be gracious to me, that the child may live? But now he is dead, wherefore should I fast? can I bring him back again? I shall go to him, but he shall not return to me.
>
> And David comforted Bathsheba his wife, and went in unto her, and lay with her: and she bare a son, and he called his name Solomon: and the Lord loved him.
>
> 2 SAMUEL 12:19–24

In spite of the challenges they faced, David and Bathsheba survived. Perhaps it would not have been possible if David had not comforted Bathsheba, but he realized that his wife didn't heal at the same rate as he.

Unfortunately, some people may never recover from your failures and may insist on holding your past against you the rest of your life. What should you do in a case like this? You must make up your mind to continue your life even if someone else opposes your right to continue and openly abhors your place on the planet!

I often tell people, "Liking me is optional, but respecting me is mandatory! If you don't like me, then you still must respect me because *I am a survivor!*" Whenever you feel trapped by the opinions of others, reserve the right to alter the grave clothes they made for you and continue to live!

If you don't change those old death rags, they will pull you back down into the same rut you just got out of. The "trappings and equipment" of the dead issue can still cause problems in many men.

For instance, the drug addict isn't just addicted to the drugs—he is addicted to the economic and social system of his lifestyle. He has been delivered from addiction to the chemical, but his life is still entangled with his lost drug friends, his drug income, and the respect he earned among his peers. These things are not the problem; the drug addiction has been dealt with. These things are the "grave clothes" that go along with the addiction problem.

The executive didn't just leave his drinking problem—he also lost the environment in which he used to conduct business. Now he must learn how to discuss business some way other than "over a drink." He used to celebrate a signed contract with a drink; he entertained prospective clients with a drink. He used liquor as a tool of seduction. It dulled his inhibitions, freed him from his Ivy League demeanor, and allowed him to loosen his white button-down collar and feel human. Now he is at a loss—his entire sociological system was associated with his drinking problem.

The adulterer isn't just entangled in the affair; he is attracted to the "game." He is excited by the adventure that is sparked by the "fear of getting caught" during the stolen moments. The planning and the elaborate lying have all become a way of life. In the end, he gives up the woman, but she is not the only addiction—the adventure is gone. He is back to normalcy, and normalcy can be boring to someone whose system is used to running on the high voltage of the illicit.

Leave your grave clothes in the grave! Those clinging garments may be just as tough to overcome as the dead thing that produced them, but you must get them off so your mind can readjust to wholesomeness. That is the miracle of salvation that causes the believer to rejoice. *The changing of the heart quickens from the dead, but the renewing of the mind is the removal of the grave clothes.* Get them off your mind and out of your life. It is a tragedy when something has taken over your life to the degree that it defines excitement and self-worth for you!

God Has a Dressing Room

Remember, you always have the right to change if the clothes you wear are tailored to *who you were instead of who you are.* Seasons change, weather changes, and the wind changes both direction and velocity. Defend your right to change with all diligence. If God has given you the grace to escape the grave, then He can give you the grace to change your garments!

Now Joshua was clothed with filthy garments, and stood before the angel. And he answered and spake unto those that stood before him, saying, Take away the filthy garments from him. And unto him he said, Behold, I have caused thine iniquity to pass from thee, and I will clothe thee with change of raiment.

ZECHARIAH 3:3–4

It has been said that clothes make the man. I don't know if that is true, but I do know that *men do change their clothes.* They can go in the dressing room one way and come out another. Thank God for prodigal sons who teach us that the Father will tailor new clothes for the same son who failed! It is the garment of the Father that we want, not what others want us to be or wear. We want to be clothed in the righteousness of God.

I challenge you to pray for the tremendous move of God that is waiting on the other side of the "change." Joshua, the high priest, changed his garment while surrounded by angels. Lazarus stripped before his family. The Sadducees didn't even believe what God had done in his life. Blind Bartimaeus left his coat on the side of the road. He knew he wouldn't need it anymore. (See Mark 10:46–52.) Whatever you need to take off, take it off— no matter who is a witness to it. Do not allow others to determine how you see yourself. The clothes they made for you reflect where you were at the time. Thank God they don't fit where you are now, nor where you are going.

I pray that God will give you the grace to discover the new garments He has prepared for you. All your social, economic, and psychological systems stripped away, you find yourself needing to get to know the "new you." You're going through an adjustment that all men face at one time or another. I pray that God will see you through it with joy. The wisest of men are those who recognize their need to change and have the courage to face the uncertainty of new beginnings with a deep commitment to succeed!

CHAPTER FOURTEEN

KNOCKED NO LOWER THAN MY KNEES!

So I want men everywhere to pray with holy hands lifted up to God,
free from sin and anger and resentment.

— 1 TIMOTHY 2:8 TLB —

Most Christian men pray like wimps and brag like warriors. The truth is that real spiritual warriors are men who pray. Prayer is the most neglected and underused resource in the kingdom of God. It is a secret weapon that Satan has hidden from men.

Prayer can be a special challenge to men because of their tendency toward nonverbal communication. Prayer requires us to express our need, articulate our pain, and describe our desire. We men avoid vocalizing our desire because we fear disappointment. We think that as long as we don't acknowledge a need or a desire, we can live free from disappointment. We say, "Well, I didn't want it anyway." Prayer makes us confess desire.

When God made us in His likeness, He planted in our nature a need to be admired. We flourish when we are praised. One of the best kept secrets about us men is how much we enjoy being complimented. Our Maker loves to be praised, and He is responsive to the praiser. We men shine when we are praised by our wives, parents, bosses, or coaches—and we gravitate to them for more. We love affirmations that suggest we are doing well.

As an employer, I was shocked to discover that many men respond better to praises than to raises or other nonverbal rewards.

Every time I acknowledged a job well done with a personal comment, I was in turn rewarded with an immediate smile and eagerness to receive more praise!

On the other hand, as a minister I have noticed that nearly every man who comes to me for marital counseling brings up his wife's words: "Pastor, she nags me; she complains all the time. No matter what I do, I can't seem to please her." These complaints are so serious that many times the man is ready to end his marriage in frustration.

Prayer is a struggle for people who need public affirmation. The praisers of men are not excited about prayer warriors. They love great preachers, but they don't acknowledge great men of prayer. My friend, this should not matter. It is more important to move God than it is to move men! Great prayer only comes forth after we have been weaned from the accolades of others. Deep prayer cannot be done in public, for it concerns private issues that should not be overheard by casual ears.

> But the Lord said unto Samuel, Look not on his countenance, or on the height of his stature; because I have refused him: for the Lord seeth not as man seeth; for man looketh on the outward appearance, but the Lord looketh on the heart.
>
> 1 SAMUEL 16:7

Don't avoid prayer because you think you are not articulate or expressive. God is not moved by vocabulary, enunciation, or articulation. He is only moved by the sincere longings of an open heart that "spills" the burdens of the day across the altar, baring every pain to the power of a God Who can! "Can what?" Can do whatever you have faith enough to believe Him for and whatever you have courage enough to beseech Him for!

The stumbling, bumbling words of a tear-stained heart ring out louder in the spirit realm than the finest resonating voice of an orator whose vocal risings and swellings have been rehearsed for the listening ears of men. When you pray about the real issues of life, your concern is not that others hear but that you have God's ear.

Pray With Passion

We desperately need to come to God with the vital issues that plague us! These usually aren't the things we want played on a loudspeaker. Often they are too private even for our wife or children to hear. Do you hear a grinding noise? It is the sound of rusted rudders being held on course by the fervent prayer of men who refuse to lose their way because they encounter the wind and surge of contrary waves!

Our greatest tragedy is that *we left the praying to the women and the intercessors* while we went off into "other areas of interest." Those interests later drained us, and we wonder why we feel so depleted. What did we expect? Since we have abandoned the prayer closet, everything is "going out" and nothing is "coming back." Prayer builds back what life has depleted. It is neither religious nor rehearsed. True prayers are spontaneous appeals by faith-filled men to a mighty God Who hears and answers.

My faith is not in my mouth's ability to speak; it is in God's uncanny ability to hear and understand my every prayer. He already knows what I am trying to say, even as I grope blindly through my inabilities looking for words that seem to evade me. Prayer is a spiritual act, and my communication is oiled by the fact that I know how well He understands.

The hymnist so aptly said, "In seasons of distress and grief, my soul has often found relief, and oft escaped the tempter's snare, by thy return, sweet hour of prayer." My brothers, *if we fail to learn the healing art of prayer, we will practice the hideous habit of worry!* If we don't learn to kneel in prayer, we will stand in frustration. Our angry ranting and raving is only a telltale sign of how long it has been since we have had fervent prayer! True prayer is not bossy, domineering, or manipulative. True prayer brings domineering men to a place of submission.

Prayer is a confession that we are still limited men, and with that confession comes the same relief a woman finds in the arms of a strong man. No, this isn't weakness. It is the wonderful privilege of turning our humanity over to a higher authority.

Many men who have tried to continue the farce of rebellious independence from God are about to collapse because their strength has come to the end of the line. Everyone dumps their garbage on them, and they have no place to release it.

Beneath their religious facade, most men are overwhelmed and stressed. Many are secretly depressed and disenchanted. They have become their own god, so they must assume responsibility for the outcome of all issues. Praying men know they are not sovereign, so even as they pray, they are joyously releasing their stresses and confessing confidence in the God Who can!

Prayer is a compliment to God. It is an admission that we believe in His competence to deal with the issues.

God Is Able

On the natural plane, you never ask someone for something you don't think he has. If you do ask, it is only because you believe he is able to deliver what you need. God is flattered and blessed when you pray. The heart of your boss is in His hand. The government is in His hand. The surgery you dread is in His hand. He is well able to intervene in everything you or your family will face, but you must learn to ask!

Therefore sprang there even of one, and him as good as dead, so many as the stars of the sky in multitude, and as the sand which is by the sea shore innumerable.
    HEBREWS 11:12

You can discuss everything from impotence to emptiness with God. He healed Abraham of impotence when his body was "as good as dead." God healed him without struggle with a promise that stirred his heart and revived his loins. God's miracle in Abraham was so powerful that even after he had fathered Isaac, the after-effects stayed with him when Sarah died! Abraham married again and fathered an entirely new family! His body had weakened, but not his faith. He was old, but he still had vision and hope.

Many men stop living as they age. They lose life and potency, and the gleam goes out of their eyes. Sometimes bitterness creeps into their hearts, or they just become bored and aloof. Nothing is really wrong medically; they just lose interest in life and living. Secretly depressed, they hide their inner death beneath work and business and other distractions. They go through the motions, but the thrill is gone. They can't remember when it left them, but they have resigned from life. The flame has gone out in their emotions, their sexual drives, and even in their spirits. Only the shells of the men remain. The hearts beat and the lungs still breathe, fooling the doctor's clinical tools.

The book of Proverbs has the accurate diagnosis: "The spirit of a man will sustain his infirmity; but a wounded spirit who can bear?" (Proverbs 18:14). This man's enthusiasm for life itself has been beaten down by stress, emptiness, frustration, and loneliness.

If you need a revival of your passion, your excitement, and your intensity, then you need to pray for a revival. No, I'm not talking about the kind of "revival" that is just a date on a calendar or a meeting time at the church. You say, "But I can't talk to God about that!" You can talk to God about *everything*. In the Bible, even *old men* kept living, giving, and feeling passion! They did it because they were men of prayer. Prayer increases passion. It is raw expectation that causes the heart to say each day, "Today either something is going to happen to me, or I am going to make something happen!"

And Isaac brought her into his mother Sarah's tent, and took Rebekah, and she became his wife; and he loved her: and Isaac was comforted after his mother's death.

Then again Abraham took a wife, and her name was Keturah. And she bare him Zimran, and Jokshan, and Medan, and Midian, and Ishbak, and Shuah.

GENESIS 24:67; 25:12

Six more children were locked up in Abraham's "dead loins." God quickened him and brought him back to life. That is what God wants—fervent men. He wants men who are alive. Yes, we will feel pain and suffer the loss of strength, of youth, and of loved ones, but by God's grace, we will not lose our life, our vitality.

If you are not dead, then live! "The effectual fervent prayer of a righteous man availeth much" (James 5:16). If the prayer of an impotent man can produce a nation of descendants, then you should know that the prayer you offer in your emptiness will produce a world of abundance and joy!

The spirit of depression and emptiness feeds on fatigue. You can't assume responsibility for the decisions of other people. The truth is that you are weary from self-enthronement. Any time you spend time worrying about things you can't change, you will fail to enjoy the gift of life. You have to stop "playing God." You are all worn out from your do-it-yourself godhood. Turn over your life, your family, and your future to God. Do it in prayer and give God the praise. He is able to lift that yoke from your shoulders and give you power over the enemy who binds you. It doesn't matter what or who the enemy is; only the answer matters. Prayer is better than counseling or therapy. Prayer is life-changing.

The Priest of Your House

Most of the things we seek counseling for are areas in need of prayer. We used to be people of prayer, but now we seek the voice of a counselor instead of the voice of the Counselor. We have returned to Egypt. We want counselor-priests to hear God for us because we don't think we can hear His voice ourselves. We must know Him for ourselves! We need men who will pray!

You are the New Covenant priest of your home. (I didn't say *boss*, I said *priest*.) You need to teach your children about their father's God. They will learn when they see you bow your knees to Him. Your greatest message to your son is the one he sees, not the one he hears. Noah's prayer life as a father saved his entire family when God warned him about the Great Flood.

By faith Noah, being warned of God of things not seen as yet, moved with fear, prepared an ark to the saving of his house; by the which he condemned the world, and became heir of the righteousness which is by faith.
HEBREWS 11:7

Do you live close enough to God to hear His warning of pending danger? Are you close enough to your family for them to have confidence in what God has spoken to you? You can't make people believe in you. Respect is not commanded or inherited, it must be earned. You can earn respect by becoming a man of prayer. You can literally change the direction of your whole family—without argument or discussion—simply through old-fashioned prayer!

Your family needs to be sheltered under the covering of your fatherly prayer life. No wonder the disciple of Jesus cried out, "Lord, teach us to pray!" The man didn't ask the Lord to teach them "how" to pray; he wanted to learn "to" pray. The "why" of prayer and the urgency of prayer are more important than the mechanics.

And it came to pass, that, as he was praying in a certain place, when he ceased, one of his disciples said unto him, Lord, teach us to pray, as John also taught his disciples.

LUKE 11:1

We are emotionally overwhelmed and spiritually depleted because we have not learned the power of prayer. Lack of prayer has left us carnal and worldly, and we blindly make decisions in business, ministry, and marriage without guidance and revelation. We can never prepare an ark in time without a warning from God. The rain is pelting us because we have not sought the direction of the Lord. Mere human weakness should never stop us from praying. In fact, it makes us pray harder when we make a manly commitment to stop running *from* God and start running *to* God!

Our epidemic lack of prayer has caused a rise in stress, hypertension, and affliction. We stubbornly insist on bearing our crosses alone! Why do angry husbands take out their wrath on their innocent families? If we will humble ourselves and pray, God has promised to heal the very things we are raging about! Anger and wrath do not heal anything or anyone. Man of God, *I dare you to kneel down and pray!* Don't ask God to fix "them"; ask Him to fix *you*, and He will heal the land.

If my people, which are called by my name, shall humble themselves, and pray, and seek my face, and turn from their wicked ways; then will I hear from heaven, and will forgive their sin, and will heal their land. Now mine eyes shall be open, and mine ears attent unto the prayer that is made in this place. For now have I chosen and sanctified this house, that my name may be there for ever: and mine eyes and mine heart shall be there perpetually.

2 CHRONICLES 7:14–16

God promised to heal the land as a result of prayer. He promised to heal the land, the situations, and the things that pertain to the man who prays. In this passage, He specifically answered Solomon's concerns about all the things that were beyond his power and authority as an earthly king. God made it clear that nothing is beyond His divine power and authority!

Pursue God in Prayer

And as for thee, if thou wilt walk before me, as David thy father
walked, and do according to all that I have commanded thee, and shalt
observe my statutes and my judgments; then will I stablish the throne of
thy kingdom, according as I have covenanted with David thy father,
saying, There shall not fail thee a man to be ruler in Israel.
2 CHRONICLES 7:17–18

God taught Solomon about the value of being a man of prayer at the same time He spoke to him about morality and character.

Would God like to speak to you about the way you live? Is it possible that God wants to release another level of blessing to you, but He cannot because of your prayerless walk with Him? You may struggle more with procrastination and "busyness" than with rank sin. Are you so overwhelmed in pursuing things that you fail to pursue God? Perhaps you are so problem-conscious and self-conscious that you fail to be God-conscious. Have you allowed the reality of God's ever-present glory to manifest in your life? Do you live as though He doesn't exist? God forbid!

Character is one of the greatest assets a man can have to "accessorize" his prayer life. His godly holiness creates a barrier that hell cannot hurdle. A man's holiness honors his commitment to God. It is a form of worship and an expression of preference. It is a lifestyle that openly demonstrates a "living sacrifice" to God. (See Romans 12:1.) Anything less amounts to empty words and miserable failure.

Do you remember the prophet Samuel's solemn warning to the disobedient and deceptive King Saul? Saul failed to destroy what God said to destroy. Instead he told Samuel that he was "saving" the sheep and oxen so he could offer them to God as a sacrifice. Samuel, being a wise man of prayer, told Saul, "To obey is better than sacrifice" (1 Samuel 15:22).

My friend, *obedience* is the highest form of praise to God! You can dance and shout, sing and raise your hands all day every day, but you have no real offering for God until you learn to conquer your flesh and obey Him! The greatest offering you can bring God as a praying man is your muffled passions that have been burned on the altar of sacrifice. God honors the man who esteems Him more important than his own selfish human need!

I beseech you therefore, brethren, by the mercies of God, that ye present your bodies a living sacrifice, holy, acceptable unto God, which is your reasonable service.

ROMANS 12:1

It feels good to live above reproach. When I fail, I feel miserable and ashamed. How about you? I have failed miserably many times. But along the way I learned how to make holiness my objective. Some men have ceased to aim for holiness. They have obtained "written permission slips" for themselves; excuses to be weak, visas to fail, and a whole list of "reasons" to justify disappointing themselves and their God. The truth is that many have become weary in the fight for righteousness. It is a long, ongoing fight, but it can be won!

Confess your faults one to another, and pray one for another, that ye may be healed. The effectual fervent prayer of a righteous man availeth much.

JAMES 5:16

I confess to you that I am made of clay that has been hardened, misshapen, and so flawed it should have been thrown away. But God, Who is rich in mercy, recycled what everyone else would have discarded! God will teach you and me how to live above our past, our fears, and our incapacities if we will confess our faults and pray for one another!

Has your masculinity been scarred and your confidence wounded by the divorce you just came through? Are you still feeling pain? Have you confessed your faults, or are you still confessing your wife's? Whether she was at fault or not, *you can never be healed confessing the faults of others!* Confess *your* faults, and God will heal *you.* The enemy knows that the most effective prayers come from the man who is fervent and honest!

One of the first things we men need to recover from the devil's thieving grip is our positions in our homes. God wants us to step back into position in our families to perform three important biblical functions. Only prayer can help us develop true strength in these areas:

1. We are to guide.
2. We are to cover or gird.
3. We are to guard.

We Are to Guide

We should be men of vision who have a God-ordained agenda! Women often take the dominant role in marriages because their husbands do not present the family with a God-ordained agenda. Men have been "in neutral" for so long that women have filled the leadership void. Now they run the whole house. Tragically, this has made men even more insecure and women even more stressed, depressed, and embittered. We will all be happier if the men of God will pay attention to Habakkuk the prophet:

Write the vision, and make it plain upon tables, that he may run that readeth it.

HABAKKUK 2:2

True masculine guidance under God's authority always respects the often keen insight of feminine perception. To be the "head of the house" does not mean to be domineering and authoritarian. It simply means that men are responsible for setting progressive agendas and being firm enough to hold their families to the track. First, godly men must be prayerful enough to hear from God. Then they must clearly communicate the vision. Write the vision and make it plain!

Once you know you have heard from God, then you must be strong enough to stand by the plan. Abraham experienced struggle, but he continued toward the vision. He and Sarah made mistakes, but they didn't deviate from the goal. Sarah is recognized for giving birth to Isaac, but Abraham is remembered for moving the family away from the known toward an unknown land of promise by faith.

You and I need to move our families forward. I can't allow stagnancy because I have been conditioned to expect progress. I believe that because I am in the house, the house should be affected. God is progressive, and He is always moving, so you and I should expect perpetual progression in our lives and homes.

Then the Lord God said, "It is not good for the man to be alone; I will make him a helper suitable for him."

<small>GENESIS 2:18 NASB</small>

Helpers are only supplied to productive people. What can a helper do if the one being helped has no plan or activity? Women have literally helped build churches, run offices, manage businesses, and much more. They are anointed to help. They have been abused because it is their nature to assist. Tragedies occur when the men that women were designed to assist haven't fulfilled their function as guides and visionaries in the homes.

Guidance includes setting standards for children and enforcing those guidelines. My wife may help, but I must set the standards. Guidance also includes being a counselor and a friend. I am the shoulder they cry on when things are tough. I am my wife's resting post and my children's compass. If I do not affect my family in a positive way, then my presence in the home is a disgrace to God!

We all want to be appreciated, but some men who read this are married to thankless spouses and rebellious children. You may need massive renovation and repair, but you won't help the problem in your home by getting out of place in bitterness. Get on your knees if you want to see change in your home and feel joy in your heart.

We Are to Cover or Gird

When Ruth came to the bed of Boaz, he covered her with the skirts or his robe as a sign that he *assumed responsibility for her wellbeing.* It was the act of a guardian. He was promising Ruth provision and redemption. When Boaz covered Ruth, she must have felt warm and safe. She knew that he was a hard-working, compassionate, and successful man who was well able to cover her and care for her. (See Ruth 3.)

Why would you come into a pastor's office with an intended bride and not be able to cover her? It will be your responsibility to clothe her and provide for her and any children you may have together. She may "help" you, but it is still *your* responsibility to provide. Be sure you have a job before you set a date for the wedding! Even if the job you find is substandard, it is important that you fight with all your might to maintain your role as the "girder" or provider in the family.

It is a tribute to me when my wife looks good and my children are dressed well. It announces to everyone, "This woman is covered. She lacks nothing. There is someone in her life who loves her, cares for her, and girds her!" I want to set a standard of excellence that is so high I won't be afraid for my daughters to marry "someone like their father." No matter what condition that woman is in when you meet her, if she is yours, *you should make it better.* Your presence should affect her for good.

Now when I passed by thee, and looked upon thee, behold, thy time was the time of love; and I spread my skirt over thee, and covered thy nakedness: yea, I sware unto thee, and entered into a covenant with thee, saith the Lord God, and thou becamest mine. Then washed I thee with water; yea, I thoroughly washed away thy blood from thee, and I anointed thee with oil. I clothed thee also with broidered work, and shod thee with badgers' skin, and I girded thee about with fine linen, and I covered thee with silk. I decked thee also with ornaments, and I put bracelets upon thy hands, and a chain on thy neck. And I put a jewel on thy forehead, and earrings in thine ears, and a beautiful crown upon thine head. Thus wast thou decked with gold and silver; and thy raiment was of fine linen, and silk, and broidered work; thou didst eat fine flour, and honey, and oil: and thou wast exceeding beautiful, and thou didst prosper into a kingdom. And thy renown went forth among the heathen for thy beauty: for it was perfect through my comeliness, which I had put upon thee, saith the Lord God.

EZEKIEL 16:8–14

If you want to know how to treat your wife, then take a lesson from God's Book. God describes how He treated His "wife," Israel. It is not wrong, but right to be good to your wife. Other men have polluted us. They have made us think we were wrong to love our wives. Giving is a statement about the giver of the gift.

"Girding" goes far beyond the provision of clothing. We should "gird" our families with wills, life insurance, and health policies. Girding means covering their needs, whatever those needs may be. It means we must cover our family's future needs as well as the needs of the present. I know it is a huge job, but don't run from it. Do it to the best of your ability. Aspire to accomplish it through God!

Many of our children never completed their childhood because they were rushed to adulthood prematurely. They didn't have the "safe feeling" that comes only from a father's secure covering. They developed a hardshell approach to life just to survive. The power of a praying father can protect his children and family from facing the chilling and destructive winds of life without protection and provision.

It is a challenge to attempt to be everyone's hero. Turn the work over to God and make yourself available to Him! He is your unlimited Source for impossible tasks. Your extremity is God's opportunity. But God won't begin to work for you until you have exhausted your own resources. Get started. God will give you miracle after miracle if you are a praying man with a goal, an agenda, and faith in His name!

You and I are called to be *effectual*. We may not be able to change everything, but we should certainly affect it. I wouldn't want to be on a job I didn't affect. I wouldn't want to belong to a church that couldn't sense a change after I joined it. I am powerful enough to affect anything I am a part of. Aren't you? Of course you are. When you join a local church, both its income and its influence should be affected!

We Are to Guard

As a father, you are the defender who must personally stop every predator who tries to attack your home. Whether the attacker is spirit, man, or beast, to gain entrance it must face the awesome power and authority of the man of God at the gate. There are no guarantees that an adversary will not come. Sometimes, despite all that we do, challenging situations still arise, but it is foolish not to take every precaution to make it as difficult as possible for a thief to break in.

Many men are ready to defend their family from physical assailants, but few men are prepared to defend their family against spiritual attacks. Although they have fought off thieves and criminals, they are still plagued by inner guilt, private perversion, and moral problems. They are poorly equipped to build defenses against depression, suicide, child abuse, or other spirits that may target their home. We can't kill these things with guns, but we can stop them cold with prayer!

The devil hates to see prayer break out among men because he knows we guard our homes through intercession. We stand in the position of impregnable authority in our home when we cover our wives and children with prayer!

Man of God, you and I are not helpless! Even when we war against spiritual forces in high places, we come to the battle with unstoppable force and unbeatable weapons.

Stand guard over your loved ones with prayer. Let your children see you ministering through prayer. Prayer is a mighty tool to protect those you love. When you pray, God often gives direction and instruction to help you safeguard your family from attack. He did it for Noah and for Joseph and Mary, and He will do it for you.

There is a difference between a good idea and a "God idea." The "God idea" is conceived and nurtured in the womb of prayer. It is not a venture or an attempt. Its birth comes by simply acting out the plan God gives you through prayer.

Once you know you have a "God idea," refuse to allow anyone to intimidate you with earthly wisdom. When you have received God's counsel on an issue, that settles it. Don't let the plans of the Lord be contaminated by well-wishers who may not have the mind of the Lord for that particular situation. Don't be confused by the manipulation of others. Some men are so indecisive that they are difficult to follow. Men who never make definite decisions allow the enemy to shift God's agenda right out of their lives!

> *If you want to know what God wants you to do, ask him, and he will gladly tell you, for he is always ready to give a bountiful supply of wisdom to all who ask him; he will not resent it. But when you ask him, be sure that you really expect him to tell you, for a doubtful mind will be as unsettled as a wave of the sea that is driven and tossed by the wind; and every decision you then make will be uncertain, as you turn first this way and then that. If you don't ask with faith, don't expect the Lord to give you any solid answer.*
>
> JAMES 1:5–7 TLB

A godly man guards his plans, his wisdom, and his family from spiritual attack. He also guards the Word of God and the godly traditions he has passed down to his family. Train your children early to understand how to walk with your God. Teach them that you serve God, not some force of energy. You don't merely "believe in some higher power" because your perception may be off-centered. Stand guard over spiritual truth. Teach your children the importance of faith. "Faith in faith" is a cheap disguise for humanism, which is man worshiping his own will. Your faith is not "disconnected energy looking for some object to attach itself to and alter." Your faith is in God, and He has a name! He is reality!

Beloved, when I gave all diligence to write unto you of the common salvation, it was needful for me to write unto you, and exhort you that ye should earnestly contend for the faith which was once delivered unto the saints.

JUDE 3

A man of God tends to have strong powers of persuasion—even a shy, stammering man like Moses. People will sometimes follow what you teach simply because *you* teach it.

Make sure your message is solid and right. Many have neutralized their witness for God by saying, "Whatever you want to believe, it doesn't matter." *How ridiculous!* Give every man and woman, every boy and girl, a clear understanding of truth. You cannot make them believe, but you can make sure you clearly understand the faith yourself, and that you clearly communicate it to others.

A praying man collects a rich heritage. It is the accumulation of all the things he has learned about God. The special things a praying father does for his family ought to be passed through the curtain into the next generation as part of a godly inheritance! This kind of wisdom puts God in the very roots of a child's being. He will not be easily shaken.

Do you have a spiritual heritage? Are there any miracles in your life? Are there any things you know God did for you? Guard this heritage of God's faithfulness and preserve it by passing it on to your sons. It may save them from needless mistakes and sorrow. They will know what you know without having to suffer what you suffered!

And he spake unto the children of Israel, saying, When your children

*shall ask their fathers in time to come, saying, What mean these stones?
Then ye shall let your children know, saying, Israel came over this Jordan on dry land. For the Lord your God dried up the waters of Jordan
from before you, until ye were passed over, as the Lord your God did to
the Red sea, which he dried up from before us, until we were gone over:
that all the people of the earth might know the hand of the Lord, that it
is mighty: that ye might fear the Lord your God for ever.*

JOSHUA 4:21–24

Finally, my brother, *guard your heart.* The enemy wants to embitter and
corrupt you. Guard your heart against contamination by lust and loneliness,
bigotry and arrogance, and everything in between. Your enemies may even
hide in good deeds done for evil motives. Only you can mount this guard
because no other man can discern your motives and intentions.

If Samson had guarded his heart, Delilah wouldn't have weakened him.
Had Samson guarded his heart with the breastplate of righteousness that
Paul talked about, he would have continued to be productive in Israel. But
in the heat of his passion and the weariness of his life, Samson "told her all
his heart" (Judges 16:17). What a tragedy! Samson's weakness caused him
to pollute his heart with lust and loneliness, and he gave it to someone other
than God.

There are some things you give to no one but God.

Many men have given their hearts to people, to careers, and to ideals
(not a God idea). They were shocked when these persons or things betrayed
their heartfelt investment. Always reserve the deepest and innermost portion
of your heart and trust for God. To go beyond borders on idolatry and will
produce a pagan's reward of failure.

God wants your heart for Himself. It was the basis of your original union
with Him. God didn't appeal to your intellect; He asked for faith. The enemy
despises your heart because it is with your heart that you believe unto
righteousness.

*For with the heart man believeth unto righteousness; and with the
mouth confession is made unto salvation.*

ROMANS 10:10

Divine peace is one of the greatest security systems you can use to guard your heart. This peace is born out of prayer. It causes you to trust what you cannot trace. It leads you to rely on the character of God. A character cannot be proven; it must be believed. Nothing you read (including this book) will replace the personal experience that evolves from prayer and praise, and from time spent learning to know the God your heart has believed. There is a realm of faith that supersedes believing, and that is the realm of knowing.

For the which cause I also suffer these things: nevertheless I am not ashamed: for I know whom I have believed, and am persuaded that he is able to keep that which I have committed unto him against that day.
2 TIMOTHY 1:12

You believe with your heart, and the process begins. Finally, your faith graduates through life's experience into a confidence called knowing. Satan wants to stop the process because he knows that the people who know their God will be strong and do exploits! Guard your heart because there may be a Samson in you that the enemy wants to destroy!

When you lose your peace and become anxious and worried, you may make radical decisions that open up the door for demonic attack and turmoil! This allows the enemy to suggest threats of impending danger and leave you terrified and shaken, causing you to lose the guard that would preserve you in a storm. Don't give up the peace of God! Peace empowers you to go through a test without the test going through you! You may lose things, but if you keep your peace, you can regain them again. If you are going to be a praying man, don't give up the peace.

Be careful for nothing; but in everything by prayer and supplication with thanksgiving let your requests be made known unto God. And the peace of God, which passeth all understanding, shall keep your hearts and minds through Christ Jesus.
PHILIPPIANS 4:6–7

The word *keep* is better translated as "guard." God's peace will guard your heart and mind. It will cause you to pick out what thoughts you will entertain. Samson entertained Delilah, and she infiltrated his heart and took his secrets. Avoid entertaining thoughts that will destroy your peace. Whenever I catch myself rehearsing problems over and over, I know I am entertaining those problems. They will "cut my hair of anointing" if I don't abort them! How can a thought be "aborted"?

> *Finally, brethren, whatsoever things are true, whatsoever things are honest, whatsoever things are just, whatsoever things are pure, whatsoever things are lovely, whatsoever things are of good report; if there be any virtue, and if there be any praise, think on these things. Those things, which ye have both learned, and received, and heard, and seen in me, do: and the God of peace shall be with you.*
>
> PHILIPPIANS 4:8–9

If life has dealt you some tough cards, don't give up. You may be down, but bless God, you are not out. Strengthen the things that remain and go on. You will never survive the challenges of life if you make decisions without consultation. God wants to teach you the significance and power of daily communion with Him.

You are in the ring with a formidable opponent who wants to take you out right now! Your enemy knows that God has predestined you for greatness. He would love to destroy you with a single blow. But he doesn't have the power to take out a man who really prays.

Make a commitment to stand in God's strength, regardless of the challenges or questions life brings, and regardless of how hard you are hit. You may feel the sting of the devil's blows, and you may even wince in pain, but give him a clear message with fire in your eyes. There will be no towel-throwing in this fight.

That snake isn't fighting a limp-wristed, emasculated coward of a man who has no stamina. You've been to hell's door and back again for yourself, for your family, and maybe even for lost souls! You have been created and trained in the likeness and image of his worst nightmare! You are a resurrected man! You have been renewed in your faith, and you are firm in your conviction. Tell the enemy, "I am a man of prayer. I will be knocked no lower than my knees!"

CHAPTER FIFTEEN

LIVING LIKE A LOOSED MAN

Jesus, therefore, six days before the Passover, came to Bethany
where Lazarus was, whom Jesus had raised from the dead. So they
made Him a supper there, and Martha was serving; but Lazarus
was one of those reclining at the table with Him.

— JOHN 12:1–2 NASB —

W hen you pass from a death or a dark valley through the birth canal of enlightenment, God releases you from old ties to live in new peace and power. *You are a survivor!* God opened your grave of failure to prove that He wants you to have abundant life! Part of the abundant life includes knowing who you are and where you are going.

Lazarus, the resurrected second-timer, set a pattern for every scarred survivor who came after him. He is an ambassador of hope for every man who ever needed or dreamed of a second chance! His flame of life was re-ignited by the breath of the Savior and he experienced rebirth after death. He is "proof positive" that God can produce a "comeback" for every mishap.

What would you do if you were Lazarus? Your life has been snatched from the cold grip of an icy grave and rekindled in a leaping contortion of supernatural domination! How do you live once you have tasted death, then been revived to tell about it?

We may never know exactly how Lazarus felt physically, but many of us believe we have experienced his death and miraculous return in the spirit! We too were buried in a tomb and abandoned for so long that our decaying lives began to stink. Then we arose to the sweet voice of a loving Savior

Whose living Word chased death from our bodies.

Jesus didn't have to speak to bring deliverance; He could have delivered Lazarus with a simple thought. But Jesus chose to speak Lazarus' name to the wings of the wind and so confound the scoffers, the doubters, and even the tearful mourners. Immediately, Lazarus' blood waxed warm in His presence!

Jesus has also called each of us from our twilight to brilliant renewed faith. If you have never needed or experienced the resurrection power of His voice, then you cannot understand these words. No treasure you possess and no degree you display can compare to hearing Him call you back from the deadness of human frivolity! If Lazarus knew nothing else, *he knew that he was alive!* Are you alive? I mean, *really alive?*

You have an appointment with God. That is why this book is in your hands, and that is why you have stuck with it paragraph by paragraph, page by page, and chapter by chapter. God is out to awaken new life in you! Quickly, I want to share some crucial lessons from Lazarus' experience that will help you to live a "loosed life"!

1. Only Show Up for Jesus!

Whenever Jesus came to town, Lazarus made it a point to be there. Once you hear Him speak, you want to hear Him again! That voice that speaks life to the deadness in you is so powerful that the things that used to move you no longer have an effect anymore! Lazarus no longer cared to run here and there to places that had once been fulfilling. His priorities had changed. One thing was certain: If Jesus was around, then you knew where Lazarus was!

Many modern men would use a "Lazarus miracle" to launch a ministry or start a sideshow. They would parade around in public as self-proclaimed "wonders" of some sort. Lazarus wouldn't have been interested. He had been through too much to toy with the vanities of selfish aggrandizement. He was too busy enjoying his second lease on life with the Author of life to prostitute what God had done for him!

If you were literally resurrected from the dead, could you resist the invitations to the late-night talk shows and turn away the magazine photographers? *Lazarus was too much in love with the Solution to glamorize the problem!*

I believe Lazarus spent more time looking at the blueness of the sky and rippling waters of the lake after his resurrection. I imagine he swirled cool water around in his mouth on a hot day more than he had before. Even the simplest things are pleasures to a once dead man!

Hezekiah was a different sort of man. He was saved from death, too, but after his reprieve, Hezekiah destroyed the good he had done by trying to impress some heathen kings! (See 2 Kings 20:1–19.) He failed to savor the moments God gave him. When judgment was pronounced upon his kingdom, he basically said, "Whew, I'm sure glad that bad stuff is going to happen to my sons instead of me!"

Learn from Lazarus and Hezekiah. Unlike Hezekiah, Lazarus invested his renewed life in the favor and presence of God, not in the favor of men.

The great multitude therefore of the Jews learned that He was there; and they came, not for Jesus' sake only, but that they might also see Lazarus, whom He raised from the dead.

JOHN 12:9 NASB

The Jews knew that if they wanted to see "the man who was raised from the dead," they had to go where Jesus was. Why? *Lazarus only showed up for Jesus.*

Among many Native American tribes, if a man saved your life, you were indebted to him all the rest of your days. Where would you be if Jesus had not stopped the mourning and rescued your decaying corpse from the tomb of failure and degradation? Honor Him with your life.

I am concerned for the many men who have received a second chance. My concern is based on the fact that they can't afford to go back to the same environment that perpetuated the problem.

If you are going to be blessed, you must avoid the associations that helped the enemy to attack you! Even at the risk of being lonely and isolated, or appearing introverted, do like Lazarus. Only show up for Jesus. If it's not for His glory, don't involve yourself! This is the dedication that accompanies a man on his second chance! It is an attitude of gratitude.

Gratitude creates a natural desire to support ministry. No one knew the value of supernatural ministry like Lazarus and his grateful sisters! Giving becomes worship when it reflects an awareness of God's blessing! Giving is an opportunity to share the fruits of your undeserved blessing with a deserving God Who has been gracious to you!

God is my favorite "charity." I will always support His work because I know firsthand that His Word is real. The media can show me a thousand failed men in their squalor, but my faith will never be swayed. I already know that God is the Lord of failed men! I support Him and His work because I cried out to Him in my despair and He answered! How can I walk away with a carnal, selfish attitude after miraculously surviving my crises? Generosity abounds where God's grace is found!

We have a God-given desire and need to exchange tangible blessings for intangible blessings. Ministry does things in our lives that simply cannot be priced or appraised.

> For it is written in the Law of Moses, "You shall not muzzle the ox
> while he is threshing." God is not concerned about oxen, is He? Or is
> He speaking altogether for our sake? Yes, for our sake it was written,
> because the plowman ought to plow in hope, and the thresher to thresh
> in hope of sharing the crops. If we sowed spiritual things in you, is it too
> much if we should reap material things from you?
>
> 1 CORINTHIANS 9:9–11 NASB

This is a commitment that boldly declares, "I am a living, giving part of this ministry because I know it works!" If people want to see me, they have to be prepared to hear about Jesus! I don't want to go anyplace where He is not welcome. He is my friend, my brother, and my bodyguard. I only feel safe when I am in His will—and I am not the only one. This attitude is shared by everyone who has felt His reassuring hand grip them when their own nerves failed them!

> If ye then be risen with Christ, seek those things which are above, where
> Christ sitteth on the right hand of God.
>
> COLOSSIANS 3:1

Only show up for Jesus!

2. Recline in His Presence.

So they made Him a supper there, and Martha was serving; but Laza-rus was one of those reclining at the table with Him.

JOHN 12:2 NASB

Once you have survived a real attack as Lazarus did, you are no longer free to be some cold and indifferent Christian who is satisfied to toy with warm thoughts about some "higher power." Your faith reaches deeper than any abstract concept of a "nonspecific force" hiding somewhere in the galaxy. Your thoughts aren't fixed on some "big guy in the sky" or some "man upstairs." Jesus pulled you out of the muck and mire of life and you know it! No one else can satisfy!

Wherever the Jews saw Jesus after the miracle in Bethany, Lazarus was there too. He was committed to the Lord Who had brought him through. Most men don't continue that long. They hang around for a while until they are out of immediate danger. Then they seem to "find other things to do." Lazarus was too smart to stop "taking treatments" just because his condition had improved. Jesus was his life, so he stayed with Him.

Lazarus didn't stink anymore. His flesh was as sound as yours or mine, but he still remembered what it was like staring out at the weeping and astonished crowd through his soiled and rotting bandages! Even then he only had eyes for One. His memory of his life of decay was enough to keep him committed to the program! He was there for Jesus.

Have you been there for the Lord Who was there for you? Someone else is teetering on the edge of a grave, and his rags stink so badly that no one is willing to touch him. How about you? You know what it was like, and you know the power of your Master's will. Will you be there to continue His work of deliverance?

Lazarus lived at his Master's side. He was so relaxed that he reclined in the presence of the Lord! He felt comfortable in His presence because he was once again resting in the power that had released him! Most men have never reclined in the presence of God. Some even think it is blasphemy to speak this way. The truth is that once we have been through traumas, new faith and hunger rise in our hearts and cause us to recklessly pursue Him at any cost.

His presence also tends to preserve our resurrection! We cannot afford to cool off; we must stay by His fire. We need worship like drug addicts need dope! We are not drawn to Him merely by the high we receive in His presence—it is the pain we feel apart from Him! We only feel normal when we are with Him. What else can compare with that? We are marked and changed. Now we can relax only in His presence.

This shouldn't seem strange. Man was created to dwell in God's presence like fish live in water! Birds were created to soar on the winds, and plants prosper in rich soil. Loosed men need God's presence. Our hunger and thirst for Him lead us to give up our cherished machismo and worship Him openly in front of total strangers. We feel after Him like blind men groping in the dark. We push toward Him like searching, thirsty roots penetrate dry ground, for we want to quench our eternal thirst with the everlasting joy that is only found in His presence!

And [God] hath made of one blood all nations of men for to dwell on all the face of the earth, and hath determined the times before appointed, and the bounds of their habitation; that they should seek the Lord, if haply they might feel after him, and find him, though he be not far from every one of us: for in him we live, and move, and have our being; as certain also of your own poets have said, For we are also his offspring.

ACTS 17:26–28

Pastor, if we are going to rehabilitate the hurting men around us, we must teach them to worship. We must help them find the secret place in the presence of God and recline there. Worship isn't effeminate. Neither is it for wimps. It is for giant killers like David! It is for men of war like Samson! Give men His presence, and they can withstand Delilah. Give them His presence before they lose their battles with lust.

The presence of God is a healing balm for businessmen whose stress cannot be resolved in a bottle of Scotch. His presence brings hope to ex-junkies who desperately need to fill their lives with God and overcome the addictive habits embedded in their souls, lest the enemy come back and find the old house cleaned but empty!

Pastor, men are emulating you. If you are cold and aloof, they will be cold and aloof. You are a surrogate father to many of them! Help them build a bond with their God that cannot be broken. Teach every young man in your care to press into God's loving presence until His impression is etched upon his character. Well-worn and completely used, we all need to recline in God's presence!

Cast all your cares, anxieties, and frustrations on Him. He didn't resurrect you to rebury you under the old worries and stresses. No one can appreciate new beginnings as well as a person who really needs one! Smell the freshness of the morning and rejoice that you somehow survived. It is time to move beyond the dismal tomb in your past! Watch the sunrise on the mountainside, and rejoice with the tender blades of grass dancing in the wind.

This is your day. There were some who never expected you to make it. But you are here. If no one bakes you a cake, throw your own party! Celebrate what God has done for you! *Recline in the presence of the Lord* in the cool of the evening, when the birds softly sing and the day closes like a curtain. He will not fail you. He can hold all your weight, so lie back on Him. He is waiting for you.

Learn from Lazarus. Rest in God's presence. There is little stress when you are living free like a *loosed man!*

3. Live Beyond Intimidation.

Much people of the Jews therefore knew that he was there: and they came not for Jesus' sake only, but that they might see Lazarus also, whom he had raised from the dead.

But the chief priests consulted that they might put Lazarus also to death; because that by reason of him many of the Jews went away, and believed on Jesus.

JOHN 12:9–11

Nothing threatens a dead man. People only fear what they have not faced, and those like Lazarus have already faced the ultimate challenges of life. *They are seldom intimidated.*

Men of less experience would have stayed in hiding. Powerful enemies were not glad he had survived, but Lazarus wasn't moved. He didn't budge.

Fear no longer worked with him because he had looked death and failure in the face and walked away into new life. He knew the cold terror of lying with other rotting corpses in the tombs. He was familiar with the stench and decay of the decomposed and the sneering grimace of skeletal remains.

Now what were these men threatening him with? Death? What planet did they come from? Lazarus had discovered a Savior Who could call him back from the grave in a split second! Threats were a waste of breath. Lazarus had been through too many challenges to take his marbles and go home just because someone didn't like him!

You are a *loosed man!* You have already passed your survival course, and you have been through boot camp. You are a combat-hardened career man complete with battle scars, memorials, and trophies of your personal survival. When you face opposition from the enemy, you don't panic anymore. You don't even think about breaking rank or running away. Things have changed this side of the grave. This time, your enemy can feel his scaly knees knocking together. There is something very familiar about the glint in your eye and the cool, underlying strength he can perceive in your heart. It is ironic that the most frightening enemy you had to face was the enemy within. Now it has become the trophy you hang high in your heart!

Once you develop the tenacity to survive, you are ready to do great things for God. You become unstoppable when you learn how to buffet your body and deny your desires. Resurrection changes the way you react to fear and death. It doesn't mean you will never fear again; it simply means you will forever react to fear differently. Survival breeds confidence.

Once the blaring scream of fear has pierced your consciousness, you will know things that others do not know. When you taste the salty tears of bitter frustration and everything within you says, "I give up; I can't go on!" you will know things that others do not. When your heart has pounded its way through numbness and continued to pump blood although it seemed to be broken by the aching pain, you will know things that others do not know.

You have survived the terror of feeling unseen weights on your chest and have fought the night armies of inner torment and wars within. I know you understand. You have stumbled and staggered from bad news to worse news without breaking pace. *You are a voice from the grave of failure sent back to speak to your generation!* You have been freed from your grave clothes and given as a living gift from God to this generation.

You and I are "proof positive" of answered prayer simply because we are alive!

No one can threaten me with death. I have already been dead. I was pulled like a cold corpse from a rushing river and resuscitated on the banks until I lived again by the breath of the one who rescued me. I will not run and hide simply because my critics are embarrassed by my progress or upset by those who surround me! Like an ex-convict, I declare that I have served my time! Release me quickly and let me go—I am loosed!

Warning: *If you love a loosed man,* then pack lightly and be prepared to move quickly! He is not likely to be afraid of many things. He may appear to be rather impulsive, and he will live radically. He has seized life with the second grip of someone who knows he nearly lost it the first time! Don't even hope to hold this man down with a threat or a scowl. He has already met his greatest nightmare face-to-face and whipped it before he ever reached you!

The loosed man you love knows himself better than other men. He has been purified on the fire like liquefied gold. He knows what is inside him. He helplessly watched all his embarrassing impurities come floating to the top for everyone to see. Yet something more than the run-of-the-mill weakness, sin, and fear bubbled to the top. The heat of the fire brought his true strengths to the top. Heat reveals faith. He saw his fervency and commitment come up through the brew like a Rambo with a sweat band tied around his head! He has kicked into survival mode—a mode most men don't even know they have!

You will only understand what I mean by "survival mode" after you have been crushed, locked in a prison, left to die, or forsaken by others. Once you have survived that, you know that if necessary you could "dig your way out of east hell with a plastic spoon" as long as God was with you!

This tenacity is what I call "living loosed." Like a rock loosed from a sling, we will go against Goliath without fear. We were buried beneath the currents of life until the Warrior chose us and revived us. Now we loudly and boisterously shout, "Let it rip! We are *loosed men.* We are going somewhere, scars and all! Some of our bandages may still be clinging to us, but they no longer bind us. We are loosed men!"

We are coming out of the tombs to be with Jesus! If the grave couldn't hold us, why do you think petty politics or unfavorable public opinion could hold us back? The only threat we fear is the possibility that we will waste this opportunity and not maximize this moment. This is raw power, uncensored and uncut! This is pure and unabashed manhood, though it may be packaged in a small-framed man with wire-rimmed glasses, or hidden in a soft-spoken accountant behind a work-strewn desk.

You may encounter a loosed man disguised as a roly-poly bear of a man with a generous girth and an overweight stance! Don't be fooled by externals. Look into his eyes. If you see fire, he is one of us! We are alive, we are revived, and we are loosed!

The loosed man's strength is not in his frame; it flows from the holy fire in his belly. He is a survivor and a strange mixture of grateful tears and cherished memories. He is almost fragile. He is more sensitive than others who have not brushed the face of death. He does everything with passion—from the bedroom to the boardroom, he wants it all. He is kind and gentle like someone who was a patient before he became a doctor. If you underestimate his kindness or mistake it for weakness, you will be shocked to find that he is a holy stone in motion, a high-flying arrow!

4. Strengthen Your Brother.

The people therefore that was with him when he called Lazarus out of his grave, and raised him from the dead, bare record. For this cause the people also met him, for that they heard that he had done this miracle. The Pharisees therefore said among themselves, Perceive ye how ye prevail nothing? behold, the world is gone after him.

And there were certain Greeks among them that came up to worship at the feast: the same came therefore to Philip, which was of Bethsaida of Galilee, and desired him, saying, Sir, we would see Jesus.

JOHN 12:17–21

The enemies of Lazarus hated him so much that they plotted to destroy him. He was a kingpin. The devil knocked him down, but Jesus raised him up again, and as a result large numbers of people were being transformed by his testimony of the authority of Jesus! Lazarus faced many abrasive attacks because his life was a catalyst that caused many men to seek Jesus!

As far as I know, Lazarus never preached a message. He was better than a sermon in words—his life was a sermon in action! He was a "walking sermon" who created turmoil all over the region. People are generally amazed to see someone they have buried walk into their yard! The naysayers were so sure they had the last word that when they saw a higher power reverse the decision and pull life out of death, they were astonished.

My brother Lazarus, the enemy did not want to surrender you without a fight because he knew that when you were delivered from death, it would be a sign to every generation that they had *another option*. Christianity is the ultimate "alternate lifestyle." When we look at Lazarus, we are reassured that serving God makes a difference.

Great pain sometimes helps us understand what the fight is all about. If you are dangling over the fire doing your best to survive the crisis in your life, you may know *what* you are going through. However, it is only in retrospect that you will understand *why* you are going through it!

Show me a man who has greatly affected his generation, and I will show you a man who has felt the pain and confinement of shackles and tribulation. The devil knew that if that man ever got loosed, he would do serious damage to the plans of hell. He was right!

It encourages me to know that I am under serious attack because I am greatly feared. When I was a little boy, I used to get into fights with other boys once in awhile. In those days, if an opponent was afraid, he would bring a lot of weapons with him to the "appointed place" after school. (Where I grew up, a weapon was a stick or a slingshot; how things have changed!) Your opponent's preparation indicates how tough he thinks you are. If you are a real wimp, he will hardly prepare for the fight because he figures you will be no problem. If Satan has sent his heavy artillery after you, take heart! You're going against a scared devil! He is deathly afraid of a *loosed man!*

Your enemy wants to have you and all that you represent, but he probably wishes he had tried to take you sooner, before you caused such a ruckus! Now some of the most unlikely men will seek Jesus because of you. Even some of your old drinking buddies and partners in crime will come around and say, "Sir, we would see Jesus!" You are the seed and they are your harvest! Don't stop until you reproduce after your own kind!

And the Lord said, Simon, Simon, behold, Satan hath desired to have
you, that he may sift you as wheat: but I have prayed for thee, that thy
faith fail not: and when thou art converted, strengthen thy brethren.
LUKE 22:31–32

Satan wanted you. He wasn't fooling around. He wanted to "take you out" and sift you in the wind. It is frightening to think how close he came to doing it! *But God,* Who is rich in mercy, saved you.

Other men had buried you under a judgment or failure. Your closest friends had given up; it was over. Then Jesus prayed and called you out of your tomb so you could sit at His table! He was so confident in His prayer that He didn't say, "*If* thou art converted," He said, "*When* thou art converted." God never says "*if*" when He talks about your destiny.

Even during the darkest moments in your life, whether you faced suicide, bankruptcy, depression, or scandal, God simply looked at you with love in His eyes and said, "*when.*" The only questions left about you lurk in the limited minds of men. God has settled it in heaven. He said, "*When.*"

Brother Lazarus, you have been through hell, but you made it! You faced a crushing challenge, but you survived. You were stinking, but God stopped the decay so you could see another day. By His grace, you are a living epistle. Every time anyone sees you, your life shouts out, "God is real!" Because you were dead and are now fully alive in body, soul, and spirit, you will see massive revival in your generation! The enemy wanted to terminate your joy, peace, and prosperity, but he has failed. Now he is in despair, for you are a loosed man with nothing to fear!

Your mission is clear: Go back into the enemy's camp! Infiltrate the office, the golf course, the country club, the basketball court, and the drunken family reunion to bring other men to the light. They saw you in your frustration, now let them see your resurrection! Let them know you made it. Tell them Who woke you out of your sleep and unraveled your problems.

Jesus told Simon, "When thou are converted, strengthen thy brethren." A loosed man always reaches back for others. He reaches back for his father, his wife, his family, and his friends. Deliverance without evangelism is just plain selfishness. Loosed men expect big harvests. You endured extreme attacks to pay the price for the harvest—it is time to reap the rewards!

There is a sharp edge of anointing on your testimony, and the fields are white with the harvest! Fear no man, fear no devil! Boldly tell the truth! Preach the gospel to the poor, heal the brokenhearted, deliver the captives, and enlighten the blind! You have nothing to lose and everything to gain—what are you waiting for? I see another Lazarus leaping into the morning light!

A FINAL WORD

As I finished writing the last page of this book, I wanted to add something even more personal, a special word from my heart to yours—man to man. I pray that it will bless you and equip you to go on, grow strong, and achieve excellence!

Dear Brother,

I admire you—even though I see you clearly. I see your strengths and your weaknesses. It doesn't matter which is which, because I admire you for accepting the challenge of life and rising to your feet in the morning light! You heard the blaring of the trumpet and you arose. You knew the night was over, and sleeping is for men who have nowhere to go.

I am writing to you about the day you face. Wake up singing. Rejoice that you are alive. Before you complain about your environment, listen closely to what you hear as you stand, stretch, and boldly enter into the brightness of the day.

Can you hear the thumping of life beating firmly in your chest? Beneath the rumbling drumbeat of your relentless heart are miles of arterial highways routing blood through every vein and filling every cell with life. Oxygen is racing beneath your skin, feeding the feverish demand of a strong body. You are the first computer, filled with a "soft" hard drive and invisible software, fueled without electricity, fully self-contained and compact, absorbing and sorting billions of megabytes of data. You are awesome and fearfully made.

You have trained in the fields of life and have been educated through hard knocks. You are an ardent lover giving tender care to the broken and fragmented. You touch the heart and caress the soul. Your arms were made to reach around the sorrows and hug the fainting. Like jumper cables hooked to a battery, you give new life and energy to those you touch.

You are a preacher proclaiming a strong work and making mighty statements. Even when your lips are closed, we hear you speak. We are convicted and instructed by the gleam of your eye. We are exhorted and uplifted by the iridescent flame that refuses to be extinguished. Man, I love to hear you!

You are an artist who doesn't need a brush. You have captured great moments without cameras and timeless thoughts without a pen. You discern with great judgment. You protect and preserve your own like a lion on the prowl. You are full of fire that cannot be extinguished.

Live long, my brother. Grow great! Do all that is in your heart. This is your moment! Please don't miss it complaining about problems. Don't be distracted by the trivial pursuits of this world. Notice the beating of your own heart and the heaving of your lungs in your chest. When in doubt, check it out: You are alive!

No matter what constrained you, no matter what tried to restrain you and keep you in the grave—death cannot hold you. Like Jesus, you have risen and you are back. So say to your soul, "Boast in the Lord!"

Why not be proud to be alive? You could have been a dead man. You could have been a drunk man. You could have been a weak man, but not you. You are too tough for that.

I admire you because when I see you raise your hands in worship, and when I see you smiling through watery eyes, I know . . . Although I may never know you personally or get to hear your story, I can see it by your praise. I can hear it in your voice. There is no doubt about it: You are a loosed man!

You are already in motion. You are already in flight. Straighten your shoulders, hold up your head, flex your arms, and with all your might and all your strength, go for it!

The world is waiting for a man. The woman is waiting for a man. Even the children are waiting for a man. They won't settle for just any man, they are waiting for a loosed man. The world is waiting for *you!*

I believe in you,

Bishop J.

P.S. Now God Himself has asked a hard question that has taken us a long time to answer. He asked the first man, "Where art thou?" He couldn't answer, and we couldn't either. It was embarrassing, but in retrospect, we have realized the truth. We have mumbled and bumbled for thousands of years, avoiding an answer that would be shockingly revealing. We wanted to answer, but were ashamed to respond because we were in such a mess. Now, after all that has happened, we are finally ready.

Thank You, Lord, for Your patience. Now we can answer what You asked us then: "Where art thou?" Our answer comes leaping up fresh from the grave! We have to stand up tall to say it, Lord. Our answer is clear in the light of our new day: "We are here!"

A SELECTION OF PRAYERS FOR MEN

Men ought always to pray, and not to faint.

— LUKE 18:1 —

Prayer For Purity

Father,

I have discovered my own wretchedness. I realize that there are areas in me that need to be corrected. I refuse to lay the blame on others, and I repent and turn from these things as a committed act of my will.

Lord, give me grace to overcome every lustful addiction that would enslave me. I need Your touch to cleanse me. I want You to wash my thoughts, my deeds, and even my memories so that I can serve You with purity and holiness.

I know You died to deliver me from every bondage, and it is my desire to be free. Thank You for Your Word, which cleanses me from all unrighteousness. I set my heart to renew my mind and hide Your Word in my heart so that I can serve You without guilt, in the freedom and power of Your Holy Spirit.

In Jesus' name, Amen.

Prayer for Salvation

Dear Lord,

Have mercy on me, a sinner. I confess my sins. I am not proud of them, but I acknowledge them. I thank You for dying to reclaim men who have fallen and are in need of forgiveness. I am a man in need of forgiveness, and I ask You to forgive me and cleanse me of my unrighteousness. Make me the man You want me to be, the man You have purposed me to be from the beginning of time.

Lord Jesus, I accept You as my personal Savior. Thank You for saving every personal area of struggle in my life. I rejoice that Your blood cleanses my sins even while I am praying this prayer, and I am filled with the strength of your Holy Spirit. I dedicate my life to You and vow to live every day according to Your Word.

Thank You for giving me a second chance. As Your Spirit and Word reign in my life, I rise up above my past, I rise up above my dilemmas, and I rise up to serve You the rest of my life, in Jesus' mighty name! Amen.

Prayer for Restoration in My Marriage

Dear Lord,

I come to You this day because I know You are a God of restoration and are able to put back into place everything the enemy has tried to destroy. I thank You, Lord, for my marriage and for giving my relationship with my wife a new beginning.

Forgive me, Lord, for my failure to be what You have always meant me to be, and take my life—every part of me—and begin the restoration there. Restore me to the level that I need to be in order to fulfill my role as a biblical husband. Restore my confidence, and heal everything inside me that says, "I can't do it."

Thank You, Lord, for giving me the strength and courage to make a total commitment to You right now to keep my marriage vows and be the faithful and loving husband my wife needs. I know that with Your help I can be the husband You want me to be and have the marriage You want me to have.

Right now, Father, I forgive my wife for the times she has hurt me, and I ask You to heal any wounds from those times. I release any bitterness and hurt to You and make a commitment never to take them back. I also pray for my wife, that she might forgive me for any hurt I have caused her, and that her wounds would be healed as well.

Thank You, Father, for a complete restoration of our marriage, a fresh awakening of our love for one another, and for giving us a powerful plan and purpose for our life together! In Jesus' name I pray, Amen.

Prayer for a Prisoner

My gracious and loving Father,

I come to You right now in prayer. I thank You, God, that even though I have made many mistakes in my life, You are a God of forgiveness. Today I ask You to forgive me and I make a commitment to dedicate my life to You, to do Your will and follow Your plan and purpose for me.

Father, I know You have forgiven me of all my wrongdoing, but I am having trouble forgiving myself. Help me, God, to understand that I can't change what has already happened but I can change what will happen in my future.

At this moment, I surrender all my bitterness, loneliness, and my low self-esteem to You, Father. I forgive all those who have hurt me and forgive myself for my mistakes and sins of the past.

By Your grace, Lord, I will use this time of imprisonment as a time of study, prayer, and personal commitment to You. Instead of allowing this time of my life to be the crushing blow of defeat, I will use it as a stepping-stone to higher accomplishments. I also ask You to prepare me to face society and assume responsibility when I am released, as one who has learned his lesson and benefited from his mistakes.

Most of all, thank You, God, for loving me and looking beyond my faults to see my need. In Jesus' name, Amen.

Prayer for the Businessman

Dear Lord,

Today I ask You to please give me wisdom in all my decisions, knowledge in all my transactions, and understanding in all my dealings as they pertain to my business. Keep me, God, from being deceived into illegal transactions, and I set my heart to walk in integrity, no matter what monetary potential is available. I know the only way I can be a prosperous businessman is to remain pure in my motives and conduct my business according to Your Word. I commit myself to do that now, Lord.

Help me to turn quay from all temptations to climb the ladder of success by stepping on others as I go up. I pray that I never become so engulfed with my work that I forget my primary purpose in You—to minister to those around me. I thank You for Your supernatural strength working in me that overcomes all stress and anxiety.

Finally, I thank You, God, for blessing my business. I know that as I put You first in every area of my life, as well as my profession, You and I stand in a covenant relationship together. Because You and I are partners, I expect the windows of opportunity to open up to my business and Your great blessings to break forth in my life. Then I can and will bless others and give toward the preaching and teaching of the Gospel.

Thank You for helping me see this great truth! In Jesus' name, Amen.

Prayer for the Backslider

Dear Lord,

I come to You today thanking You for Your loving-kindness. I thank You that, even though I have made some wrong decisions in my life which have led me away from You and caused me to be unfaithful, Your faith still abides in me and You still love me.

Though my fellowship has been broken with You, Jesus is still my Lord and Savior. I am sorry for all of my sins. I am tired of living in remorse for what I have done, and I repent of my sins and ask your forgiveness. I thank You that Your forgiveness and mercy do not depend on my good works, but are available to me simply through Your grace. I am so glad Your mercy endures forever and is new every morning!

Thank You, God, for forgiving me and receiving me back into fellowship with You. I make a wholehearted commitment to You and to Your Word this day. Thank You for giving me Your Spirit, Who gives me the divine strength and grace to stay away from those things in my life that caused me to fall before.

Help me to take one day at a time, trusting Your grace and mercy to see me through every moment, every temptation, and every trial. Thank You for restoring the fullness of Your joy to my heart and soul. As I walk in fellowship with You, I know every weak area that I feel insecure and unfulfilled in will be made strong by Your courage and wisdom.

Thank You, God, for restoration of our fellowship and for giving me back my joy as Your child. In Jesus' name, Amen.

Prayer for the Single Man

Most gracious and loving Heavenly Father,

I come into Your presence today thanking You that I am "somebody" in Your eyes. I thank You that I am happy and prosperous as a single man because of Your favor and blessing on my life.

I ask You, Lord, to totally saturate my life with Your presence, to give me direction, and to help me find my purpose in You. I feel a destiny and a future deep inside me that is just waiting to manifest itself in my life, and I am completely secure and confident in who I am in You.

I thank You, Father, for Your Holy Spirit, Who lives inside me and gives me the supernatural strength to abstain from any type of premarital sexual relationship, which would only destroy the intimacy and fellowship I enjoy with You and hinder my future relationship with my wife.

Help me always to be open-minded concerning all relationships and to find Your will and do what is right in them, particularly in the marriage relationship. I pray that if the day should come for me to marry, You would bring me the wife You want me to have, just as You brought Eve to Adam.

Until that day, Father, I thank You that whenever I get lonely I can talk to You in prayer and read Your Word. Thank You, God, for being my friend! In Jesus' name I pray. Amen.

T.D. Jakes

SO YOU CALL YOURSELF A MAN?

CONTENTS

GETTING TO JESUS . . . NO MATTER WHAT IT TAKES!

TIME FOR A NEW LEVEL OF RECONCILIATION AND HEALING!

And they sung a new song, saying, Thou art worthy . . . for thou wast slain, and hast redeemed us to God by thy blood out of every kindred, and tongue, and people, and nation.

REVELATION 5:9

The church that I pastor is multiracial and multicultural. I believe that is part of God's plan for reconciliation in these last days. I don't believe you can have multiplication if you only have duplication of like elements. Multiplication is born of reconciliation among those with differences.

God loves a multiplicity of people and He blesses people in a multiplicity of ways. We must be willing to accept the different ways in which people receive blessings and then thank God for them. We must be willing to accept different ways of worshiping the Lord Jesus Christ—one may dance, another may bow, yet another may stand and shout. He is One Lord, but He has created many people.

We must never bring people to Christ and then insist to them, "Now, be just like me." We need massive diversity in programming, in our praise, in the expression of our spiritual gifts. In the church, we have divided ourselves in just about as many ways we can be divided. We have divided ourselves by denomination . . .

means of baptism . . .

timetables related to the tribulation . . .

types of services . . .

and meanings for communion. It's time we recognize that the Lord meant what He said when He inspired Paul to write:

- "For we being many are one bread, and one body: for we are all partakers of that one bread" (1 Corinthians 10:17).
- "There is neither Jew nor Greek, there is neither bond nor free, there is neither male nor female: for ye are all one in Christ Jesus" (Galatians 3:28).
- "There is one body, and one Spirit, even as ye are called in one hope of your calling; one Lord, one faith, one baptism, one God and Father of all, who is above all, and through all, and in you all" (Ephesians 4:4–6). .

Fads come and go in the church, just as they come and go in society. Prophecy is big right now—people are all looking for the "prophetic word." Some only want to go to services that are labeled "healing services." This one will lay hands on the sick, that one will call out diseases, another one might throw holy water on those with sickness.

The methods and fads don't matter. We serve One Lord. He is faithful to remain the same yesterday, today, and forever. He works through a multiplicity of ways and through all manner of gifts.

It is only when we feel truly free to be ourselves, however, that we allow other people to be truly free to be themselves. The person who enjoys the unique ways in which God has created him, is a person who is likely to appreciate and enjoy the unique way in which God has created others.

Our goal is to preach, teach, and experience truth—not culture.

There's more than one way to skin a cat.

There's more than one way to bake a cake.

There's more than one way to praise the Lord!

It's not just Satan who has bound God's people in their praise. We have bound each other in order to promote our own causes, agendas, and preferred styles.

You may not like the way another person expresses his faith in Christ. You may not agree with it fully or choose to adopt it as your means of expression. But you *must* value his right to express his faith in Christ the way he believes the Lord is leading him to express it. And don't waste your time criticizing him and become a prisoner in your own mind . . . heart . . . emotions!

There are many ways to praise the Lord. A person might dance, walk, stand with his arms raised, fall on his knees, lie flat on his face before God. He might sing, shout, talk, cry, laugh. What's important is that a man find a way to open up and express himself to the Lord. There's no "right" position or "right" form of expression for praise—the only thing that must be right before God is a man's heart, humbled to praise Him from the depths of his emotions.

When the world sees Christian men dropping their differences and coming together, the world is going to want what Christians have.

Politicians, educators, economists, scientists, and corporations—they have all tried unsuccessfully to bring the world together and to bridge the gaps that divide nation from nation, tribe from tribe, people from people.

But only God can build that bridge.

And the good news is that God does build that bridge by His outpoured Holy Spirit.

True Pentecost comes when devout men come together from every nation under the one anointing of the Holy Spirit. Regardless of their backgrounds . . .

races . . .

cultures . . .

and denominations. You cannot have a genuine Pentecost outpouring of God's power in the presence of segregation, alienation, or separation among God's people.

When the world sees Christian men coming together under one anointing, it is going to run to our upper room to hear the Gospel.

Yes, indeed. When we are loosed in our hearts of all prejudice . . .

loosed from our emotional bondage . . .

loosed in our praise and worship . . .

and loosed in our ability to love others as God loves them . . .
the world will begin to turn to Christ for forgiveness, deliverance, and healing. It will *run* to the cross.

Loose that man inside you—and let him be free in Christ Jesus!

GETTING UP FROM YOUR LAME POSITION

WAITING ON MAN TO GET INTO POSITION

*These are the generations of the heavens and of the earth when they
were created, in the day that the LORD God made the earth and the
heavens, and every plant of the field before it was in the earth, and
every herb of the field before it grew: for the LORD God had not caused
it to rain upon the earth, and there was not a man to till the ground.*

GENESIS 2:4–5

T hings must be in place before God will act. The Bible tells us that at
the beginning of creation, God had not caused it to rain upon the
earth. This does not mean that the earth was without water. Up to this time,
God had caused a mist to come up from the earth to give moisture to the
earth. There had been no downpour, however, from the heavenlies.

Why? Because there was not a man to till the ground.

There are some things that God has planned to do, has made provision
for doing, and desires to do that He will not do until man is in place to
receive what God intends to give.

The blessing is there . . . in God's safe keeping.

The need is there . . . insistent, resistant, persistent in its pain and suffering.

But the blessing won't be applied to the need until man's heart is in a
position for God to act according to His own laws of redemption, healing,
and deliverance.

There are some things that God has in the heavenlies that will not be
released to you until you are in the proper position spiritually, relationally,

emotionally. Oh, you may be experiencing a "mist"—but in your spirit, you have a restlessness that there must be something more. You have an inner knowing that you aren't fully where you ought to be. You have an uneasiness, a frustration that causes you to say, "Why am I no further than this in my life?"

Rather than blaming your wife, your parents, your boss, or your race . . . you are wise to ask yourself, "Is God waiting on me to be in a different spiritual position before He pours out a blessing on my life?"

When you are in alignment with God and His purposes, He *will* open up the heavens and cause it to RAIN on you! You'll experience such an outpouring of God's blessings that you won't know how to contain them.

Ask God today WHERE He wants you to be spiritually so that you might receive the downpour of His heavenly blessings.

RECOGNIZING THE LAME AT THE GATE

Now Peter and John went up together into the temple
at the hour of prayer, being the ninth hour. And a certain man
lame from his mother's womb was carried, whom they laid daily
at the gate of the temple which is called Beautiful.

ACTS 3:1–2

The lame man who was brought to the Beautiful Gate was incapacitated, and because he was in that condition, he needed special care. While other men walked in and out of the temple area, this man was carried to the temple.

There was nothing wrong with this man in many areas of his body—he could see, hear, touch, and speak. He could move his arms and upper torso. In fact, there was only one thing wrong with this man—his ankles had no strength.

If there is something wrong in only one area of life, however, and that area of weakness is severe enough, a man's entire life can be affected. The "operation" of a man's life—the function, the activity—can be so impacted that it will feel to that man as if *everything* has gone wrong. That was the case with this man. Only one thing was wrong with him, but that one thing created a whole-life problem.

When a man is handicapped, he needs to be carried. He cannot support his own life, pull his own weight, or operate in his own strength. This has nothing to do with whether or not the man is a good man in his heart and motives. It has to do with his having a bad problem.

The lame man's problem had made him dependent upon other people. His problem interfered to a certain extent with their lives—he had to be carried by other men to a place where he could beg, and then carried home at the end of the day. He could not get to where he wanted to be on his own.

This man no doubt felt discouraged and low in self-value. When a man has to be carried about, unable to move about on his own, he feels demeaned. When a man has to beg for a living and is not allowed to participate fully in the activities of other men, he feels diminished.

Not only was this man lame in his ankles, he had a lameness in his emotions and his spirit. One area of weakness had created another in his life. Not only were his ankles lame; he was lame.

Virtually all men are in that position today. We each have a weakness in our lives that keeps us from functioning as a whole person. But what do most of us do? We deny our own lameness. And we pass by others who are lame because we don't have either the courage or the compassion that it takes to stop and help them.

It's time we quit kidding ourselves. We each have a need for God's healing power. Others have needs, and they need for us to help them experience God at work in their lives. Yes, we are all lame at the gate at some point in our lives, in some area of our lives.

The good news is that God sends people to the gate where we sit to help us receive what God has for us to receive. Watch for that person in your life. Look for that person to come. And be very aware that *you* may be the person that God is sending to bring deliverance to a lame man.

---

*Be on the alert for a person who may be sitting at a gate
through which you will pass today.*

WHAT ARE YOU EXPECTING?

And a certain man lame from his mother's womb was carried,
whom they laid daily at the gate of the temple which is called Beautiful,
to ask alms of them that entered into the temple; who seeing
Peter and John about to go into the temple asked an alms.

ACTS 3:2–3

What do you want when you go to church? Why are you really there? What is it you are seeking? Are you present only so that you can tell others that you go to church? Are you there so that you can play a role that you think gives you some kind of status in your community? Are you there just to keep peace in your family and to avoid the nagging and pleading of your wife or your mother or your children?

Jesus once asked a group of people concerning John the Baptist, "Who did you go out into the wilderness to see? A reed shaken with the wind? A man clothed in soft raiment? A prophet?" (See Matthew 11:7–15.)

It's an important question for us to ask ourselves: Who are we going to church to see and hear?

If we are going to church just to hear the choir sing or to hear a preacher speak, we are making the same mistake that the lame man made when he was carried to the Beautiful Gate that day. He was looking for the wrong thing. He was seeking alms. He wasn't expecting healing.

We also need to ask ourselves some serious questions about the way we regard the people we meet on a day-to-day basis: How are we looking at other people? What do we expect from our encounters with them?

So often we approach people the same way this lame man did. We are looking for what they are going to do for us. We are looking for what we can get from them. We aren't looking for what it is that God wants to do in us or through us.

I call this a "get-over" spirit. The person with a get-over spirit is always looking for some one or some thing to help him get over his problem. He's looking for what he can take from others, or what they will give to him freely—which is no different than alms-begging—without any effort or responsibility on his part.

People with a get-over spirit are users. They use people, but don't really love them. They latch onto people and seek to take from them what they desire or lust after—it may be sex, it may be money, it may be fawning adoration. They have little interest in other people apart from what they can get from them that will help them make it from today to tomorrow.

God calls us to see Him when we see other people. He calls us either to give to other people as He would give to them, or to receive from other people as if we are receiving from the Lord Himself.

When we go to church, we are to go with an expectation that *God* is going to speak to our hearts and heal our lameness.

When we encounter other people, we are to regard them with love and compassion—open to receive what good thing they may say to us to encourage us in the Lord, and also open to say and give to them whatever the Lord prompts us to say and give.

In this way we live in freedom—freely receiving and freely giving. (See Matthew 10:8.)

Identify precisely what you are expecting from God today.

WHY ARE YOU WHO YOU ARE?

A certain man lame from his mother's womb. . . .

Have you ever stopped to think about who you are and how you got to be who you are? Have you wondered how it is that you got through all the things you have been through? Have you ever thoroughly considered your own life?

So many men are so busy looking at their lame ankles—their problems, their needs, their area of weakness—that they fail to see the big picture of their own lives. They don't have an awareness of where they are in their lives, primarily because they don't have a clear picture of where they have been.

This man who was carried to the Beautiful Gate had not become crippled as the result of an accident or an illness. He hadn't fallen from a rooftop or been thrown from a horse or been run over by a cart. He had been born lame. He had never known anything other than lameness all of his life. His lameness was not a disease, but a *weakness*. The bones of his feet and ankles simply had never gained strength.

This man actually had two advantages that many men do not have today.

First, the lame man knew that he had a problem. His lameness was obvious—not only visible to others, but visible to himself. He had to face his problem; there was no way to avoid it or ignore it.

Many men today haven't faced their lameness. They think that because they can look in the mirror and not see any major flaws, or get through a social event without making any major mistakes, or keep a job without getting fired . . . things must be all right. The fact is, we *each* have an area of lameness in our lives. It's there—even if we refuse to face it, even if it isn't obvious.

Second, the lame man knew the reason for his lameness. He knew the cause of his problem. He knew the "why" for his life being the way it was.

One of the things we each must do about the area of weakness we have in our lives is to trace it back to its origin. We need to ask, "*Why* am I like this? *Why* do I do what I do?"

Until we know why we are so angry . . .

so filled with hate . . .

so resentful and bitter,

we cannot understand fully what it is that we need to do to get beyond our problem.

Why do I come home from church where I've been acting like a saint and leaping about in praise like David . . . only to act like a wild gorilla with my wife and children?

Why don't I know how to communicate? Why am I unwilling to learn how to communicate better?

Why do I feel an inner rage all the time? Why do things often spin out of control?

Why am I not succeeding more at work?

Why do I feel depressed at times?

Why am I not growing more in my spiritual life?

Why am I not further along in my walk with the Lord?

Why am I who I am?

Get your own résumé and read it to yourself. Look back over your life. Face your life. Find out why you have been camping out in a state of lameness for so long.

Taking a look at your own life can be depressing if that's the point where you *end* your search of self. But if you use your new understanding to say, "This is how I got where I am, and here's what I am going to do about it," then your self-exploration can be highly positive.

When we look closely at our lives, we each discover that we need a Savior, we need a Lord, and we need relationships with other Christians who will teach us God's Word and build us up in Christ Jesus. That's one of the greatest discoveries a person can ever make.

There's a reason that you are who you are. But there's an even greater purpose for your life. You may be who you are, but you are not yet who you will be! God has bigger and better things ahead for you. We each are called to be a "partaker of the glory that shall be revealed" (1 Peter 5:1).

Consider today not only your problem and its cause,
but your calling in Christ Jesus and its result!

ALIVE AND AVAILABLE

Now is the accepted time; behold, now is the day of salvation.

2 CORINTHIANS 6:2

W here are you on God's agenda? Do you know?

The Bible doesn't tell us how long the lame man sat at the Beautiful Gate, but I feel certain that being carried to the gate was his daily habit. He had no reason to think that the day he encountered Peter and John was any different from any other day in his life. To him, it was probably "just another day" of begging alms.

Most of us don't know what day it is on "God's calendar." We don't know the day that is *the day* that God has marked on His timetable for us to receive our miracle. We very often aren't aware that God has a life-changing, mind-altering, spirit-redeeming, soulcleansing miracle for us . . . today.

The challenge to us is to be aware of our miracle moment when it comes. And the only way I know to be aware of that moment is to stay aware always. We must be available *continually* to receive from God *continuously*.

Being ALIVE is the first requirement for being available. The good news is . . . *you ARE alive!*

In spite of the pain and weakness in an area of your life . . .

in spite of not being able to do what other men are doing . . .

in spite of not being able to move about like other men move about, walking and leaping about with full freedom of mobility . . .

the fact is,

you are still here! You have survived to this moment.

No matter how broken

or wounded

or frustrated you may be, you are alive!

And as long as you are alive, a miracle is possible. To receive a miracle of any kind, however, you must be *available* for a miracle.

Miracles happen to those who know they need them and make themselves available to receive them. So the devil would much rather see you so active and busy that you never give God or your life or your weakness a moment's thought. The devil would much rather see a man become completely involved with contracts and opportunities and business trips and too-full schedules than to see a man be brought to a place of being available should a servant of God walk by or should a servant of God come to speak a word from the Lord.

Being available means that we are . . .

- *alert*. We're looking for a miracle.
- *ready*. We have our hands lifted in praise, ready to receive.
- *excited*. We have a sharp, eager anticipation about what God is going to do.

Jesus said to His disciples—including us—"Your time is alway ready" (John 7:6). Let's live with that degree of availability!

Stay available today to receive the miracle that God has on its way.

GUARDING YOUR MOST PRECIOUS SPIRIT

The thief cometh not, but for to steal, and to kill, and to destroy:
I am come that they might have life, and that they might
have it more abundantly.

JOHN 10:10

M any people have security systems for their houses, or alarms for their cars. They know they have something of value. And they also know that there are thieves loose in the world who are likely to want the valuable possessions they have.

While this is true for material possessions, so many men do not have a security system for their emotional and spiritual lives. Part of the reason is that they don't know *they* are valuable to God. And another part of the reason is that they don't know that a thief is loose in the world who wants to steal, destroy, and kill everything of value that they possess.

You can put bars on the windows of your house ... You can put an alarm system on your car that will cause sirens to sound and lights to flash on and off ... You can put video cameras and silent alarms in your store ...

You can put padlocks on your bicycle or on trunks filled with things you hold to be valuable ...

You can put your most prized possessions in sealed vaults with highly sophisticated security systems ...

But are you putting something in and on and around yourself to guard your precious emotional and spiritual life from the ravages of the thief who wants to steal from you your very life?

You were created in the image and likeness of God. That's the only reason the thief needs to want to rob you of *who you are*. He knows that first and foremost you are an offspring of the omnipotent, omniscient, omnipresent, all-loving God.

You are a spirit . . .

that has a soul . . .

and lives in a body that was formed from the dust of the earth. Your spirit comes from God's "isness," and therefore you can know God in your spirit.

In your spirit you have God-consciousness. You have an awareness of Him and a desire for Him.

In your soul you have self-consciousness. In your mind, your psyche, your memories, and your emotions you know who you are and what you are supposed to do.

In your body you have world-consciousness. In your body, you know if you are hot or cold, hungry or satisfied, comfortable or uncomfortable.

The thief is after you solely because you have a part of God's eternal Spirit in you.

Guard your spirit. It's not only the most valuable part of you, it's the eternal part of you.

How do we guard our spirits?

First, build your relationship with Jesus. Spend time communicating with Him. Draw your identity from Him.

Second, build yourself up in God's Word. Read your Bible. Study it. Bind the Word of God to your mind.

Third, build up yourself spiritually in praise. Worship the Lord. Serve Him in every way you know.

Stay on guard. The thief never sleeps.

Look for the abundance that is found in Jesus. He has come to RESTORE whatever the thief may already have taken from you.

WHEN YOU KNOW WHO, YOU CAN FIND OUT WHY

The spirit of God hath made me, and the breath of the Almighty hath given me life.

JOB 33:4

When God blew from His own breath into the dust body of man, man came alive and knew who he was and Who God was. Your understanding of yourself and your understanding of God are intricately intertwined. You cannot know fully who you are until you know Who God is. Until you recognize that God is the One Who has given you your life—the One Who has formed and fashioned you with a specific plan and destiny in mind—you cannot find either peace or a sense of purpose. It's time we stopped letting other people breathe on us their plans and start looking close into the face and heart of God for our identity.

Until we allow God to breathe upon us and breathe into us His Spirit, we will be vulnerable to any person and anything that comes along that seeks to define us, and in defining us, manipulates and controls us.

There are many men who get up every day "just swinging," just beating the air. They are in a fight, but they don't know what they are fighting about. The person who is just flailing away is a man who is without purpose or goals, without direction or impact. He senses he is in a struggle but he doesn't know who with. The result is that at day's end, he is exhausted, frustrated, and angry. He has virtually no ability to win.

But the man who gets up every day knowing who he is battling is a man who can fight with purpose and intelligence and direction.

In order to win you must know that God is the Source of your life and that you have an enemy of your eternal spirit, and that God your Source will help you *defeat* your enemy. It is only when you come to that awareness that life makes sense.

If you don't know that God is your Source and the devil is your enemy, life can overwhelm you. There are too many issues and situations that just don't make sense, don't connect, don't produce as they should, or don't fit.

Say to yourself today, "The Spirit of God has made me. The breath of God is giving me life."

Don't let anyone breathe his or her identity
or plans into you except God.

PLEASING TO THE FATHER

This is my beloved Son, in whom I am well pleased.

MATTHEW 3:17

When Jesus stepped down into the Jordan River to be baptized by John the Baptist, He stepped into the fullness of God's purpose for His life. Jesus' step into the Jordan waters was symbolic of His perpetual death and resurrection.

Have you ever stopped to think that by the time Jesus stepped into the waters of the Jordan River that day, they were teeming with the sins of mankind? John the Baptist had baptized countless people in the Jordan, their sins figuratively passing from them into the sea of God's forgiveness, just as the waters of the Jordan River end up in the Dead Sea.

From the shores of spiritual blindness, one might think, "How awful! Jesus was wading into sin." Jesus was doing so, however, to fulfill the purpose of God—redemption from sin. Jesus was *exactly* where God wanted Him to be, doing *precisely* what God wanted Him to do.

As Jesus stood in the very place God desired for Him to stand, God opened up the heavens, the Spirit of God descended upon Him, and a voice spoke from heaven saying, "This is My Son. This is My seed, My Son, Who pleases Me!"

Don't expect God to speak up for you—or to cause others to see you for who you really are—until you are willing to step into the place where God has called you to be. When you step into that place where you are supposed to be, you don't have to speak up for yourself, fight for yourself, or demand anything of others. God will speak for you. He'll command whatever forces are involved to yield to you, give to you, honor you, listen to you, obey you.

Don't expect God to open up the heavens and pour out His Spirit of power and truth and wisdom and righteousness onto your life unless you are where you are supposed to be. When you step into the place God has destined for you, you won't have to take on your own battles, grope about for the right decisions, or wonder if something is right or wrong. God will give you every ability you need. He'll put into your path what you need to have. And you won't have any doubt that it's God Who is providing for you or working in you.

To please the Father . . . obey Him. Even if it means wading into someone else's muddy waters.

Go only where God calls you to go. Once there, do only what He commands you to do. You will be pleasing to Him!

THE ENMITY BETWEEN YOU AND THE DEVIL

And the LORD God said unto the serpent . . . I will put enmity between thee and the woman, and between thy seed and her seed; it shall bruise thy head, and thou shalt bruise his heel.

GENESIS 3:14, 15

A re you fully aware that the devil is after you? Do you have a keen sense that the devil is on your trail?

Yes, you.

You.

You.

YOU.

We sometimes think, "Oh, yes, the devil is alive and lurking about today, but he's not after *me*. I don't have anything he wants. I'm nobody. I'm not called by God to do anything spectacular. Why would the devil want me?"

He wants you because you are a potential seed for producing a harvest for God in this earth!

God prophesied to the serpent that had seduced Eve into sin that He was going to put enmity between the *seed* of the woman and the serpent. This word for seed, *zera* in Hebrew, is also a word used for semen. Women don't have semen. The seed of the woman, therefore, was to be a "man-child" descendant of Eve.

This prophecy was fulfilled in Jesus Christ, but that fulfillment in and through Christ is ongoing in *us* until the day God brings this age to an end. The devil is a defeated foe in the context of eternity, but he has not yet been defeated fully in the context of earthly time. He still has access to men, women, boys, and girls to tempt them into sin. He still has an opportunity to lay a claim on the souls of mankind.

Therefore, there's enmity between you—one of the human seeds born down through the centuries from your great ancestor Eve—and the devil. Paul wrote to the Romans: "The God of peace shall bruise Satan under your feet shortly. The grace of our Lord Jesus Christ be with you" (Romans 16:20). The devil's hate is still raging against you.

Enmity is a state of ill will or hostility. It doesn't come and go. It remains the devil's intent to destroy you no matter what you do. His nature is the nature of a violent murderer who is on the lookout for his next victim. In 1 Peter 5:8 we read, "Be sober, be vigilant; because your adversary the devil, as a roaring lion, walketh about, seeking whom he may devour."

The devil is stalking you. He hates you. He is in a state of perpetual ill will, hostility, and conflict with you whether you know it or not. He is after your self-esteem, your identity, your mind, your emotions, your wife and children, your job or your business, your church, your well-being, your witness, your productivity, your health. He's after everything you value and hold as being good. Ultimately, his goal is the destruction of your eternal spirit.

Throughout the centuries, this warfare of the devil has been aimed primarily at the man-child. The devil's primary battles have been against men. When Pharaoh looked at the Hebrews and determined that they were becoming too numerous and too powerful, he didn't authorize the killing of all the Hebrew babies—no, only the male babies. (See Exodus 1:22.) Pharaoh didn't have an understanding that the Messiah would one day be a man born to an Israelite virgin. The one who knew this fact was the devil; Pharaoh was simply one of his pawns. And therefore, Pharaoh's order was that any time a manchild was born, the midwives were to kill him.

The devil is after you. He wants you. He seeks to kill you.

The devil doesn't mind your coming to church. He just doesn't want church—the Spirit of God—to come into you.

The devil doesn't mind your holding a position. He just doesn't want you to occupy *the* position you're supposed to hold in the kingdom of God.

The devil doesn't mind your having a title. He just doesn't want you to operate in your divine calling.

I have traveled the nation in recent years and have seen the power of

God work in marvelous ways. Let me assure you, when men begin to move into the positions that they are called to occupy in the body of Christ, things happen! They happen both individually and in churches.

Are you in the position you are supposed to be in with God?

Being in the right place with God is the only way you can remain secure in the face of the devil's assault against you. To stay alive, stay connected to God as the Source of your life.

To stay alive in your spirit, stay alive in God's Spirit. That's the only way you will defeat the devil every day.

DON'T LET THE DEVIL DESTROY YOU!

Man that is born of a woman is of few days and full of trouble. He cometh forth like a flower, and is cut down: he fleeth also as a shadow, and continueth not.

JOB 14:1–2

Y ou don't have long on this earth. Even if you live to be a hundred years old, or older, you are going to look back on your life and think, "It's only been a few days that I've been alive."

In some communities and among some groups of people in our nation today, man's days are especially few indeed.

All around us we see man killing man.

Man gunning down his fellowman on the street . . .

Man lying lifeless in crack houses . . .

Man curled up on street corners, homeless but too drunk to do anything about it . . .

Man suffering in a hospital bed, HIV positive, until he breathes his final breath.

All around us we see men killing their seed, their *zera*. Men making babies and then not having the desire or taking the time to be fathers to them . . .

men impregnating women and then not
marrying them or caring about their *zera*,
encouraging women by their lack of
involvement and provision to get

abortions . . .

men abandoning their children and teenagers,
leaving their sons to struggle with finding
their own identity in a godless world.

If there ever was a mission field in need of a missionary, it's the mission field of the men in our nation. It's easier to get ten women to come to church, and then to love and serve God, than to get one man to do so.

What are we doing to God's seed? How are we destroying our lives? Wars and plagues don't need to cut down our men anymore. We are cutting down ourselves!

Who molested our boys and girls?

Who raped our women?

Who beat our toddlers?

Who abandoned our babies?

If the devil can't destroy your seed, he will do his best to damage your seed—to make it lame in some way, to make it weak in the ankles, to limit the effectiveness and strength of the seed.

We've all hurt some people . . .

betrayed some covenants . . .

made some mistakes . . .

blown some money . . .

missed some opportunities . . .

and sinned against God. But thank God, He is merciful. The good news—the very BEST news—is that God forgives. He forgives the molester . . .

He forgives the abuser . . .

He forgives the addict . . .

He forgives the liar and the thief . . .

He forgives the SINNER.

And He doesn't stop there. He heals the situation that sin created. He restores men to wholeness and changes their circumstances into a blessing.

The devil may be out to defeat you, but God is out to defeat the devil. Stay on God's side. Receive His forgiveness. Walk in His commandments. Praise His holy name. In staying on God's side, you are staying on the winning side.

Make every day you live a day that
you CHOOSE God's life over the devil's death.

ARE YOU STUCK AT THE GATE?

A certain man lame from his mother's womb was carried,
whom they laid daily at the gate of the temple.

Acts 3:2

This lame man was laid daily at a gate that was so beautiful it had Beautiful as its name! If a man has an ugly problem, it matters very little that he is in a beautiful place. A person with an ugly problem has very little ability to enjoy beauty or appreciate it.

Not only that, but this man was living in the Promised Land. Yet he had very little ability to receive the fullness of the promises that others were receiving. As a lame man, he was not allowed into the temple. According to the law, his condition made him unworthy to participate in the rituals that able-bodied men kept.

So many men are close to being in the right place, but they aren't yet fully there.

They are just close enough to the church to know what's going on—to know who's who and what's being preached. But they are not all the way into the body of Christ so they can experience the fullness of God's power and provision in their lives.

They are stuck at the gate.

Some of them even know when to kneel and when to raise their hands. They know the songs in the hymnal and precisely what time the service should start and end. They've heard more altar calls than they can count. They know all the protocol. They take all the ritual of the church in stride and from a distance . . . but they never get all the way into the place where they can receive God's blessing.

What keeps them stuck at the gate? Their attitude.

They have the same attitude that they have in the world, an attitude that says, "I'm like this because nobody will help me. I'm the way I am because nobody will help me 'get over' to the place of blessing."

They bring their unrenewed minds into the church. They expect the church to change them and do for them in the same way they expect their bosses, or the government, or the neighborhood social worker to change their world and do for them.

Now you don't have to be poor or financially destitute to have a get-over spirit. You can be rich and still blame your problems on somebody else who you believe is failing to do for you what you think they should be doing for you. You may be a very wealthy business owner and still have a get-over attitude, blaming your employees or your competitors for keeping you from the success you think you should have. You can be a church pastor and have a get-over attitude, blaming the members of your church for not appreciating you the way you think you should be appreciated.

The worst attitude in the world is a get-over attitude regarding God—that you are expecting somebody else to provide for you what God alone can provide for you, and then blaming that other person or group of people for failing you and causing you to fail.

Nobody can be your Source but God.

And nobody can put you into a right relationship with God but *you*.

If you are stuck at the gate today because of your own bad attitude, repent of that attitude! Go all the way into the place where you can receive God's blessings for YOURSELF . . . DIRECTLY from God. The way to that place is praise and worship.

CREATED FOR WHOLENESS

This is the book of the generations of Adam. In the day that God
created man, in the likeness of God made he him; male and female
created he them; and blessed them, and called their name Adam,
in the day when they were created.

GENESIS 5:1–2

God created man in His own image—whole. So often we get into a numbers game in the church. We get all wrapped up in determining if God is one or three—a single entity or a committee, a unity or a trinity. The Hebrews didn't have this conflict about God. Moses said, "Hear, O Israel: The LORD our God is one LORD" (Deuteronomy 6:4). The Lord is whole. And that is the only perspective that is necessary. The Lord isn't fragmented or divided. God is full and complete, lacking nothing whatsoever.

God has never faced a question He couldn't answer. He has never faced a need He couldn't supply.

He never had a desire He couldn't fulfill.

He is altogether self-sufficient and perfect.

And God made man in His likeness and image—*whole*. Male and female created He *them*. He called *their* name Adam.

This first whole man had dominion over everything. He had a position granted to him by his Creator.

One of the great differences between men and women is rooted in this: Man had position with God before he had a relationship with another human being. Woman was birthed in relationship.

We see today that men are positional and women are relational. Men are concerned about power and status far more than women. Men love titles. Women are concerned about their relationships: their children, their spouses, their friends. When men get together they ask one another, "What do you do for a living?" In the course of the conversation, they expect to find out what position another man holds in his company. When women get together they ask, "Are you married? Do you have children?" In the course of their conversation, they pull out pictures of their family members and give details about every one of them.

Man's first job was naming. If he called a giraffe a giraffe, it was a giraffe! He had dominion over his world. But when man looked around, he didn't find a mate for himself. God said, "This situation isn't good. Man is too much like Me. He's too self-sufficient, too self-contained."

When God made Eve He didn't reach down into the earth again. He reached into man. He said to Adam, "I'm going to reach into you and pull out of you something that I've already placed in you." Man was created with woman inside him. And out of the inner emotional and spiritual womb of man, Eve was created.

Jesus approaches us in the same way today. He says to us, "I've placed My faith and My Spirit and My life in you. I'm going to pull out of you something that I've placed in you. I'm going to bring My desire for your wholeness to a reality that you can fully experience."

Jesus said time and again to those He healed and delivered: "Be thou made whole." He saw people as being whole entities—spirit, mind, emotions, psyche, body, relationships—all linked together so tightly that it was impossible to separate or fragment the elements of man.

Wholeness is God's plan for you. Jesus came to make you whole in His way, His timing, and for His glory. His wholeness for you includes *whole* relationships.

Ask God to make you whole today and to reconcile you to wholeness in your relationship with your wife, children, and brothers and sisters in Christ.

WALKING IN WHOSE LIKENESS?

Adam lived an hundred and thirty years, and begat a son in his own likeness, after his image; and called his name Seth.

GENESIS 5:3

After Adam and Eve had fallen into sin and were expelled from the Garden of Eden, we read that Adam fathered a child, and the boy was just like him. Adam's son was born "in his own likeness" (Genesis 5:3).

Adam had been created in the image of the wholeness of God. Seth was created in the image of his fallen father.

And throughout the generations, we men have been born in the image of fallen men. We bear their sin nature. How many times have we heard it said about ourselves, "He's just like his daddy"? In some cases, we are too much like our daddies. History repeats itself over and over and over again.

Daddy was angry and frustrated . . . now look at my temper.

Daddy couldn't stay with Mama . . . now look at my string of divorces.

Daddy was an alcoholic . . . now look at my drug addiction.

Daddy had girlfriends . . . now I'm involved in a relationship I have to hide.

Daddy was a workaholic . . . and now I spend fourteen hours a day at work.

Daddy wasn't affectionate with his children . . . and now I don't know how to hug and kiss my children.

We have an interesting and clear example of the way in which sin tendencies are passed along from father to son in the stories of Abraham and Isaac.

And Abraham journeyed from thence toward the south country, and dwelled between Kadesh and Shur, and sojourned in Gerar. And Abraham said of Sarah his wife, She is my sister: and Abimelech king of Gerar sent, and took Sarah. (Genesis 20:1–2)

Sarah looked so fine as an old woman that Abraham knew that when he entered the south country of Gerar, King Abimelech was going to take one look at Sarah and want her as part of his harem. And Abraham was right. Abimelech did come and take Sarah to be his concubine.

Abraham told Sarah, "Tell him you are my sister." Abraham knew that if Abimelech thought Sarah was his sister, he would treat Abraham better. But if Abimelech thought Sarah was his wife, he would kill him so he might have sole right to Sarah. Abraham was willing to tell a half-truth and allow his own wife to be raped by a heathen king in order to save his own skin. And not only that, in the process he was jeopardizing his own future, since Sarah at that time had not yet given birth to Isaac, Abraham's *zera*, his destined seed.

Abraham passed on his tendency toward deceit to his son.

In Genesis 26 we read that Isaac, the son of Abraham and Sarah, faced a famine where Isaac lived, and he went south in search of food. He also went to Abimelech, king of the Philistines, and "Isaac dwelt in Gerar" (Genesis 26:6). History was repeating itself.

In Genesis 26:7 we read:

And the men of the place asked him of his wife; and he said, She is my sister: for he feared to say, She is my wife; lest, said he, the men of the place should kill me for Rebekah; because she was fair to look upon.

Isaac wasn't even alive when his father had made the same statement about Sarah. And yet there it was—the sin tendency of his father appearing in his life.

We see the pattern again and again in the Scriptures.

When you receive Jesus as your Savior, you become a son of God. Paul says, "Wherefore thou art no more a servant, but a son; and if a son, then an heir of God through Christ" (Galatians 4:7).

No longer do you need to walk in the likeness of your earthly daddy. Rather, you are called to walk in the likeness of your heavenly Father, your eternal Abba, Daddy God. Determine that you will be more and more like *Him,* day by day!

Choose today to WALK in the image of your ETERNAL Father.

THE IMPORTANCE OF A FATHER'S BLESSING

And it came to pass after these things, that one told Joseph, Behold, thy
father is sick: and he took with him his two sons, Manasseh and
Ephraim. And one told Jacob, and said, Behold, thy son Joseph cometh
unto thee: and Israel strengthened himself, and sat upon the bed. . . .
Now the eyes of Israel were dim for age, so that he could not see.
And he brought them near unto him; and he kissed them, and
embraced them. . . . And Israel stretched out his right hand,
and laid it upon Ephraim's head, who was the younger,
and his left hand upon Manasseh's head.

GENESIS 48:1–2, 10, 14

The blessing was passed down from generation to generation among the Israelites when fathers placed their hands upon their sons and spoke God's words over them.

Jacob was on his deathbed when Joseph came to him with his two sons so that Jacob might bless them. In blessing them, Jacob prophesied their identity.

Father to son.

Father to son.

Father to son.

The people of Israel understood who they were largely because individual men learned who they were from their fathers and their grandfathers.

In the last few years as I have traveled this nation ministering in conferences of men, I have encountered literally thousands of men who do not know who they are. They never have had fathers who would lovingly lay their hands upon them and tell them who they were—either in their human family, or in the eyes of God.

A man who grows up without a father grows up not knowing his name, his identity. A boy who doesn't have a father figure after which to pattern his life will run the streets looking for father figures to give him a sense of identity and a name. He'll find one eventually—most likely a gang. He'll take on their name and become a Red or a Blue or a Cryp or a Blood. He'll take on the identity of his "older brothers" in the gang who actually operate in the role of a father to him, telling him who he is and what he is destined to be and do.

If that boy doesn't run into the arms of a gang, he's likely to run into the arms of the corner dope dealer or crime boss. He'll give him a name— Freakin' Freddy or Jumping Jim or Slick Sam.

Every man-child needs a name. He needs an identity.

He can't get that from his mother. Mothers are capable of giving great love and encouragement to their sons, but they cannot give them their identity. Only a father can do that.

Jacob refused to die until he could lay his hands on his sons and grandsons and tell them who they were and what they were destined to do.

We must follow his example today. It doesn't matter if our sons are five or fifty years old. We need to put our arms around them and tell them that they are loved by us. We need to tell them who they are in God. We need to quote Scripture over them and tell them—

- *You are a lion's whelp, and your hand shall be in the enemy's neck. (See Genesis 49:8–9.)*
- *You are more than a conqueror. You can do all things through Christ who strengthens you. (See Romans 8:37, Philippians 4:13.)*
- *You are a son of the Most High God. You have been purchased by the shed blood of Jesus Christ on the cross. You are a joint heir with Christ—a prince of the King of kings. There's greatness in your bones and in your bloodline. (See Galatians 4:6–7.)*

One Sunday in our church, I called all of the young boys who had no fathers to come forward so that I might lay hands on them and prophesy over them and tell them who they are in the Lord. I looked up and found that a thirty-year-old man had come forward and fallen at my feet. He said, "Pastor, I know I'm not a boy, but nobody ever told me who I am. Will you lay your hands on me and tell me who I am? I'm hurting because nobody has ever blessed me like that."

Call your sons and your grandsons to you today. Lay your hands upon them and tell them that you love them and that God loves them and has a purpose for their lives. Give them an identity.

If you are a grown man, find someone who can truly be a spiritual father to you. Ask him to bless you and tell you who you are in Christ Jesus.

Give a blessing to your children today. Talk to them about their identity in Christ Jesus. Encourage them with your love and faith.

RELYING ON GOD TO REVEAL YOUR TRUE IDENTITY

And Jacob was left alone; and there wrestled a man with him until the breaking of the day. . . . And he said, Let me go, for the day breaketh. And he said, I will not let thee go, except thou bless me. And he said unto him, What is thy name? And he said, Jacob. And he said, Thy name shall be called no more Jacob, but Israel: for as a prince hast thou power with God and with men, and hast prevailed.

GENESIS 32:24, 26–28

Y ou are not who the devil or sinful people say you are. You are who God says you are. And sometimes you have to go directly to God to get your real name and your real identity.

That was certainly the case in Jacob's life.

All of his growing-up years, Jacob had been called a supplanter, one who got what wasn't rightfully his. Jacob's very name means "trickster."

Schemer, where's your coat?

Schemer, come into the kitchen.

Schemer, put on your overshoes.

Schemer, take out the trash.

Can you imagine as a boy growing up only to hear every time somebody called your name what they believed to be the most negative aspect of your character?

Hey, con man!

Hey, fat boy!

Hey, worthless slob!

Hey, bastard child!

Hey, doper!

Hey, crook!

Hey, unwanted baby!

Hey, crippled man!

Jacob grew up believing what others said about him—that he was a schemer, a plotter, a manipulator, a con man. And Jacob lived true to what was said.

He believed the lie about him until he became the lie. He tricked his father into giving him the blessing and the inheritance that was rightfully his older brother's. He tricked his uncle Laban in his care of Laban's flocks, and he hoped to trick his brother Esau in the way that he returned home to face his family.

And then all alone in the dark of night, Jacob had an encounter with God. He wrestled with God until daybreak and finally cried out to God, "Bless me!"

The Lord asked him, "What is your name?" Jacob replied, "I am who people have said I am. I am Jacob, the trickster, the con man, the schemer."

And God said, "No, you are not. You are Israel. You are a prince, the child of God, and you have power with God."

You may have done what people say you did, but you are not what people say you are.

When you start praising God, He'll tell you who you are. When you get into God's Word and ask God to reveal to you your identity, He'll show you who you are. He'll show you that you are—

The head and not the tail. (See Deuteronomy 28:13.)

Above only, and not beneath. (See Deuteronomy 28:13.)

Chosen for this generation. (See 1 Peter 2:9.)

More than a conqueror. (See Romans 8:37.)

Part of a royal priesthood. (See 1 Peter 2:9.)

A peculiar treasure. (See Exodus 19:5.)

The citizen of a holy nation. (See Exodus 19:6.)

Look to God to reveal your true identity. He alone knows ALL about you.

Who is God saying that you are . . . right now?

THE RIGHT NAME AND
THE RIGHT ACTION TO GO WITH IT

Peter said, Silver and gold have I none; but such as I have give I thee:
In the name of Jesus Christ of Nazareth rise up and walk. And he
took him by the right hand, and lifted him up.

ACTS 3:6–7

W hen Peter and John came to the temple at the hour of prayer, they
fixed their eyes on the lame man by the Beautiful Gate and Peter
said, "Look on us." Peter didn't want this man to be distracted. If a person
gets distracted, he can miss what God has for him.

Peter wanted this man to pay close attention to what he was about to
do. He wanted him to *really* hear him. I believe he got right down into the
face of that man and locked his eyes on that man's eyes so that everything
else in that lame man's awareness was shut out. That's the way we need to
deal with people who are in pain.

If we are the ones who are suffering, that's the way we need to look at
Jesus. We need to get so close to Him, and look so directly into His eyes,
that we don't see anybody else, we aren't aware of anybody else, we don't
hear anybody else. We only hear and see Jesus.

And then Peter spoke to him with a name. Every one of us needs a name
that is stronger than the devil's name . . .

a name that is stronger than your problem . . .

a name that is greater than your need . . .

a name that is more potent than your pain.

That name is the name of Jesus.

Paul wrote, "At the name of Jesus every knee should bow, of things in heaven, and things in earth, and things under the earth; and that every tongue should confess that Jesus Christ is Lord, to the glory of God the Father" (Philippians 2:10–11).

It is the name of Jesus that is higher than any other name. The writer of Hebrews says, He is "holy, harmless, undefiled . . . and made higher than the heavens" (Hebrews 7:26).

There is no other name that can make whole the part of you that is lame. Only the name of Jesus.

But then Peter went beyond words. He did what needed to be done. This lame man by the Beautiful Gate heard what Peter said, but the words themselves had no visible effect on his life. You may hear a sermon and in your mind say amen, and then find that nothing changes in your life. People in great need all around you may hear about the love and mercy of God, the blood of Jesus, and the power of the Holy Spirit, and yet not experience any of it for themselves.

Peter put the name of Jesus into action. He reached down and took this lame man by the right hand and lifted him up. And it was *as* Peter pulled this man to his feet that the lame man's feet and ankle bones received strength. (See Acts 3:7.) This man who had never walked, didn't need any help walking. No, he only needed help getting up on his feet. Instantly, he was standing, walking, and leaping about as he praised God.

There are people around you today who need for you to speak the right name into their lives—the name of Jesus—and they need for you to help them get to their feet spiritually and emotionally, and in some cases, physically and materially. It is your hand reached out in love and compassion, with genuine help that is not born of sympathy but which is born of faith, that will help them stand. You don't need to be their crutch. You don't need to spend the rest of your life helping them. But you do need to pull them to their feet so that God can heal and strengthen the lameness in their lives.

If you are the one who is being helped to your feet by a Christian brother, then rise up in faith on the inside even as you are helped to rise. Don't place your confidence in the person who is lifting you or praying for you. Put your trust in the name of Jesus. He is the One Who will heal you of your lameness, strengthen you in your weakness, and cause you to walk in boldness. He alone is the One Who can make you whole. *God is desiring to work in you and through you today.*

———————————————

Speak boldly and act boldly when He reveals to you the person you are to help.

NO MORE HIDING OUT

DYSFUNCTION IS NO EXCUSE

And Cain talked with Abel his brother: and it came to pass,
when they were in the field, that Cain rose up against
Abel his brother, and slew him.

GENESIS 4:8

In Genesis, the book of beginnings, we find the first fight in the first family between the first two brothers. We find our first example of dysfunction. You can hardly turn on a talk show today without hearing people give this justification for their abnormal and often sinful behavior: I came from a dysfunctional family. As if that's supposed to be a legitimate excuse!

Oh, the words sound good and they ring true. The *excuse*, however, is lame. The reason the words ring true to us is because we all have a degree of dysfunction in our lives. The reason for the lameness of the excuse is this: we are *all* from dysfunctional families. *Every* family has an element of dysfunction to it. We are all the descendants of Adam and Eve, our great ancestors who fell from a state of perfect function. So, if *any* person is able to rise above dysfunction, then *all* people are able to rise above dysfunction.

Adam and Eve became the parents in the first dysfunctional family. They gave birth to a dysfunctional son, Cain. Murder and mayhem broke out among the first two brothers.

That same murdering spirit exists in the world today. We seem perfectly oblivious to the fact that we are all brothers—that we all have the same blood flowing in our veins. We allow ourselves to fall into the same competitive, jealous, angry spirit that Cain first manifested.

People sometimes have a "get him first" killing spirit, while at the same time they give an appearance of being courteous and cooperative.

You must face the reality every day that some of your problems stem from the fact that there is *somebody* who doesn't like your success. International wars have resulted from the jealousy of one man over another man's success or possessions. Is it any wonder that the minor skirmishes we face in the daily battles of our personal lives come from the same root of jealousy?

Your attitude today is something that is totally under your control. You choose. You choose whether you will be

prejudiced . . .

    angry . . .

        hateful . . .

            bitter . . .

                resentful. It is in your power to make a decision about what you will think and how you will act.

Don't blame your actions on your dysfunctional family. Base your actions on an attitude born of functional faith. "The grace of our Lord was exceeding abundant with faith and love" (1 Timothy 1:14).

Rather than have a "get him before he gets me" attitude, choose to have a "give to him first" attitude. Such an attitude will be far more beneficial to you . . . not only now, but for all eternity.

———————

Refuse to blame your circumstances on the dysfunction of men.
Instead, place your circumstances in the path of the function
of the grace and love of Christ.

WE ARE ALL THE CHILDREN OF OPPRESSION

God anointed Jesus of Nazareth with the Holy Ghost and with power:
who went about doing good, and healing all that were oppressed
of the devil; for God was with him.

ACTS 10:38

Nearly every person who came to America from another nation came to this nation as a wounded person—someone who was oppressed in the land where he or she lived before coming to America. Every group of people has a horror story to tell as part of their personal cultural heritage. The oppression may have had some distinctive qualities, but oppression in general is a common denominator for every group of people who came to America.

Oppressed people readily become oppressors. We know that molested children are the most likely children to become molesters, abused children are the most likely to become abusers, and so forth. Every victim can easily become a victimizer. Those who have had no control in their past are the most likely to seek the most control in their future.

Oppression is nearly always by "family." When the Jews were sent to the concentration camps, they were sent as families. When the Indians were put on reservations, they were put there as families. Our problem is never ours alone. It is by "family."

As a result, an attitude of oppression is passed down family by family, tribe by tribe, people by people. Just about every "family" thinks it is more oppressed than all other families!

A man can be oppressed but not be able to identify his feelings as being oppression. He only knows that he feels trapped and he's angry about it.

Any time a man thinks that he cannot change things and that he has no options, he becomes filled with rage and becomes abusive or violent . . . or he becomes despondent and depressed.

Some men who are filled with rage are talking encouragement but walking defeat. They try to convince themselves that things can be better, but they only give lip-service to such change. In their hearts, they feel trapped.

The man who feels trapped has no tolerance for people who tell him things that he needs to do or points out to him things that he has left undone. He has no capacity for hearing that the trash needs to be taken out, the children need to be disciplined, or the room needs to be painted.

The fact is, however, if you don't like your circumstances or your situation, you can change it.

Whatever is oppressing you—people, habits, addictions, circumstances—whoever or whatever your slave master happens to be . . . you are mightier with Christ than the thing that is oppressing you!

Jesus came to heal "all that were oppressed of the devil" (Acts 10:38). And that, sir, includes *you*. He came to set you free, and he whom the Son sets free of oppression, is free indeed. (See John 8:36.)

Accept God's healing today. Walk in the freedom
that Christ Jesus gives to you!

YOU HAVE BEEN FAVORED BY GOD

By this I know that thou favourest me, because mine enemy doth not triumph over me. And as for me, thou upholdest me in mine integrity, and settest me before thy face for ever.

PSALM 41:11–12

One of the things that Satan wants to keep you from knowing is that the favor of God is upon you and that you have been touched by Him and allowed to become the success that you are. Satan doesn't want you to give any of the credit to God. In fact, he doesn't want you to think that God has ever done anything for you at all.

Satan's lie is that a man has no purpose, power, or potential. The enemy does his utmost to get a man to buy the lie that he is broke . . .

busted . . .

disgusted . . .

oppressed . . .

depressed . . .

and confused.

The enemy will try the race card, and if that doesn't work, he'll try the childhood memories card. And if that doesn't work, he'll dredge up all of your past sins and run them by you. He'll remind a man of broken promises and broken dreams.

Satan works continually to build a case *against* God, never a case *for* God. The result is that some people have such low self-esteem that they don't believe God has touched them at all or that they have any possibility for success in their lives. Others are so arrogant that they think they've achieved all of their success on their own and that God hasn't had anything at all to do with it. Both groups of people are sorely wrong.

No matter how small your area of expertise or accomplishment may seem to you in your own eyes—that degree of success has been made possible because the Lord is on your side. You can't even hold up your own pants without the Lord giving you the strength and knowledge and ability to do so. You certainly can't raise a God-fearing family or contribute your talents to a job without God's assistance.

The irony is that often others are about to stab us to death—emotionally, spiritually, mentally, in our jobs, in our churches—and we don't even know why! We don't know that it's because others are perceiving the favor of the Lord on our lives and are jealous of it. We don't know that we have been blessed by God. We don't know that others are motivated to a great extent to act against us because they are jealous of what they see in us. How sad that they see what we don't see in ourselves!

Refuse to walk in ignorance of your own *God-given* blessings.

Praise God today for His FAVOR shown to you.

THE PROMISED LAND OF
YOUR LIFE RIGHT NOW

Be strong and of a good courage: for unto this people
shalt thou divide for an inheritance the land, which I sware
unto their fathers to give them.

JOSHUA 1:6

You can be in the right general area for your success, but until you claim that area and move into it, you cannot possess the fullness of all that God has promised to you.

Are you in your promised land? Are you in your field of dreams?

If you answer no to those questions, it may very well be because you have a false concept of what it means to be in a place that bears the marks of God's favor and blessing.

Many of the old hymns in our churches talk about "Beulah Land," "Canaan Land," or "the promised land"—they all speak of a wonderful land "over there," one that we will experience in the "sweet by and by." Many of these songs came right out of a slavery mindset, but they have been sung for decades by both white and black people. Even today the idea is deeply engrained in us that we can only experience God's promises and blessings in the future, and very specifically in heaven.

That thinking is erroneous from a Bible standpoint.

When the Israelites went through the wilderness and arrived in the Promised Land, they encountered the Canaanites, the Jebusites, the Amorites, the Hittites, and a whole lot of other "ites" that didn't want them to settle in their area, much less take control over it. The Israelites had to do serious battle in order to *claim* the Promised Land that God had for them—the land to which God had called them, the land God had promised to them, and the land that God was going to help them conquer. The Promised Land wasn't a land they were going to enter after their death. It was a land they were expected to conquer during their life!

When you stepped through the blood of Jesus that flows from the cross, you stepped into your promised land.

Somebody else presently may be occupying the territory that God has for you—they may be in the job that God has destined for you; they may be living in the house that God has planned for you to own; they may be holding the office that God expects you to win in an upcoming election; they may be occupying the store or warehouse that God is going to help you purchase. Nevertheless, you are *in* your promised land. The Lord has led you to the place where He wants you to manifest His power and His greatness.

Keep in mind that you didn't arrive in the promised land of your life today by yourself. Neither did any Israelite man who crossed the Jordan River with Joshua to take claim to the land God had designated for them arrive there on his own. Each man came to that Promised Land with his family—either with his parents or with his wife and children. He came into the land with all of the other Israelites—his tribe and the other eleven tribes, as a whole, his people, his "church community."

The same is true for us today. You don't come into your promised land alone. Your acceptance of Christ involved other people and the claiming of your promised land still involves others. Factor in your family. Move as a whole family to the territory God is calling you to claim.

Take an inventory today of the things that God has promised to you. You'll find those things in the many promises that God has made to His people in the Scriptures. Every promise that is in the Bible is for you and your family *today*. Those promises are not for the hereafter. They are for NOW.

Target and then conquer a portion of your promised land today.

THE WAY WE COME INTO BLESSINGS

The kingdom of heaven suffereth violence,
and the violent take it by force.

MATTHEW 11:12

S anta Claus isn't going to come and drop large bundles of God's blessings into your life. If you are sitting at the base of your fireplace with a glass of milk in one hand and a plate of cookies in the other just waiting for his arrival, you are going to be sorely disappointed.

Neither does God drop blessings out of nowhere. He doesn't sprinkle them around on the unsuspecting like so much fairy dust.

Receiving God's blessings into your life is a matter of warfare. This is not warfare waged with guns or knives or bombs. It is not warfare that is rooted in jealousy, anger, bitterness, or hatred. It is warfare against the true enemy of your soul—warfare in the spirit realm, warfare that is very real.

So many men are lacking in so many things today—things that must be won first in the spirit realm and then manifested in the natural realm—because they are lazy. I'm not talking about being lazy physically, or being lazy mentally, or being lazy on the job. I'm talking about being lazy spiritu-ally. They don't want to have to *do* anything to bring about God's blessing in their lives. To get what you want you have to want it badly enough that you are willing to fight for it.

In the last several years, I've ministered to large groups of women and to large groups of men, and I've noticed a significant difference in the two groups. Women aren't at all reluctant to get into the trenches of spiritual warfare. I invite women to praise and worship the Lord, and then often I have to tell them when to quit so I can get on with my next point! They have no problem at all crying out to God or weeping unashamedly for the desires of their hearts—even if it means that their eye makeup goes streaming down their faces. They have no problem with raising their voices in prayer or laying hands on their sisters and rebuking the devil off their lives.

But when I invite a group of men to enter into the warfare of praise and worship, sometimes I'm lucky to get a couple of hallelujahs. If some men stand and praise the Lord for longer than thirty seconds, they think they've sacrificed a great deal of time and energy. Even under a strong anointing, some men find it difficult to enter into fierce spiritual battle.

Oh, they feel the anointing. You can't convince me that they don't feel what the Holy Spirit is doing. And they sense the power. You can't convince me that they aren't aware of the power of God or have a knowledge of what it is that God is desiring to do. The difficulty they have lies in their unwillingness to *express* what they feel and in their inability to *yield* their own pride to the power of God.

Unless a man is able to cross this hurdle and humble himself before God and engage in genuine praise and worship, he won't win the battles that are necessary for him to win in the spirit realm. He won't be able to lay claim to his promised land.

Be prepared to fight today in the spirit realm for the territory of blessing that you desire.

GIVING TO GOD WHAT HE WANTS

And the Lord had respect unto Abel and his offering:
But unto Cain and to his offering he had not respect.

GENESIS 4:4–5

Have you noticed that Superman is out? Clark Kent is the one everybody wants. If you are offering Superman results to a woman today, you may attract her attention, but you won't be able to keep her affection. You may as well hang up your cape back in the closet.

If you are choosing to be a stoic, strong superhero to your sons and daughters, you may impress them, but you will not fulfill them. Your children would rather be caressed by you than impressed by you.

The strong, silent type is out. Some of our fathers were so silent they never told our mothers that they loved them . . . they never told us they loved us. Some of them were so strong they never learned how to express themselves except through rage and abuse.

If you use accomplishments and power to replace affection and availability, you are not going to be regarded as a "king" by your wife and children. You are going to be considered as a heartless robot.

Machoism is dead. It's the sensitive and caring and vulnerable and available man who is desired today. If you are still offering machoism to the world, you are offering a product that nobody wants. Including God.

Your machoism placed against the standard of God's holiness and righteousness and compassion is about as impressive to God as a feather on the back of an elephant is impressive to the elephant.

God isn't remotely impressed by our approaching Him and asking, "What's up?" He isn't impressed by your résumé or your fancy suit. He isn't impressed by your expensive new wristwatch or your recitation of church history. He isn't impressed by your degrees or your pedigree. God is responsive only to those men who are willing to fall on their faces before Him, completely yielding everything to Him, and placing themselves in utter reliance upon Him.

An amazing thing happens when we learn how to bless the Lord—how to praise, worship, and exalt His name. We become more willing and able to bless our wives and children! In giving God what He wants, we are better able to give others what they truly need and desire from us.

God accepted Abel's offering because Abel gave God something that God wanted. Are you willing to give God what He wants from you today—a humble, open, loving heart filled with praise and worship?

Give God an ACCEPTABLE offering of praise today.
He WILL receive and respect your sacrifice.

MOVING THE HEART OF GOD

And the Lord your God, he shall expel them [your enemies] from before you, and drive them from out of your sight; and ye shall possess their land, as the LORD your God hath promised unto you.

JOSHUA 23:5

U ntil you learn how to move the heart of God, you will never be successful in spiritual warfare, and until you are successful in spiritual warfare, you cannot be completely successful in your life.

You may look like who's who and know what's what, but you will never possess all that God desires for you to have until you move the heart of God to "fight for you" and win the territory for you that He desires for you to have.

The first and foremost step for moving the heart of God is to break down the old man inside you and give him up. We dismantle the old man in us when we say with a genuine heart, "It's not about me, God. It's about You."

You can tell a lot about a man by listening to him pray.

I pray that You will endow us with all such endowments that may matriculate from Your throne, and cause us to enter into various dimensions of glory. Even now as I stand on the crystal shore, I pray You will lead me into a place. . . .

Who are you trying to fool?

God doesn't need or want your egotistical, intellectualized image. In fact,

He doesn't desire anything that is man-engineered or man-contrived. Including your flattery.

If a woman came to you and, measuring you up like a specimen in a lab, said to you, "You are a wonderful example of the male physique, with huge biceps and tight abs and a great smile," you might be impressed that she's impressed with your body. But her objective appraisal of your body is not going to be what would make you want to snatch her and hold onto her for the rest of your life. In your heart of hearts, you want a woman who knows the inner you and loves you anyway. And the same goes for God.

God desires for you to come to Him not with lofty words that express theological and historical facts about what He has done, but with a heart that is *dependent* upon Who He is and what He does and will do in order for you to take your next breath. He wants you to come with a desire to know Him, and with a willingness to lay your entire life bare before Him so He can heal you and restore you and create in you the likeness of His Son, Jesus Christ.

Cain tried to impress God—and Cain failed miserably. Cain gave to God something that he felt he had accomplished on his own. After all, he had tilled the earth and planted the seed and gathered the harvest. He came proudly to God, saying in his heart, "Look what I've done. Bless me on the basis of what I have accomplished."

Abel came to God and said in his heart, "I didn't do a thing. You caused this lamb to be birthed. You caused it to survive and grow. You provided the water for it to drink and the grass for it to eat. You are the Creator of all life. I'm giving back to You what *You've* done. I trust You with my life."

Ask yourself, "Is God receiving what I am giving to Him?" If you are giving Him a good front or a good line about yourself, He won't receive it. If you are giving Him your heartfelt praise and worship, He will receive your sacrifice of praise and bless you in return.

Look at yourself in the mirror today and say to yourself about your own egotistical pride, "Give it up." And then start praising God for Who He is and who He desires for you to become and who He is making you to be.

WHERE ART THOU . . . REALLY?

And the Lord God called unto Adam, and said unto him,
Where art thou?

GENESIS 3:9

A re you in touch with where you are? How you feel? Can you accept your own progress? Have you faced your faults, and also your great assets? When God called to Adam in the Garden of Eden, He wasn't trying to find Adam. God knew where Adam was. Nobody and nothing can hide from God. No . . . God wanted for Adam to *admit* where he was. He wanted Adam to recognize fully who he was and what he had done.

One of the most important questions you can ever ask yourself is this: Where am I in my life?

Men get into trouble when they don't know where they are.

So many men I've encountered are in one stage of their lives and acting as if they are in another. They have entered into marriage and fatherhood, and therefore, they have certain responsibilities, but they are still living as if they are boys playing in the park.

Even if you don't tell your wife . . .

Even if you don't tell your children . . .

Even if you don't tell your boss . . .

Even if you don't tell your pastor . . .

At least tell *yourself* where you are in your life!

When we hide, we turn phony. We act out a charade. We put on a "face" and participate in our own masquerade. Only two things are worse than

65

being phony with other people: being phony with yourself and being phony with God.

If you haven't faced up to who you are and what you have done, you will find it very, *very* difficult to enter into praise and worship. Furthermore, you'll find it very difficult to relate to other men, or to their wives and children.

If you are feeling lonely and deprived, in all likelihood you are emotionally intimidated by other people. You can't open yourself up and give them a hug or pay them a compliment or look them in the eye with compassion because you are *afraid* they may look inside your heart and see the real you. Why are you afraid? Because you haven't looked there lately and you are afraid of what you might find if you do!

Until you face up to your flaws and failures—openly admit them to yourself and to God, and accept the fact that you aren't perfect—you'll never be able to allow other people to know, much less accept, your imperfections. If you aren't open to that kind of sharing, you will feel forever cut off, estranged, isolated, lonely, deprived, and alienated from other people.

Many men spend a lot of time and energy asking about the other men around them, "Where are they?"

What does that man have that I don't have to get that kind of woman?

What does that man do to be able to afford that kind of car and live in that kind of house?

How is it that HE has that kind of job and authority and power?

These are all variations of asking, Where is *he* at? The answer to that question leads to a dead end. It results in jealousy and competition and hatred and distrust and suspicion . . . all of which result in a murderous attitude.

Instead, ask *yourself*, "Where am *I* at?" That's the question that can lead to life. That's the question that will lead you to repentance before God, to an ability to get close to other people, and to fulfillment and true satisfaction in life.

Face yourself today. Answer God's question: Where ARE you?

YOUR ANSWER TO GOD'S QUESTION

And he said, I heard thy voice in the garden, and I was afraid,
because I was naked; and I hid myself.

Genesis 3:10

God called to Adam and asked him, "Where art thou?" And here's how the first man answered the first question that God had asked him: "I heard . . . I was afraid

. . . I was naked . . . I hid."

Most men don't like open confrontation. I have known some physically big, powerful men who were afraid to go home to their five-foot-two-inch wives because they knew they would be facing a confrontation with her the minute they walked in the door.

In my years of counseling men who had a long history of being physically and emotionally and sexually abusive, I discovered that abusers are among the most fearful men I've ever met. They come across to their victims as being totally unafraid, but the fact is, they are *very* afraid of themselves and of being confronted with who they are. They rarely face themselves—they don't know who they are or where they are at—and they are highly fearful that somebody else might discover the darkness that they secretly know is inside them.

Men tend to talk very easily about things that don't really matter. But most of us men clam up when the talk turns to the things that matter the most. We hide.

You can't have a relationship with someone if you are hiding from a person.

Not a relationship with God.

Not a relationship with your wife.

Not a relationship with your child.

Not a relationship with the brother who stands next to you in the pew at church. Relationships are built when we stop hiding and face ourselves, and then allow ourselves to be vulnerable and open with other people.

A man sometimes acts as if he can't hear, or hasn't heard. The fact is, he heard—he just didn't like what he heard.

He heard his wife when she said she needed more time, attention, or consideration.

He heard his child when he complained that Dad wasn't around very much. He heard his daughter when she said, "I love you, Daddy," and he heard her sigh when Daddy didn't say anything back.

He ran and hid emotionally because he didn't know how to give to other people what they said they needed.

A man who is afraid and doesn't know what to do is a man who feels exposed. He feels undone. He'll go to great lengths to hide himself—to bury himself in his work, to get involved in an affair that doesn't require any vulnerability on his part, to put up a brick-wall facade around his heart to hide his true emotions.

So men end up afraid, frustrated, whimpering inside, locked up, impotent. And all the while, they are doing everything they can to cover up their inner feelings and emotional inadequacies.

Truth requires that you open up and share who you really are. It requires an honest answer to God's question, "Where art thou?" rather than an excuse rooted in your own fear.

Ask the Lord today to give you the courage to know yourself and then to reveal yourself to others.

ACKNOWLEDGE YOUR EMOTIONAL NEEDS

My heart is like wax; it is melted in the midst of my bowels.

PSALM 22:14

What is the harm in keeping your fears and your emotional needs to yourself? Because what you use to hide your fears and needs from others will eventually become a prison to you. It will lock you up, freeze you up, bottle you up . . . and keep you from moving in to claim all that God has for you in your life. Some men turn to alcohol or drugs in an effort to hide themselves from their fears and emotional needs.

Some turn to prostitutes—they won't trust their wives with their emotions, but they'll trust a total stranger with their bodies, their potential *zera* (seed), and their reputations.

Some turn to overwork—putting all of their energy into the job and burning the midnight oil—in an effort to avoid the need to relate to people.

Eventually, each of these escapes—and any other escape—becomes a prison. It traps you even further into a cycle of silence, because once you are entrapped by your escape mechanism, you won't want to tell anybody about that trap either. Your fear only grows greater as your silence grows deeper.

The fact is, God created you with emotions. He created you with a need to feel, to touch, to express, to have an emotional outlet and release. Look at a little boy. He's free to express himself, to vent his feelings, to hug and kiss and be hugged and kissed in return. He hasn't learned to hide yet.

What happened to you on your way to becoming a man?

Where art thou?

What caused you to feel that you need to run and hide?

There's another you behind the facade.

You need to be touched just as much as the next guy.

You need to be held.

You need to hear loving words, spoken in a gentle way.

Don't deny your emotional needs.

David wasn't afraid to admit to himself and to God that he was weak, afraid, sorrowful, angry, or in need of love. He even said that his heart melted like wax! (See Psalm 22:14.) In fact, the entire twenty-second psalm is *filled* with emotions. Read it!

The Bible says about Jesus that He was a man "who in the days of his flesh . . . offered up prayers and supplications with strong crying and tears" (Hebrews 5:7.) Jesus was a Man Who knew how to express His emotions.

Tell God you need Him.

Tell Him you love Him.

Tell Him you are in trouble in your life.

Tell Him where you ARE.

Express your emotions to God today.
He created you to pray with FEELINGS.

BREAKING THE SILENCE OF THE LAMBS

Hear my cry, O God; attend unto my prayer. From the end of the earth
will I cry unto thee, when my heart is overwhelmed: Lead me to the rock
that is higher than I. For thou hast been a shelter for me,
and a strong tower from the enemy.

PSALM 61:1–3

G od knew that Adam not only needed to know where he was at, but
that he needed to say so. Are you a man who turns off the lights at
night, only to lie in the darkness of your own bed, unable to say to your
wife, "I love you"?

Are you a man who, when your son comes to you, you respond with
"Hey, what's happening, man?" instead of putting your arm around your son
and giving him the hug that he really desires?

Many of God's men—God's sheep, His beloved lambs—are silent today.

They know who they are and what they have done, but they have lock-
jaw when it comes to talking about it, even in private confession to God.

They *know* they need to be held, but they'll never *admit* that they need
to be held. Instead, they'll come home and say to their wives and children . . .

Why haven't you cleaned the house?

Why aren't you making better grades in school?

Why didn't you catch that fly ball that came your way?

They are scared that they are about to lose their job but they'll never say
a word about it. Instead, they'll march around with a chip on their shoulders, as if to say . . .

What are you doing in my way?
Who gave you the right to tell me what to do?
Why are you showing favoritism to everybody but me?

They are afraid that if they tell what they feel, others will lose respect for them or will take advantage of them.

Our fears can erupt in anger and in criticism. But most of the time, they lie just under the surface of our stone-cold silence. As long as they remain there, they will foment and brew . . . unhealed, unchanged, unresolved. We will remain weak on the inside even though we may seem strong on the outside.

David said, "O LORD my God, I cried unto thee, and thou hast healed me" (Psalm 30:2). Hasn't the time come for you to break your silence so God can heal *you*?

Make today the day that you break the "silence of the lamb"
in your life. Tell God what you are feeling. Tell your wife
and children today how you feel about them. Express to them
what you need emotionally—first, that you have emotional needs,
and second, what they are. Open yourself up to receiving
from them the love they will give you.

LAYING YOUR HEAD ON JESUS' BREAST

Herein is love, not that we loved God, but that he loved us, and sent his Son to be the propitiation for our sins. Beloved, if God so loved us, we ought also to love one another.

1 John 4:10–11

During the Last Supper, as Jesus was eating His final meal with His disciples before going to the cross, we read that John was "leaning on Jesus' bosom . . . lying on Jesus' breast" (John 13:23, 25). Can you imagine what people would say about a man who did that today? Even if we knew the person was very spiritual, we'd probably raise an eyebrow.

But John had no problem with it. He knew that he was loved by Jesus. In fact, throughout the gospel of John, we find John referring to himself as the "disciple whom Jesus loved." (See John 13:23.)

John was open in his devotion to Jesus. Of all the disciples, only John is mentioned by name as being at the crucifixion. He is the only disciple to whom Jesus spoke directly from the cross. Jesus gave John the responsibility for Jesus' own mother. Jesus no doubt knew that, of all the disciples, John was the one most capable of expressing love to His mother.

I once did a study of the life of John and I discovered that John was the youngest disciple. Peter, James, and the others were probably in their forties at the time of Jesus' ministry, but John was very likely in his early twenties. John hadn't been corrupted yet into denying his emotions. He wasn't hiding. He wasn't afraid.

Love and showing love one to another is the hallmark of John's letters.

(See 1 John, 2 John, 3 John.) It is the theme of John's gospel—"For God so loved the world, that he gave his only begotten Son" (John 3:16).

Are you aware that John is the only disciple that we know with certainty died of old age? All of the other disciples, about whose deaths we know, died in martyrdom. But John died peacefully at more than a hundred years of age. I personally believe that was because John had learned how to love people and how to express his faith with loving words backed up by loving actions.

If you want to live a long life and die in peace, I suggest that you lay your machoism down and lay your head on Jesus' breast.

Voice your love to God today. Then swallow your pride and fear and say to your wife, your children, and your friends, "I love you."

THE DOMINO EFFECT OF YOUR PRAISE

[I] will yet praise thee more and more.

PSALM 71:14

There's a domino effect that starts to manifest itself when you praise and worship God. When you open up yourself to tell God how wonderful He is and how much you love Him and enjoy spending time with Him . . . you are very likely to find that your wife starts telling you how wonderful *you* are and how much she loves you and enjoys being with you.

When your wife starts talking to you like that, your children are going to overhear her at some point . . . and very likely they are going to start telling you what a great dad you are and how much they love you and enjoy spending time with you.

What happens to you in the process?

Your loneliness—that ache in your inner man that feels alone and isolated and hurting—is going to be healed. You're going to feel more courage and strength than you've felt before.

As you continue to go to God in open, free-to-be-your-self vulnerability and continue to praise and worship Him with your entire being, your love for Him is going to grow . . .

your love from and for your wife is going to grow, your love from and for your children is going to grow, and

your love for *yourself* is going to grow so that you can appreciate the good things that God is doing for you and in you and through you.

But as long as you starve God of the praises due Him, you are going to be starving yourself of the praises that you need. You'll find yourself living in an emotional wasteland, without love and deep appreciation from the very people with whom you *should* have the most loving relationships.

David said, "O magnify the LORD with me, and let us exalt his name together" (Psalm 34:3). The end result of your magnifying and praising the Lord is that your entire family is going to want to join you in magnifying and praising Him, and as they do, they will magnify and praise one another so that your home will become a haven of peace, rest, and emotional strength.

It's time we start saying to the Lord—

You are wonderful. There's nothing You can't fix. There's nothing You can't do. There's no problem You can't solve. There's no need You can't meet. There's no issue too great for You. I'm casting all of my care upon You. I'm giving it all to You. I'm giving all of ME to You. I'm laying my head upon Your breast, Lord. I know You love me and I'm relying upon You to provide for me every-thing I need! I'm not going to have this depression. I'm not going to stress out. I'm not going to have this nervous breakdown. I'm going to trust You to defeat my enemies for Your glory. I'm trusting You to break down the doors that are locked and to wax great on my behalf. I'm relying upon You to win the victory!

When we praise the Lord, He opens up the gates of His kingdom and sends forth His warriors to fight and win the spiritual battle you are facing. They ride on the wings of our praise.

It's time to break the silence!

**Give voice to your feelings, to your needs, and to your praise.
Lay your head on Jesus' breast today!**

REFUSE TO PLAY THE BLAME GAME

And the man said, The woman whom thou gavest to be with me,
she gave me of the tree, and I did eat.

GENESIS 3:12

G od asked Adam, "Who told you that you were naked? Have you eaten of the tree whereof I commanded you not to eat?" (See Genesis 3:11.) Adam didn't answer either question. Oh, that he would have! Oh, that he could have been honest enough with himself to cry to God, "I have sinned. Have mercy on me!"

Instead, Adam tried to justify what he had done by blaming someone else. He said to God, "It's the fault of the woman you gave to be with me. She gave me of the tree, and I ate of it." (See Genesis 3:12.)

How many men try that same line today?

I'd be a better husband, Lord, if my wife would just . . .
I could be a good father, Lord, but my wife . . .
I'd be further along in my life and in my career, Lord, if only my wife would . . .
I wouldn't get so angry and lash out with so much hatred, Lord, if my wife . . .

And if it isn't his wife who gets the blame, he might try to lay it on someone else.

I'd be more honest in my business dealings if my partner . . .
I'd have better control of my temper if my boss would just . . .
I wouldn't be like this if my parents . . .

I wouldn't have all these troubles if the people in the government . . .

The "blame line" didn't work for Adam, and it won't work for you. The situation in your life is not the *fault* of someone else. It's *your* responsibility.

Deal with yourself. And you'll probably find that those you have been blaming are not nearly the problem they were!

Come before God today and with an honest heart admit, "God, the problem is with me. Fix ME, Lord. Show me what it is that I must do in order to be forgiven and healed by You and to be free to forgive others and to heal my relationships with my wife, my children, my friends, and my co-workers."

YOUR WRESTLING MATCH WITH GOD

THE ENEMY IN-A-ME

*And even as they did not like to retain God in their knowledge, God
gave them over to a reprobate mind . . . being filled with all
unrighteousness, fornication, wickedness, covetousness, maliciousness;
full of envy, murder, debate, deceit, malignity.*

ROMANS 1:28, 29

I n any group of men, I know in my heart that every kind of problem is
present . . .

every kind of need . . .

every kind of weaknesses . . .

every kind of struggle.

I also know that *today* is the time when we need to confront those problems, needs, weaknesses, and struggles.

It's time that we begin to challenge and confront ourselves about what
we hold within ourselves.

I am not too concerned about the witches or witchcraft, or about
demons, demonology, sorcery, or astrology. As bad as crime is, I'm not too
concerned about the mugger, the rapist, or the con artist. What I am concerned about, however, every day of my life is *the enemy in-a-me*. If there's
anyone you need to confront continually, it's yourself.

When a man ignores the commandments of God and refuses to turn to
God and acknowledge Him as Lord, the worst punishment God gives to that
man on this earth is to turn him over to himself—to give him over to his
own reprobate mind.

A popular advertising slogan in recent years had as part of its slogan— "have it your way." The problem is that when we seek to have it our own way, we literally self-destruct.

I am always amazed at how a man can look at another man and arrogantly say, "I'm better than that person." I'm not talking about racial or social distinctions here—I'm talking about the distinctions that we make about another person's sinfulness. When we make a claim that we aren't as sinful as the next person, we are, in effect, claiming that one type of sin—and in particular, *our* type of sin—isn't as bad as another type of sin. The man that draws such a conclusion doesn't know his Bible. The Bible says, "All have sinned, and come short of the glory of God" (Romans 3:23).

The fact is, the capacity for *every* type of sin resides in each one of us. We may not have done it, but chances are, we've thought about it! We each know that there are lots of things in our imaginations that we don't talk about. And if we haven't thought about it *yet*, given the right situation and circumstance, we *will* think about it and possibly even do it.

If you were pressed . . . or under certain stresses . . . or faced with certain alternatives, you'd have no problem at all in committing every sin in the book.

> *If a murderer entered your house and was heading for your child's room, would you have any second thoughts about stopping that man no matter what it took to do so?*
>
> *If you and your family were starving and you came across a cart filled with food, would you have any hesitation about becoming a thief?*
>
> *If you were told that you had to have sex with a certain person in order for your baby's life to be spared, would you say no?*

In our human nature, we are totally depraved. We have an equal capacity to sin. And we each must face that capacity within us. We must confront our sin nature.

Thank God today that He has not turned you over to your own self, but that in His great mercy, He is still present in your life.

YOUR LIFE HAS BEEN PRESERVED

And Jacob called the name of the place Peniel: for I have seen God face to face, and my life is preserved.

GENESIS 32:30

God isn't finished with you yet. You haven't arrived. There's still more to be done by you, and therefore, still more that needs to be done in you. God still needs to work on each one of us.

That truth doesn't scare me in the least. I'm just grateful that He's kept me alive long enough so that He *can* work in me! I'm grateful that He's poured into me what He's already poured into me, and I'm looking for anything else that He wants to pour into me because what He pours is always good!

We each know, if we're honest with ourselves, that the Lord has protected us or we wouldn't be at the point we're at today. We have to admit that His hand was on us long before we were saved.

When you were driving around drunk, an accident just waiting to happen . . .

When you were slapping your wife around and she was on the verge of calling the police . . .

When you were lying to that girlfriend to get her to do what you wanted her to do . . .

God was there. Even then. He had you in His grasp. If God hadn't been merciful to us when we were sinners, we'd all be dead! So often I see men who have been through so much in their lives that I am amazed they are still alive. Anybody else would have self-destructed. Some of their school classmates died. Some of their teenage friends were murdered. Some of their adult friends overdosed on drugs. Through all of their troubles, they are still alive! The devil has tried to take me out on numerous occasions, through one means and another, but I'm still here. And before I'll let him take me out completely, I'll tie a rag around my head and put a knife in my teeth and wait for him in the bushes! I'm prepared to do battle with the devil.

Some people get depressed too easily.

They become discouraged too easily.

They become suicidal too easily.

You've got to have a little Rambo in you!

I'm not giving up. I'm going to FIGHT. I'm going to HOLD ON. That's what Paul wrote to Timothy when he said, "Fight the good fight of faith, lay hold on eternal life, whereunto thou art also called" (1 Timothy 6:12). I refuse to give in!

Thank God today that He is still at work in you. Refuse to give in to the devil. Fight him every step of the way.

REFUSE TO REMAIN A WELL-MARKED TARGET

He was manifested to take away our sins.

1 JOHN 3:5

I f you don't confront your own frailties and your own capacity for sin, you remain a well-marked target for the devil. If you don't admit that you are vulnerable to committing sin in a certain area, you remain vulnerable in that area. Why? Because in being so sure that you'd never commit the sin in question, you take no safeguards against it. And without safeguards, you are wide open to the devil's attack.

You never thought you could get that angry.

You never thought you could be that hostile.

You never thought you could have an affair.

You never thought you could be that weak.

You never thought you could cheat in your finances.

You never thought you could leave your family.

And because you never thought you could . . . you did. Look at yourself in the mirror and admit, I *could* commit every sin. I'm capable of it in my human flesh. People may be saying to you, "You're going to have to deal with your problem." They see your problem as being drugs, or alcohol, or an affair. They may see your problem as being your temper, your hatred, your prejudice, your bitterness.

But I'm telling you, "There's a problem *behind* your problem." And that REAL problem is sin.

What is it that makes a thirty-five-year-old married man try to act like he's seventeen and single?

What makes a man want to drown his troubles in alcohol or use drugs to give himself a high?

Why does a man feel a need to prove himself by doing daredevil stunts?

The bottom-line answer is this: man's sin nature.

Your sin nature is your tendency to want to do what the devil tells you to do, more than you want to do what God tells you to do. It is your sin nature that is changed when you believe in Jesus Christ and accept Him as Savior, and then follow Him as Lord. John wrote, "He that committeth sin is of the devil; for the devil sinneth from the beginning. For this purpose the Son of God was manifested, that he might destroy the works of the devil" (1 John 3:8).

If you have never asked God to forgive you of your sins and change your sin nature, do so right now! God stands ready to forgive you. As 1 John 1:9 promises, "If we confess our sins, he is faithful and just to forgive us our sins, and to cleanse us from all unrighteousness."

Face your own sin capacity and then accept God's capacity to forgive you and transform you.

GOD HAS RESERVED A PLACE FOR YOU

God, who quickeneth the dead . . . calleth those things
which be not as though they were.

Romans 4:17

A re you aware that God has made a statement about you in eternity? God exists in eternity. We exist in time. When God says something, He says it in the context of eternity. That means that it *will* happen and it *will* last forever.

What has God said about you? God has taken a chair and placed it in the midst of His angels in eternity. Then, pointing directly at you, He has said to them, "This chair belongs to that man. I'm going to bring him right here for an encounter with Me. I'm going to do My best to love him until he receives My love and My forgiveness. I am going to make him into one of the jewels in My crown."

And when God speaks, He doesn't listen to any of the arguments that oppose His will.

But that man is a liar.

God says, "A liar is a bad thing to be, but it doesn't stop Me from loving him. I'm going to bring him into My presence. This chair has his name on it."

But he's a thief.

God says, "That's not good, but it doesn't stop Me from reaching out to him. I'm going to bring him into My presence. I love him and I want him here."

But he's a molester.

God says, "That's a very hurtful thing to be, but nevertheless, I'm going to bring him into My presence so I can tell him I love him and desire to forgive him."

Murderer . . . homosexual . . . rapist . . . drug dealer. God says, "I've got a chair with his name on it in My presence. I've got a plan for bringing him here to Me so I can love him and forgive him and live with him forever."

But he's a man who is violent emotionally and physically to everybody he meets.

"Yes," says God, "but when *I'm* finished with him, he's not going to be that way. In fact, he's going to be a deacon in his local church and he's going to be sharing the Gospel with men who are violent emotionally and physically."

I know men today who, ten years ago, would never dreamed of attending one of my conferences, much less praising and dancing and shouting before the Lord.

God calls those things which were not as though they were, because He knows He has the power to make them become what He says they will be. God does not have any doubts about His own ability to save, redeem, deliver, or transform a human life.

Furthermore, the seat that God is holding for you is *your* seat and nobody is going to sit in it but you. You don't have to worry about someone else getting your gifts or taking your place or earning your rewards.

Your enemies never thought you'd be there.

Some of your friends never thought you'd be there.

There were moments that even *you* thought you'd never be there. But the time came when you sat down in God's presence and He sat down with you, and you had an encounter with God and it changed your life.

His right hand and holy arm pulled you out of the place you were and placed you where you are. He has done, is doing . . . and *will do* . . . ALL that He has planned and purposed for you.

That's why God can call a person holy, blameless, and righteous while they are still confused, in trouble, in turmoil, and tied up. He knows His plan and His power. He knows that He *will* accomplish His purposes.

Thank God today for holding a seat for you—for making you an advanced reservation in His kingdom. Trust Him to do in you all that He has planned.

GOD WRESTLES WITH YOU . . . ALONE

And Jacob was left alone.

GENESIS 32:24

G od maneuvers each one of us into a place where He can deal with us
directly. He calls us to a state of "aloneness." He doesn't deal with us
in the context of other people. Cliques, clubs, groups, and all sorts of
entanglements, societies, and mentalities can keep us from hearing God as
much as they can help us to hear from God. When God gets you to the
point of dealing with the deep issues of your life, He does so one-on-one.
Just you and God. Just me and God. Just each one of us alone with God.

Who are you really?

When nobody's looking . . .

    when you aren't "prepared" . . .

        when all the camouflage has been removed . . .

            when you don't have an ego to

                defend or anything to prove . . .

                    when you aren't bogged down in imitations or con-
                    cerned about status?

Who are you?

Anytime you are surrounded by people who don't know the real you . . .

Anytime you are in a situation where you can't fully be yourself . . .

Anytime you have to camouflage who you really are to be accepted . . .

You are alone. You will feel isolated, as if you are watching people through a glass wall.

When God is ready to do His divine surgery on you, He brings you to an "alone" place. Nobody invites guests into an operating room. Neither does God. His work on you is private.

When God begins to move in on your life and starts setting up His one-on-one appointment with you, you may feel very uncomfortable. In fact, I believe the first response of nearly all of us at that time is to try to surround ourselves with more and more people. We feel restless, frustrated, lonely in our spirits. We feel a greater need to have somebody with us, to protect us, shield us, wrap their arms around us, join us, walk with us. We soon discover that the presence of other people doesn't meet the need. The loneliness and restlessness we are feeling in our spirits is God's call to us. He is reeling us in to our one-on-one encounter with Him.

You can be surrounded by people . . . and still be alone.

You can have intimate relations with your wife . . . and still be alone.

You can have dozens of close friends . . . and still be alone.

It's when we admit that we are lonely and need something that people can't supply—we need Someone to fulfill a part of us that nobody else seems to be able to fulfill—that's when God steps in.

When you say that you are left alone, it means that somebody that you thought you could count on for protection has disappeared. You feel isolated, separated, apart. Alone.

When we feel left alone, therefore, our hope is usually that someone will come along and comfort us. In fact, we expect from our human standpoint that "comfort" is what a loving God would do to a man who is left alone. God says, however, that He is not coming to comfort, but to *confront*. God came to challenge Jacob, to wrestle with him. Jacob's first reaction was, no doubt, "Oh, no, not You too!"

Everybody is wrestling me.

My wife is wrestling with me.

My children are wrestling with me.

My boss is wrestling with me.

My creditors are wrestling with me.

My co-workers are wrestling with me.

My church is wrestling with me.

My own mind is a wrestling match.

And now, You, too, God?

The Bible says, "Faithful are the wounds of a friend" (Proverbs 27:6). A true friend is one who "wounds" you for a good reason. What he says may hurt you, but in the end, it helps you. What he does may seem painful to you, but in the end, you'll thank him for doing it because it was for your good.

A really good friend doesn't agree with you all the time. No matter how brutally you roar, a good friend will stand right up in your face and say, "You're still wrong."

You don't have real help until you have someone who will confront you about what needs to be changed in your life.

God comes to each one of us . . .

To stand up to us, and to force us to face our sin.

To confront us about our lies.

To make us uncomfortable about our bad habits.

To move us away from mediocrity.

To challenge us to excellence.

Are you ready today for your private appointment with God?

WHY GOD CHOOSES TO WRESTLE WITH YOU

Seek, and ye shall find.

MATTHEW 7:7

God wrestles with you so that you will discover what you are made of. He already knows what He created you to be and He knows what you've done with His creation. He's waiting for you to discover who you are. He wrestles with you so you will know His power and your weakness, His wisdom and your error, His strength and your frailty.

God wrestles with you to make you realize that you are wasting your life . . .

that you are mistreating your wife . . .

that you aren't the "greatest" or the center of the universe . . .

that you aren't the "least" and unworthy of anything good.

God wrestles with you to make you see that you need to keep this job and not quit it like you did the last three jobs . . .

you need to stay involved with this church and not back away from it like you did the last three times you say that you "got religion" . . .

you need to stay in your marriage and not wander off like you did the last time.

God wrestles with you until you face the facts of your life. He doesn't sugarcoat anything. He gives it to you straight. He wrestles with you until you admit . . .

Yes, I'm unstable.

Yes, I'm making excuses.

Yes, I was wrong.

God also wrestles with you so that you will start searching for Him and hunting for what He wants you to find.

Man is a hunter by nature. God's commands to man at his creation were to "be fruitful, and multiply, and replenish the earth, and subdue it: and have dominion . . . over every living thing that moveth upon the earth" (Genesis 1:28).

To subdue means to conquer, to have dominion means to maintain one's conquest. Somewhere as part of the masculine nature is the need to subdue, the need to conquer, the need to track down and bring something into dominion. There's a hunter inside every man.

We may be hunting for a contract or business deal.

We may be on the hunt for a woman.

We may be hunting for the perfect new car.

Sometimes we don't even really want what we are after, we are just hunting because it is our nature to hunt. Fishermen often catch fish, unhook them, and throw them right back. They say, "Look what I caught." And then they toss that fish back into the lake. That doesn't make the man any less a fisherman. It means that he is merely fishing for the sport of it, not for dinner. He is "hunting."

Unless we allow God to step in and give us the right goals and guide our "hunting" instinct, we can spend our entire life hunting for the wrong things.

Jesus said, "Seek ye *first* the kingdom of God" (Matthew 6:33). And He promised that if you seek for it, you'll find it. (See Matthew 7:7.)

Wrestle with God today until the night ends, the dawn breaks, and you can see His face, feel His love, and know His purpose.

THE URGENCY OF GOD'S PURPOSE

Return ye now every man from his evil way, and amend your doings,
and go not after other gods to serve them, and ye shall dwell
in the land which I have given to you.

JEREMIAH 35:15

R eturn NOW.

There is always an urgency in God's call for us to repent of our sin and to return to Him.

There is also a persistence in God's wrestling with us. People will sometimes tell us what they think, but then they abandon us. God doesn't give up. He wrestles with us *until*. He isn't swayed from His purpose.

There's an appointed time for the wrestling match in your life to end. God wrestled with Jacob "until the breaking of the day" (Genesis 32:24). God wrestled with urgency, with insistency, with greater and greater strength. He knew that if Jacob didn't confront who he was in that night, he was going to miss the prime opportunity to become who he was destined to be.

You may be running out of time, too.

A lot of things you perhaps could get away with in times past . . . you no longer can get away with. A lot of excuses you've used in the past . . . you no longer will be allowed to use.

God's urgency must not be ignored. He knows something about your life and your encounter with Him that you don't know. He knows when Satan's assassins have been launched against you for your demise. He knows when the death angel is allowed to do his work. He knows when He is returning again.

Before you lose your life . . .

Before you lose your integrity . . .

Before you lose your wife . . .

Before you lose your son or daughter . . .

Before you lose your future blessing . . .

Before you lose what God has given to you . . .

God's urgency is for a *purpose.* Don't ignore Him.

You don't have time to fool around.

You don't have time for detours.

You don't have time for childish things.

You don't have time for your rebellion.

You don't have time to play games.

You don't have time for an affair.

You don't have time for meetings and committees that aren't important.

If you're going to experience the place God has reserved for you, you are probably going to have to cut off some relationships . . .

give up some things . . .

dig deeper into God's Word . . .

learn how to pray for yourself . . .

and truly become the priest of your home.

If people ask you why you can't do what you've done in the past, tell them, "I don't have time. I'm going someplace and I've got to get there."

Look at your watch right now and say to yourself, "NOW is the appointed time for me to serve God so I can dwell in the land He has prepared for me!"

THE TOMB IS NO PLACE TO LIVE

THE REALITY OF THE SPIRIT REALM

We wrestle not against flesh and blood, but against principalities,
against powers, against the rulers of the darkness of this world,
against spiritual wickedness in high places.

EPHESIANS 6:12

There is a world about which many of us are unconscious, or unaware. It is real nonetheless. In fact, it is more real than the world we can see, touch, taste, hear, or feel. It is the realm of the spirit.

The most real part of you is your spirit. You *are* a spirit. Many men seem to think the real part of them is their body, but no matter how much you build it up, manicure it, dress it, or feed it, you are not first and foremost a body. You *have* a body. You live in a body. It is a temporary home.

You also have a soul. The soulish area of man is where most of the problems occur; this is the area of the mind, the emotions, memories, appetites, desires. The mind of man, including the mind of the Christian, is often trapped between the physical and the spiritual—flashbacks to memories of the former life in the flesh can fill the mind. The result can be a tremendous wrestling match, with each force, spirit and flesh, trying to dominate the other. In fact, it is only when a man receives the Word of God and engrafts it to his mind that he is able to save his mind from the clutches of the flesh.

Demons are disembodied spirits. They don't have a body, and they don't have a soul—they have no mind of their own or will of their own. Their will is totally subjected to Satan. They are vessels and carriers of Satan's nature. They are filled with his desires, his lusts, his passions, and his unclean thoughts.

Because demons don't have bodies, they are seeking one. They are seeking a vehicle through which they can express their lusts and passions for evil.

Jesus once said to Simon Peter, "Simon, Simon, behold, Satan hath desired to *have* you, that he may sift you as wheat" (Luke 22:31). He was saying to Peter, "Satan desires to possess you, to have you, to dominate you." Men know what it means to lust after a woman in order to *have* her. That's the way Satan looked at Peter. He lusted after him, that he might completely *take* Peter's mind and body—to satisfy his cravings through him.

Satan's demons desire the same thing today regarding you—

To use your body, your temper, your lust, your passions.

To work through the broken places of your childhood to fulfill their ravenous desires.

To possess you so that he might sift you.

Before Satan makes a move to have you, he studies you. He learns all he can about you—your moods,

your attitudes,

your background,

your past hurts and

painful memories,

your desires.

He has stalked you. He has put you under surveillance, watching always for an opportunity to move in to take you. He *longs* to possess,

dominate,

control,

rule over,

and act through you.

That's the reason you must walk *closely* by the side of Jesus. Cling to Him. Never for a moment believe Satan's lie that you can go it alone or make it on your own strength. David—one of the bravest and most capable men who ever lived—cried out to God, "Hide me under the shadow of your wings." (See Psalm 17:8.) Tucked under the wings of God . . . that's the only place you will ever feel fully secure.

Trust in the Lord today. Ask Him to give you the courage and faith to withstand Satan's sifting.

WHO IS IN CONTROL?

Lead us not into temptation, but deliver us from evil.

MATTHEW 6:13

E very act of your life is motivated by a spiritual force.
Who is controlling you?

What is motivating you?

What spirit is being satisfied through your body?

If it is Satan's spirit that you are allowing to work in you—manifest through his demons—then you are grieving the Holy Spirit. Any time you allow the enemy to work his will through your mind or body, you grieve the Holy Spirit.

The Holy Spirit also desires to use you. But He wants to use you for God's glory and God's service. You will feel satisfied and have great joy when you live for God's glory. The Holy Spirit's purpose is not to dominate you or crush you, but to fulfill you.

Satan desires to use you for his own purpose, as a pawn in his hand to laugh in God's face. He desires to use you, abuse you, and then refuse you. You are in a state of living death when you succumb to the devil's purpose. He defies God as he works in you through his demons, saying in effect, "Is this someone You wanted, God? Well, I'm here first and I'm not moving. You called this man Your son? Look who's really in charge of his life. Look what I am making Your son do."

Temptation is Satan's tool for getting you to do things that you really don't want to do. Deep inside your spirit, you know that what he is tempting you to do is wrong. The worst and most hardened criminals in our world today know they have done wrong—they may blame others for their actions, they may act as if they don't care about the fact that they've done wrong, been caught, or are facing serious consequences—but deep inside, they know. They knew when they were doing wrong that what they were doing was wrong.

Satan's lie is that you have a *right* to do wrong.

Society is at fault. You have a right to get even with society.
Your daddy is at fault. You have a right to rebel against him.
Your boss is at fault. You have a right to steal from him or cheat him.
God is at fault. He made you this way. You have a right to act the way you
    do because He made you with this temper, this anger, this lust, this desire.

God's Word says that you have a right to choose. Joshua said to the Israelites, "Choose you this day whom ye will serve . . . as for me and my house, we will serve the LORD" (Joshua 24:15). You have a right to choose, a free will, a mind that can make a decision. But you have no right to sin.

Make sure today that you are yielding the control of your life *only* to God.

Make it your prayer today: "Deliver me from evil!"

DON'T LET SATAN DIVIDE AND CONQUER YOU

If we say that we have no sin, we deceive ourselves,
and the truth is not in us.

1 JOHN 1:8

One of Satan's foremost tactics is the tactic of "divide and conquer." When Jesus encountered the man with an unclean spirit, He found him dwelling among the tombs. He was outside the city, away from family and friends. He had been "divided," and then conquered.

Satan always and relentlessly will attempt to move you away from community, family, and ministry. He will do anything in his power to convince you to break away, because he can conquer you more easily if you are isolated.

The enemy will move you to break away from others by feeding you lies, some of which are that . . .

You're exceptional. You're not really LIKE these people. You are better than
they are.
Your situation is different. You grew up in conditions that weren't like those of
anybody else's.
Your childhood has molded you in certain ways that cannot be altered.
Your problem is unique. Nobody can relate to your problem because nobody
has had it as bad as you had it. They can't relate to how you feel.

These lies become your excuses. They become your false premise for your taking license to act or speak in ways that are contrary to God's commandments. If you think that you aren't like other people, then it's only one step further for you to come to the conclusion that you don't have to abide by the same rules as other people.

If you find yourself saying . . .

I wouldn't be like this if my mother hadn't given me away . . .

if I'd had a different father . . .

if I had a more loving wife . . .

if I had a better job . . .

if I had not faced so much opposition . . .

. . . wake up! You are giving yourself a passport to failure, a visa to flunk. You are hardening your attitude so that no matter who preaches to you, you whip out your yeah-but card and say, "This is why your message won't work for me."

If you adopt an attitude that you are "different," then you mentally and emotionally begin to separate yourself from other people. You disconnect from your foundation and from the fundamentals of truth. There's grave danger in that, especially if you are disconnecting from people who truly know God and are serving Him.

Once you are disconnected mentally and emotionally, you are also disconnected in other areas of your life whether you intended to be or not. You'll find it impossible to keep a job . . .

hold a marriage together . . .

relate in good ways to your children . . .

or make any long-term commitment that requires self-discipline.

The reason that you offer to others is always a *good* reason. It makes sense to you. It may even make sense to other people. It just doesn't fly with God.

Your excuse may keep you from being disgraced. But it will also keep you from being convicted and from changing.

Don't buy into Satan's lies. Don't give yourself license to lay in the cesspool of sin. Get rid of your excuses!

Refuse to be separated from God's people, God's plan for righteousness, or God's purpose for your life.

When Satan comes around with his lies,
confront him with God's truth.

BEWARE: MAN OUT OF CONTROL

There met him out of the tombs a man with an unclean spirit . . .
no man could bind him, no, not with chains.

MARK 5:2, 3

One of the indications that a person is bound by Satan's influence is that "no man could bind him, no, not with chains."

The issue is one of control.

Now, I'm not talking about whether this man was possessed or oppressed. In either case, a person is being controlled by Satan. Even a Christian can be so oppressed that he operates under Satan's control.

A little boy might be sitting on his daddy's shoulders, pulling at his left ear and saying, "Daddy, go this way," and then pulling at his right ear and saying, "Daddy, go that way." And in play, the daddy does what the little boy demands. This little boy isn't *in* his father, but he is *controlling* his father's actions. And that's the way demons operate. They seek to fuel our desires and direct our passions, and in so doing, exert such tremendous influence on our behavior that it's almost as if we no longer have a will of our own.

You can be so oppressed that you might as well be possessed. The result is that you are a lascivious man.

Lasciviousness is unrestrained action. It is being "out of control." No limitations. Whatever flesh says, flesh gets.

If you are angry, you tear up everything in the house.

If you are lustful, you'll even try to date your sister-in-law.

If you are filled with hate, you'll break every stick of furniture in sight.

The man who is lascivious might as well wear a sign around his neck, "Man out of control." He does things he may not even like to do solely because they are *possible* to do. He can't be trusted. He can't fulfill responsibility.

The lascivious man can't be bound. He doesn't pay any attention to the restraints of others or to the normal conventions of society or to the normal restraints of his own conscience. He certainly doesn't pay any attention to the commandments of God.

Domestic violence is "man out of control." It's a man beating what he ought to be protecting, it's a man beating his own body.

Sexual and physical abuse is "man out of control." It's a man turning on his own *zera*, his seed, so that his own children can't feel comfortable sitting on his lap.

Lasciviousness knows no boundaries. It infects every race, every culture, every nation. Rich and poor. Educated and uneducated. It doesn't care if a man is wearing a pinstripe suit with a red paisley tie or a plaid flannel shirt and jeans or a torn T-shirt and baggy pants.

Nobody tries to get close to a man out of control. They want to, but they are afraid to.

Daddy's drinking.

Papa's high.

Father's in a bad mood tonight.

Honey's not at home and it's midnight.

It's not a matter of temptation. All men are tempted. It's a matter of self-control and self-discipline. Can God trust you to control your own *self*, to put boundaries on yourself?

One of the indications that this man had an unclean spirit was that nobody could get him to stop doing what he was doing. And what is it that he was doing? He was "crying, and cutting himself with stones." He was hurting *himself*.

The Bible says this man "had been often bound with fetters and chains, and the chains had been plucked asunder by him, and the fetters broken in pieces: neither could any man tame him" (Mark 5:4).

This man had been caught in the past, but he got away. He had made New Year's resolutions, but he broke his commitment to himself before January was over. He had been to the altar before and told God, "never again," but he had lied to God. He had done the very thing he had vowed never to do again. And you know, once a person has lied to God, he has no trouble at all lying to his wife, his children, his pastor, his friend, his boss.

> *Oh, you're so slick. You can slip past anybody if you want to. You can get away with anything.*
> *Oh, you're so discreet. You're just sitting idly by, hunting with your eyes. Nobody knows what you're thinking, nobody knows the fantasies that you are living out in your mind.*
> *Oh, you're so clever. You have a justification for everything, an excuse for every action, an alibi for every hour.*

The reality is, you are hurting yourself when you break through all barriers. You are cutting short your own potential. You are breaking chains that were in place for your own good.

Is there an area of your life today that is out of control? Ask God to bind it up—and to give you restraint by the power of the Holy Spirit.

Say no to your flesh today and say yes to the Spirit of God.

STOP LIVING IN THE TOMBS

And always, night and day, he was in the mountains, and in the tombs.

MARK 5:5

The fact is, we're killing ourselves. Countless men are living in the "tombs." I'm not talking about murder in the streets. That's there, and it's real, but that's the "outer world." I'm talking about the "inner world," the world that's just behind the facade that you put on.

You can kill a person with your words, your attitude, your absence. You can kill a relationship without any other weapon than your tongue. You can murder an association or a relationship without exploding any bomb; you can destroy it by neglect.

We are a people living out in the tombs. We're surrounded by death, and much of it is death that we have inflicted upon ourselves.

How many aborted babies were yours, and you didn't even know it because you weren't *around* to know it?

How many of those boys in the 'hood are running in gangs because you refused to be a father to them, and perhaps didn't even know you *were* their father?

How many women are in counseling offices every week because of what you said you'd do that you didn't do, or because of what you said you didn't do that you did do?

How many chains have you broken?

How many people are bleeding from wounds that you inflicted?

How many of your children are going to need serious pastoral counseling?

How many people are suicidal or messed up in their minds because of the lies you told?

How much death and destruction have you caused in your life? What tombs are you living in?

Jesus said, "I am the way, the truth, and the life" (John 14:6). Turn to Jesus today and ask Him to forgive you for all the deaths you have caused. Ask Him to lead you into the FULLNESS of His life.

Today can be your resurrection day in Christ Jesus!

THE VICTIMS OF SPIRITUAL AIDS

*This poor man cried, and the Lord heard him,
and saved him out of all his troubles.*

PSALM 34:6

A IDS.
It's a deadly disease.

But there's something even worse than acquired immune deficiency syndrome and it's this: "Spiritual AIDS."

A spiritually acquired immune deficiency syndrome has some of the same hallmarks as AIDS:

- It is *acquired*. You get it, catch it, or buy it. You become infected with it. You pick it up and it stays in you.
- Its presence in you is related to the broken-down barriers in your life. Just as your immune system keeps you from becoming sick from every germ or virus or bug that comes close to you, so your *spiritual immune system* keeps you from falling prey to every trick and temptation of the enemy. When your immune system breaks down, you get sick. When your spiritual immune system breaks down, you are an easy target for the devil.
- It is *deficiency*. You are lacking the spiritual immune system you are supposed to have. The barriers that once kept you from sin have been torn down in your mind. You know, people sometimes say they are scared to be around people with AIDS. The reality is, people with AIDS

should be a lot more scared of you, a person without AIDS, than you should ever be of them. Why? Because you have immunity and they do not. You are carrying germs and viruses in your body that aren't affecting you because of your healthy immune system, but those germs and viruses can be deadly to them.

The person with spiritual AIDS catches everything that passes by him. The Bible says, "He that hath no rule over his own spirit is like a city that is broken down, and without walls" (Proverbs 25:28). Without immunity, without defense, without walls.

- It is a *syndrome*. Spiritual AIDS becomes a habit. It sets itself up in the spirit and it becomes a man's identity.

The man with an unclean spirit had a spiritual disease that was out of control, and it was killing him. He was already living in the tombs. He wasn't far from death himself.

The man with AIDS is a man who is living with a time bomb in his body. Death is stalking him. The man with spiritual AIDS is also living in a state of death—and his state is much worse because it is a state of *eternal* death.

The cure for spiritual AIDS is found in Psalm 34:14, 17—"Depart from evil, and do good; seek peace, and pursue it. . . . The righteous cry, and the LORD heareth, and delivereth them out of all their troubles."

Ask God to give a boost to your spiritual immune system today.

HUNGERING FOR RIGHTEOUSNESS

Blessed are they which do hunger and thirst after righteousness:
for they shall be filled.

MATTHEW 5:6

The man with an unclean spirit looked strong. He caused fear in others. Nobody wanted to get close to him because they were afraid of his strength that could "pluck asunder" fetters and leave chains in pieces.

But when this man was alone, he was anything but strong. He was crying. (See Mark 5:4–5.)

Countless men are crying today because deep down inside their hearts, they have become something they didn't *want* to become.

Not wanting to be who you are is the key to your deliverance. It's not what you've *done* that makes you a candidate for God's forgiveness; it's how you *feel* about what you have done and how you *feel* about what you want to be.

Jesus did not cross the Sea of Galilee on a stormy night to meet this man simply because he had an unclean spirit. No doubt there were people with an unclean spirit on the shore where Jesus was. No . . . Jesus was led by God to this man because this man was in the tombs "crying." He didn't want to be the man he had become. He didn't want his future to be the same as his past.

Thank goodness, Jesus didn't say, "Blessed is he who *IS* righteousness." That would eliminate all of us from God's blessing! Thank goodness, Jesus said, "Blessed is he who still wants to be righteous—who still has an appetite for doing the right thing, who still thirsts to be a better person, who still wants to be whole even though he knows he isn't whole . . .

who still wants to be the good husband he knows he isn't . . .
who still wants to be the father he believes he can be but isn't right
now . . .
who still wants to change and grow,
who still desires to be holy."

Deliverance begins with desire, a PASSION in you that challenges the PROBLEM in you.

I do not want to live like this anymore.
I do not want to be like this.
I do not want to act like this.
I do not want to be a drunk, a drug addict, a homosexual.
I do not want to be this angry, this critical, this cold, this indifferent, this
destructive, this lazy, this trite.
I do not want to be jealous, suspicious, or distant.
What is it that you *don't* want to BE anymore?
What is it that you *don't* want to DO anymore?
What is your cry to God?

God can and does hear you when you cry. He doesn't condemn you for crying out to Him. Rather, He moves toward you when you cry. He comes to you with deliverance and forgiveness.

Cry out to God today for the changes you want in YOUR life.

STOP CUTTING YOURSELF DOWN

He was . . . in the tombs . . . cutting himself with stones.

MARK 5:5

This man with an unclean spirit is a classic example of a man with extremely low self-esteem. He didn't value himself. He was cutting his own flesh with stones. Countless men today are "cutting themselves" in their own minds. They may put on a brave front to the outside world, but when they are alone, they wound themselves and bleed—they dissipate their own energy, their own life force.

They are insecure about themselves, hating themselves. The man who hates himself cannot love another person. How can you give to another person what you can't even give to yourself? It's not possible. The man with low self-esteem can't build up other people—not his wife, or his children, or his employees, or those he is asked to supervise at work.

Self-image is the most important thing in the world that you need to have next to your faith in God. It doesn't matter what others think of you. It matters only what *you* think of you based upon what *God* thinks of you.

When you start cutting and gnashing at yourself, you become preoccupied with self-hatred.

We each treat other people out of our own reservoir of self-dignity and self-respect. If you don't have respect for yourself, you won't have genuine respect for other people. Jesus taught, "Love thy neighbour as thyself" (Matthew 19:19). If you don't love yourself, you can't love your neighbor.

The Bible also says that a man should love his own wife as he loves himself. (See Ephesians 5:28.) If you don't like yourself, you can't love your wife.

Most men who abuse their wives are self-haters. It is out of their own anger and frustration that they lash out at their wives. They aren't overflowing with hatred for their wives, but for them*selves*. If you truly want to know how you feel about your*self*, look at how you treat your wife. She is your body, one with you. She is "bone of your bone and flesh of your flesh"—the feminine expression of your masculinity. The way you treat your wife is the way you treat your*self*.

If you are physically, sexually, emotionally, or verbally abusing your wife, you are abusing yourself.

You are denying,
>   screaming at,
>   lashing out at,
>   ignoring in your silence,
>   cutting to the core of . . .
>   *your very own self*.

You cannot receive the esteem of your son or daughter if you do not esteem yourself.

The man with an unclean spirit was cutting himself, doing far more damage to himself than any other person had ever been able to do to him. The same holds true for us. We do far more damage to ourselves than others do.

Self-esteem has to come from self. You won't believe the good things that anybody else says about you unless you first believe those things about yourself.

I like me. I'm glad if other people like me, but I don't do what I do *so* that other people will like me. I'm not dependent upon whether other people like me or not.

If I come across anybody who doesn't like me, I am very happy to say to them, "I disagree with you." I don't give in to the way they feel about me and like myself less. I simply disagree with their opinion. I like me! I have a right to my own opinion.

I know all about me . . . and I still like me. I know all my faults, but I still like me.

I like me in part because I'm still here—I've survived. I've lost some friends, some jobs, some cars, some things . . . but I'm here. If you have no other reason to like yourself other than the fact that you are a survivor of life's problems, like yourself for that reason.

Be who you are and be proud of it.

Not a lot of blacks live in West Virginia, especially in the rural areas. Sometimes when I am out in the remote regions, I encounter little white children who have never seen a black man. I recall this one little boy who just stared at me, aghast. He had never seen anything like me in his life. He said, "Lord, mister. Are you that color all over?"

His mother almost turned purple in embarrassment. I said to him, "Yes, I think I am. Everywhere I can see and everywhere I can see in the mirror, I'm this color. It seems to be all over me."

I'm not at all ashamed of being a black man. That's who God made me to be!

Start believing in the *you* that God made *you* to be. He loves you and that's all the reason you need for loving yourself.

Compliment God today on the fine job He did when He made you.

WORSHIP AWAY YOUR PROBLEM

When he saw Jesus afar off, he ran and worshipped him.

MARK 5:6

This man with an unclean spirit saw Jesus from afar off and his response was to worship Him. I want you to note that this man didn't get delivered first and then worship Jesus. He worshiped Jesus and *then* was delivered by Jesus.

Some men today aren't delivered from the oppression they are experiencing from the devil because they haven't learned how to *worship away their problems.*

Even the devil has to bow down and acknowledge that Jesus is Lord of all. The Bible tells us that *every* knee must bow to Him: "of things in heaven, and things in earth, and things under the earth; and that every tongue should confess that Jesus Christ is Lord, to the glory of God the Father" (Philippians 2:10–11). Every system, government, and society must bow to the Lord of lords and King of kings.

Every hex, every curse, every evil work must BOW to the name of Jesus. That includes every satanic power and generational curse. "No weapon that is formed against thee shall prosper; and every tongue that shall rise against thee in judgment thou shalt condemn. This is the heritage of the servants of the LORD, and their righteousness is of me, saith the LORD" (Isaiah 54:17).

Your childhood hurts . . .

your painful memories . . .

your addiction . . .

your past sins . . .

must BOW to the name of Jesus. You must condemn anything that rises up in you to destroy you and your ministry—your lust, your anger, your hate, your bitterness, your rebellious spirit, your job-quitting, church-hopping spirit—and say to it, "*BOW* to the name of Jesus."

Bow in worship.

When this man began to worship Jesus, the demons in him cried out, "What have I to do with thee, Jesus, thou Son of the most high God? I adjure thee by God, that thou torment me not" (Mark 5:7).

The fact is, demons have NOTHING to do with Jesus. They have nothing in common with Him, no association with Him, no alliance with Him. And Jesus has NOTHING to do with them except to cast them out. The very presence of Jesus torments demons.

If you are in a truly anointed worship service, demons scream out and flee from people who are calling out to the name of Jesus. Nobody has to touch a person or pray a long prayer over a person with unclean spirits. The very atmosphere of worship is a torment to demon powers.

Worship is the key to your deliverance.

Run to Jesus today and worship Him!

BREAKING THE DEVIL'S STRONGHOLD

Deride every strong hold.

HABAKKUK 1:10

D avid was a good man. He was creative, strong, courageous. He was a man of musical and songwriting talent. He was a natural leader. But he had a generational curse on his life—a lust problem that cropped up from time to time.

Everybody around David apparently knew he had this problem. In fact, the Bible says that when David was an old man and he could not get warm, his servants brought a young virgin to lie in his bosom, that "the king may get heat." (See 1 Kings 1:1–2.) His servants said, in effect, "If being with this young woman can't get David's circulation going, nothing can! He probably *is* dying if he doesn't feel anything when he's with her."

The generational sin in David was passed on to Amnon, who had a lustful spirit for his sister, Tamar. He lured her to his bed and raped her. The Bible tells us that when David heard what Amnon had done to Tamar, he was very angry . . . but he didn't say or do anything to Amnon. What could he say? His son was just like him. His own spirit of lust had passed on to his son. (See 2 Samuel 13.)

Lust is not a craving,
    a fancy,
        or a whim. It's sin.

When a pattern of evil passes from generation to generation, it becomes what the Bible calls a spiritual "stronghold." A spirit of evil is passed from generation to generation until it truly has a *strong hold* on a man's life. He can't get free of it simply because he wishes to be free or hopes to be free. Only Jesus can set that man free.

Many men can look back at their family history and see a bad spirit at work in their family, generation after generation.

> *Daddy drank too much . . . and granddaddy drank too much . . . and great-granddaddy drank too much.*
>
> *Dad cheated on Mom, and Grandpa cheated on Grandma, and Great-Grandpa wasn't even around to cheat on Great-Grandma.*
>
> *Father had a bad temper . . . and so did grandfather . . . and so did great-grandfather.*

Sometimes a man can look and see a pattern of abuse and sin and evil coming at him from both sides of his family tree. It isn't only his grandpa on his father's side who was filled with anger, but his grandpa on his mother's side. Or, a man may know nothing about his grandparents or great-grandparents—and perhaps not even his father's behavior—but he may see a particular pattern of behavior rampant among his brothers, uncles, and cousins. His *family* has been infected with a bad spirit.

When Jesus commanded the demon who afflicted the man in the tombs to tell Him his name, the demon replied, "Legion: for we are many" (Mark 5:9).

Very often, the demonic oppression on our lives has many facets—it has many names, simultaneously. The spirit is not just one of lust, but of anger. It is one of emotional deprivation and one of poverty. When you combine various types of demonic oppression they multiply in their hold on a person's life.

A spiritual stronghold is not something that you can drink out of your life . . .

smoke out of your life . . .

curse out of your life . . .

argue out of your life . . .

or plead out of your life. BUT you can CAST it out of your life!

Before you go to the judge . . .

Before you go to the rehab center . . .

Before you go to the counselor . . .

Go to God.

Get to the altar and ask God to break that stronghold from your life. You may still need help to learn *how* to express yourself, but first and foremost, you need God's help in breaking the spiritual oppression that has you in its clutches.

If you don't break the spiritual strongholds on your life, your own sons and daughters will be victims of it. Lay your hand on your son and your daughter and say . . .

Don't let the same things that infected me, infect another generation.

Don't let the same abuse be passed on to my children.

You could be a great husband.

You could be a great father.

You could be an outstanding employee.

You could be a very effective witness.

What keeps you from it? Name that stronghold and ask God to break it off your life.

Make Jesus the Lord of anything that is lording it over you.

BREAKING THE CURSE OF POVERTY OFF YOUR LIFE

Bring ye all the tithes into the storehouse, that there may be meat
in mine house, and prove me now herewith, saith the Lord of hosts,
if I will not open you the windows of heaven, and pour you out a
blessing, that there shall not be room enough to receive it. And I will
rebuke the devourer for your sakes, and he shall not destroy the
fruits of your ground; neither shall your vine cast her fruit
before the time in the field, saith the Lord of hosts.

MALACHI 3:10–11

J ust recently I heard a report about a young child who went to school wearing a $400 pair of shoes. This child was the son of a woman who was selling drugs. I thought to myself, if that woman can trust the devil and his demons to clothe her baby like that, how is it that Christian men refuse to trust God to take care of them and their families.

And yet I see it all the time: Christian men jealous of other men. Mostly they are jealous of their *stuff.* They are jealous of their house, or their car, or their wristwatch, or their clothes, or their gold jewelry, or some other possession they have.

Then, to compound matters, they try to cover up and justify their jealousy by saying, "We shouldn't have nice things or own the best that is available to purchase." They turn their jealousy into a stingy, angry spirit. They complain about the kind of car their pastor drives, although when they were in sin, they never once complained about the gold jewelry and big diamond rings and fancy cars that were owned by the man who ran the local bar or the corner pool hall.

I refuse to give in to the jealousy of other people. I want to say to any person who might be jealous of something I own, "I paid for what I have, and I paid first of all in the spirit realm."

God said that He would bless me if I brought my tithes into His storehouse. He said He would open up the windows of heaven and pour out a blessing on me and my family that was so great I wouldn't have room enough to receive it. He said He would rebuke the devourer from my family. He would cause us to be fruitful in every area and that others would see our blessing and call us "delightsome." (See Malachi 3:12.)

I broke the spirit of poverty over my house by giving my tithes and giving my offerings. I beat the devil out of my checkbook and pleaded the blood over my finances. I scraped and crawled my way up out of poverty and into God's prosperity by doing what God said to do! And you can, too.

I refuse to listen to those who have spent the money that should have been their tithe and offering to God, who are bound up in a spirit of poverty and stinginess toward the things of God, and then complain that I shouldn't receive or enjoy God's blessings. The simple fact is, I have done what God has said to do. They haven't.

Do what God says to do in His Word. And then . . .
Let God bless you! Enjoy what He gives to you!

Take authority over your finances today. Rebuke the devil from your finances in the name of Jesus, give your tithes and offerings—as the man and priest of your house, and then look for God's blessings to be poured out from heaven on you.

CASTING THE DEVIL OUT OF YOUR FAMILY

[Jesus] said unto him, Come out of the man, thou unclean spirit.

Mark 5:8

J esus' response to the man who was living in the tombs was to speak to the evil spirit in him, "Come out of him." (See Mark 5:8.) Jesus didn't condemn the man. He condemned the evil spirit that had attached itself to the man.

This was a good man who had a very bad spirit in him. The bad spirit needed to be pulled out of him, the power of the evil spirit broken in his life.

When Jesus rebuked the devil in this man's life, the demon started pleading. He didn't plead about leaving the man, but about leaving the "neighborhood." It was as if he was saying to Jesus, "I've been assigned to this territory. Don't make me leave my post."

The devil may not mind your being free. But he will mind being cast out of your family. He may say, "If I can't have you, at least let me have your son." The devil will do his best to drive a wedge between you and your son so you can't communicate and so that he will come to a conclusion that you don't love him.

The devil may say, "Fine, if I can't have you. Let me have your brother, your cousin, your neighbor." He wants to stay in your neighborhood.

Your answer to his compromise must always be NO!

Shout it at him. Refuse to give an inch. NO to his having your son. NO to his having your daughter. NO to his having your brother or sister. NO to his having your neighbor. Shout it LOUD.

There was so much demonic power in this one man that when Jesus commanded the power to leave, He sent it into an entire herd of swine. They broke their natural instinctual tendency and leaped into the sea.

If the devil can't have you, he will make a bid for your family. Don't allow it.

Pray that the blood of Jesus will cover your entire family today. Claim your wife, your children, your brothers and sisters, your nieces and nephews, and your grandchildren for God.

DIRECTING YOUR DELIVERANCE BACK HOME

*And when he was come into the ship, he that had been possessed with
the devil prayed him that he might be with him. Howbeit Jesus suffered
him not, but saith unto him, Go home to thy friends, and tell them how
great things the Lord hath done for thee, and hath had compassion on
thee. And he departed, and began to publish in Decapolis how great
things Jesus had done for him: and all men did marvel.*

MARK 5:18–20

When a man is truly delivered by Jesus, everybody can tell. You can't
keep it a secret. When the man with an unclean spirit named Legion
was delivered, everybody in both the city and the surrounding countryside
knew it. They all went out to see what had happened.

When you are delivered by God . . .

Your old girlfriends are going to know it.

So are your old running buddies.

And your old drinking buddies.

And your co-workers.

The people in your old neighborhood are going to hear about it.

And for some of you, the people in your church will be able to see a
difference!

Don't be ashamed to be a witness!

Be happy about what God has done for you.

If all God wanted was your salvation, He would have heard your pleas
for forgiveness, saved you, and then killed you. No! God wants you to be
His witness.

Where?

First, to those who are right where you are.

This man wanted to go with Jesus as He departed by boat to go to the other side of the lake, but Jesus said no. Why? He intended for this man to be a witness *to the people who knew him best.*

His ministry wasn't to be in the tombs or in the mountains where he had withdrawn in his torment. It was to be in the cities of the Decapolis, the place no doubt where this man had first become oppressed by evil.

God never intends for us to live apart from the world, but to be witnesses *to* the world.

Have you ever been to a meeting or a conference that was so wonderful, you never wanted it to end? Have you ever been on a retreat in a place so beautiful that you never wanted to go home?

That's the way the unclean man felt after Jesus had delivered him from the demon power that was oppressing him. He didn't want to leave Jesus' presence.

God frequently gives us "mountaintop" spiritual experiences—leading us to times and places where we can experience a powerful anointing of His presence—but then the time comes when He says to us, just as Jesus said to this man, "Go home."

Ask God today where He wants you to witness for Him. It very likely will be the place you know best.

Today, tell somebody who is CLOSE to you
about the love and power of God.

GETTING BACK INTO YOUR RIGHT MIND

[They saw him] that was possessed with the devil, and had the legion,
sitting, and clothed, and in his right mind . . .

MARK 5:15

When God does a work in your life, He does it in calmness. He brings about a peace in your life. All hell may be breaking out against you, but you can sit back and whistle.

This man with an unclean spirit sat calmly at Jesus' feet after his deliverance. He had been ranting and raving, roaming through the mountains and tombs—restless in his outward actions, just as he was forever restless in his inner spirit. After his deliverance by Jesus, he knew the peace that only God can give.

This man was clothed, where he once had been naked. The Bible tells us that those who overcome the enemy shall "be clothed in white raiment"—they will be in God's eyes as if they have never sinned. Peter tells us that we are to be "clothed with humility," completely submissive to God so that we will hear what God wants us to hear, see what God wants us to see, and then say and do what God wants us to say and do. (See Revelation 3:5 and 1 Peter 5:5.)

Have you thought about the fact that once this man had been delivered and forgiven by Jesus, it was as if he had *never* been under the influence of a demon power named Legion? It was as if he had never walked around with torn chains hanging from his arms and legs, slashing himself with stones and living in the tombs. He was *clothed* with righteousness. God saw him only as *forgiven*. He had no "past" with God, only a bright future.

The assurance of forgiveness is what gives a man peace. When you truly know you are forgiven, you feel a calmness born of trust, a peace born of assurance. Paul described it for the Philippians as a peace that "passeth all understanding" (Philippians 4:7).

Every man I know needs this kind of peace.

You cannot be the head of your house and be hysterical at the same time. You can't fall apart just because your wife has fallen apart. You can't lose your cool just because your kids have lost theirs. Somebody has to keep their wits about them and say, "We're going to come out of this." As priest of your home, you are called to be a stabilizing, protecting force in your home. When you walk in the front door of your house, everybody in your family should feel safer. You are called by God to have a "right mind." "Let this mind be in you, which was also in Christ Jesus" (Philippians 2:5).

Having a right mind means being aware of your responsibilities and accepting them.

I know many men who let their wives deal with all the stress of the family, including anxiety over the family finances, worries over the spiritual life of each family member, and concerns over family provision. That's not her role. You and your wife must share the responsibility for your children and work together to make a plan for your family. It's a cop-out for a man to say to his children every time they ask for a decision, "Go ask your mama."

Can you answer these questions about your children?

Where are your children?

What time do they go to school?

What time do they get home?

Where are they in the evenings?

What time will they be back?

You should know!

Having a right mind means being responsible in providing for your family.

I see absolutely no excuse today for a man not to have a job. If there isn't a job available in your community that's suited to your educational level, find a job that's lower than your educational level and fill it until a better job opens up. If it's not illegal, and it's not sin, go for it! Pick up a shovel and dig a ditch if you have to. You may say, "Bishop, have you ever done that?" I certainly have. I have dug ditches until my hands were bleeding in order to get $100 to buy groceries to feed the children for another week. As long as I am in my house, I am responsible for providing for my household.

If you can't provide everything you *want* to provide for your family, do what you *can* do. You may not know everything, but you can find people who can teach your children the things necessary for them to know. You may not understand the Bible fully, but you can get your children to church and Sunday school and to youth group programs where they can learn the Bible, experience the power of God, and learn how to apply the truth of God to their lives. You may not know everything about prayer, but you can pray for your children with a humility of heart and a love that speaks volumes.

Ask the Lord to transform you by the renewing of your mind. (See Romans 12:2.) The Lord Jesus Christ *is* your sanity.

Ask God to give you a clear, pure, right mind today.

GUARD, GIRD, AND GUIDE

For this God is our God for ever and ever: he will be our guide.

PSALM 48:14

As husband and father, your role is threefold:

- *to guard your family*, which includes practical safety, but also spiritually guarding against evil.
- *to gird your family*, which means to provide for your family the support it needs—including food, shelter, clothing, and general well-being.
- *to guide your family*, which includes having a plan and direction for your family—setting goals, developing your family's witness and outreach efforts, and guiding your family into a greater understanding of God's truth.

Guarding means that if there's a strange noise in the night, *you* get up. If your child is having serious trouble in school, *you* go there. If somebody comes to the door, *you* answer it. Guarding sometimes means simply showing up. For you to be there when your child needs you, you need to be sensitive to their needs.

Girding means that your children have shoes on their feet and clothes on their back. It means making sure your wife has what she needs. I do everything in my power to make sure my wife looks good. She's a reflection on me! I do everything I can to make sure that she's happy and content. She's my best sermon! In fact, I expect to live in such a way with my wife that if I die before she does and she remarries, her next husband will *hate* me. He'll have to work overtime to do for her as much as I have done—including writing songs and poetry just for her, blowing kisses to her across the room, buying her nice things, giving her the compliments she deserves. He's going to get very tired taking care of her in the way that she is accustomed to.

Guiding means having a plan. For example, as you face your family's finances, do so with a plan. Then, share that plan with your family. Make it an all-family effort. Say to your wife and children, "Things are tight right now, but here's what we are going to do. In three months, this is where we should be. In a year, this is our goal. In three years, we should have our finances fully under control." Give your children a future to anticipate with hope. They can't have hope if you haven't spelled out a plan and set a direction toward a circumstance that will be better than what they know today.

Have an agenda for your family's spiritual growth. Plan with your wife what you are going to do together to raise your children up to know and love God, His Word, and His church.

Guard.

Gird.

Guide.

Make that your motto!

Even as you choose to guard, gird, and guide your family,
trust God to guard, gird, and guide YOU.

GETTING TO JESUS . . .
NO MATTER WHAT IT TAKES!

THE UNTAPPED POWER OF CHRIST

For thine is the kingdom, and the power, and the glory, for ever.

Matthew 6:13

One of the things that needs to be better understood within the body of Christ is the power of Christ. In many cases, the church needs to understand this as much as the world does. Christ is not a weak, impotent, unresponsive force. Our God is a God of power—He impacts every situation and circumstance He is allowed to enter with revolutionary, life-changing power.

One Christian can chase a thousand, and two can chase ten thousand because our God allows it to be so. (See Deuteronomy 32:30.) The church bears all the power necessary to heal marriages and to heal those who are sick—physically, emotionally, mentally, and spiritually. The real psychologist's couch resides in the Word of God. The church can impact every community—its families, its economy, its health.

When Jesus came to a city, the magistrates and all of the city leaders knew it. He worked in such a way that everybody knew He was there. He *changed* things.

It's time that more of us in the body of Christ be noisier about the power of Christ—to be movers and shakers who will go into the enemy's camp and take back what he has stolen from us.

We have the answer to domestic violence,

racial tension,

immorality. His name is Jesus. We don't need to look to the White

House, but to the church house. We don't need to take over the ballot box; we need to kneel before the altar.

This is not to say that the church today is so perfect that it couldn't be amended or improved. But what is wrong with the church is of man, not Christ. His power is absolute, unchanging, and perfect.

The power of Christ can be criticized . . . but not contained. It can be frustrated or thwarted . . . but not stopped. It can be hindered . . . but not quenched. If God is behind even the smallest thing, it becomes mighty, effective, and powerful to the tearing down of all types of strongholds.

It's time we used the name of Jesus to declare that the enemy no longer has any authority over our own lives, or the lives of our families. We must force the issue with the enemy. We must be radical enough to "make" him loose us and let us go.

Say to the enemy today, "In the name of Jesus, loose me. Loose my family. We belong to God and to Him alone!"

MAKING A "NOISE" AND A DIFFERENCE

*And again he entered into Capernaum . . . and
it was noised that he was in the house.*

MARK 2:1

When Jesus arrived in Capernaum, He turned the city upside down.
Whatever you enter today . . .
Whatever you belong to . . .
Whatever you participate in . . .
Whatever you are in . . .
Your presence ought to be felt.
*If you're on the usher board, every usher ought to be blessed because you're
on the board.*

*If you're on a neighborhood committee, every other person on the committee
and every person your committee touches ought to be blessed because you are
there.*

*If you're on the job, your boss, your co-workers, your customers and clients,
your vendors and suppliers, your employees . . . everybody with whom you do
business ought to be blessed. You are God's agent for making a difference for good.*

Your presence also ought to provoke change. Wherever God is present,
change happens. Things grow. People's attitudes are altered. Situations are
turned around. There's no way you can be filled with God's presence and
then be incapable of altering your circumstances.

I recently was asked, "Bishop, what do you think about the hopelessness
in our nation?" I said, "What hopelessness?" I don't believe in hopelessness.

I believe that as long as you have a thumping of your heart in your chest, you should have hope. As long as you are a blip on a monitor and your skin is warm you *must* have hope! I don't care how bad you blew it or what you have done, as long as you can say, "Jesus," you have hope.

You have hope because you serve a God Who has the power to change things, and to call into being things that are not.

Make some noise today about Who God is and what God does. Do it by your love in action as much as by your words of hope!

Be God's agent for change wherever you go today.

WHAT HAS YOU BOUND?

Bringing one sick of the palsy.

MARK 2:3

This man who was sick of the palsy was in an immobile state. Palsy is a term that was applied to a number of diseases at the time of Jesus. It was used to describe the condition of any person who was unable to command movement in an area of his body. This man apparently was incapable of commanding movement that enabled him to walk.

In palsy of this type, the muscles, tissues, blood vessels, bones, nerves, and every other physical attribute necessary for movement are present. But for some reason, flesh rebels against command.

I should be able to move from where I am, but I can't. I'm stuck.
I want to move on, but I can't. I'm stuck in this place.
I don't want to live like I'm living, but I can't seem to change. I'm stuck in this condition.
I want a better life for my family, but I can't seem to make it happen. I'm stuck where I am.

Men get angry when they feel "stuck." They feel as if everybody else is moving and free. They have all of the physical, mental, and emotional attributes necessary for change and growth—they can still think, still feel. They still have talents and skills. They still have opportunities and possibilities. But their inner spirit does not respond to command. They are in a state of inner rebellion.

Stress turns into pressure, and pressure into rage, and constant rage creates a state of weariness. Webster defines weary, in part, as having "your sense of pleasure exhausted." When you are weary, nothing is exciting. Everything seems bland. You become numb, unable to act or even to believe for change. Every day seems like the day before.

It doesn't matter if you live in a ghetto or a penthouse, if you are not liberated in your mind and encouraged in your spirit, you will feel as if you are in a jail cell. You will feel stress.

Stress, anger, and prejudice are not linked to any one race or level of income. They infect nearly every person. And if they become severe enough, they bring a person to a state of weariness, of numbness, of immobility.

Such a person is sick of inner palsy.

A man can get stuck in childhood memories.

He can get stuck in teenage issues.

He can get stuck in an adult problem.

While one type of palsy leaves a person "frozen," incapable of movement, another type of palsy leaves a person with spastic motions—the person can't coordinate his movements, or hold onto objects he desires to hold.

Some men can't hold a job.

They can't hold a relationship together.

They can't seem to hold onto their finances or save money. They can't keep their word. A part of their lives is out of control.

Lust out of control . . .

rage out of control . . .

bitterness out of control. The man with this type of palsy knows something is wrong with him, but he can't seem to do anything about it.

A third type of palsy comes from sheer muscle exhaustion. A man's muscles become so worn out he can't move. The mind, the emotions, and the spirit also can become exhausted.

If you have everyone around you drawing from you, you can quickly become depleted unless you have another means of making deposits into your life. That's true in your finances, your emotions, your ministry, your health. If you don't give something back to yourself, you will soon have nothing to give out. It simply isn't possible to be a continual encouragement to others, and not become discouraged, drained, or depleted in the process. You must avail yourself of conferences, meetings, seminars, and retreats that will build you up and give something back to your spirit.

Whatever the cause of this man's palsy—frozen muscles, spastic muscles, or exhausted muscles—Jesus was his Great Physician! Whatever your palsied state today, Jesus holds the key to your vibrancy, freedom, healing, and an abundant life.

The Bible tells us that when David's family was taken captive at Ziklag and David was "greatly distressed," he "encouraged himself in the LORD his God" (1 Samuel 30:6). Jude speaks of our "building up" ourselves on our most holy faith. How? By praying in the Holy Ghost and by keeping ourselves in the love of God, looking for the mercy of our Lord Jesus Christ unto eternal life. (See Jude 20–21.) Build yourself up in Jesus!

Refuse to live in a frozen, out of control, or exhausted state.
Ask Jesus to impart to you His LIFE.

BE PREPARED FOR A HEAVY LOAD

They come unto him, bringing one sick of the palsy,
which was borne of four.

Mark 2:3

L et me assure you of this, if you ever decide to carry another person, you will discover that he is heavy. It took four men to carry the man with palsy to Jesus and he no doubt was a heavy load for even four men to carry.

Anytime you pick up the weight—the problem, the need—of another person, you'll likely find that it is a heavy load. Don't ever be duped into thinking that ministry is easy. Genuine and effective ministry to another person is always a great challenge.

First, you must be sensitive to a person's need to be carried. In any church service you are in, there's somebody close to you who is lying on a "stretcher" on the inside. He may act as if he has his life together, but he knows he's putting on a facade. He knows he has a need, but he may have trouble telling you about it. He's hurting . . . he's out of control . . . he's paralyzed in some way . . . and he knows it. In all likelihood, his wife and children know. You will have to be very sensitive to the Holy Spirit if you are to know it, too.

Don't be fooled by the prayers he prays when others are listening. When he's alone, he's praying a different way.

He's mumbling and groaning and crying into his pillow. He's crying out, "Lord, if You don't help me, I'm going to lose everything I have."

Don't be fooled by his fancy clothes or big smile. On the inside he's crying, "Help!" Don't be fooled by his race, his denomination, or his status in society.

Black man . . . gotta get to Jesus.

White man . . . gotta get to Jesus.

Brown man . . . gotta get to Jesus.

Red man . . . gotta get to Jesus.

Baptist man . . . gotta get to Jesus.

Pentecostal man . . . gotta get to Jesus.

Rich man . . . gotta get to Jesus.

Poor man . . . gotta get to Jesus.

Big-shot executive . . . gotta get to Jesus.

Down-and-outer . . . gotta get to Jesus.

Don't be put off by his "dirty" reputation or by his sin.

Man on crack . . . get him to Jesus.

Man abusing his wife . . . get him to Jesus.

Man abandoning his family . . . get him to Jesus.

Don't pick up another person only to drop him. If you commit to helping another person come to Christ, make sure you bring him all the way to Jesus, no matter what it takes.

Many times we only want people delivered if it's easy on us. We don't want to have to sacrifice to see the deliverance or healing of another person.

Hold him steady.

Hold him tight.

Hold him until Jesus touches him with His power.

As you carry him, reassure him . . .

You have an appointment with a miracle. God has set a time for you to experience a complete makeover . . .

a massive turnaround . . .

a total reconstruction. You may not be able to help where you have been, but you can do something about where you are going. God has something better for you than anything you've known to this point!

Once you get a man to Jesus, you no longer have to carry him. Make sure you get him there, but once you have him in Jesus' presence, leave the work to Jesus. David said, "In thy presence is fulness of joy; at thy right hand there are pleasures for evermore" (Psalm 16:11).

If a person who is hurting is brought to Jesus, he isn't bashful about asking for what he needs. He knows that he may be experiencing his last chance to cry out to God and be heard. David cried out, "Lead me to the rock that is higher than I" (Psalm 61:2). The hurting man WANTS you to take him to the One Who can meet his needs.

Helping another man get to Jesus is the greatest thing you can do in this world. Be a lifesaver, a soulwinner, a family-healer, a community-changer. It will happen as you get those with palsied spirits to Jesus, the Healer and Deliverer.

Join with a Christian friend today in praying and believing for a man who needs to be healed by Jesus. Be sensitive to what God tells you to do for him and say to him.

BRINGING THE NEED TO JESUS

And they come unto him. . . . And when they could not
come nigh unto him for the press, they uncovered the roof
where he was: and when they had broken it up, they let down
the bed wherein the sick of the palsy lay.

MARK 2:3, 4

These friends of the man with palsy brought him to Jesus. They didn't bring him to church—not to the bureaucratic power structure of the church or to a cold, dead church service. They brought him to the direct power of Jesus.

They brought him to the One Who could heal him. They brought him on a stretcher because he couldn't walk on his own power.

Every time I hold a men's conference, I know that there are some who come because they want to be "seen" at the conference . . .

others come because their friends are coming and they don't want to be left out . . .

some come simply because they have a new suit and they are looking for a place to wear it . . .

still others come because they say they don't have anything better to do . . .

but there are also those who come on a stretcher. They may be brought by others who saw a need in their lives. They may be bringing their own needs into the conference as if bringing their inner man on a stretcher.

Those who have spiritual palsy—paralyzed in their need or sick with needs that are out of control—are the ones who get the most help. You see, they don't care if their names are called or who sits next to them. They are present to receive from Jesus all that He has for them. They need help . . . and they know it. They aren't embarrassed to reach out and receive all the help Jesus offers to them.

One of the things every person has to do in coming to Jesus is to get through the "press."

So many men come into the church today and they can't get to Jesus for the "press"—the press of all the church politics and the press of all the she-say, he-say, they-say hearsay. So many people are in their way, they can't see Jesus, even though He's the One they came to see and the One they need to see the most.

Some people have become so "professional" in their approach to church, they've forgotten why they are in the church. They've forgotten how they once felt, who they once were. They've lost sight of Jesus for the "press" of knowing who's hot and who's not. They've been around so long they've lost the pure motive of worship—of humbling and casting themselves before Jesus in total submission.

Don't let anything or anyone stand in the way of your bringing your need to Jesus.

Don't think about what other people might think of you . . . or what they might say to you. Don't worry about how you look . . . or about how you sound. The thing that matters is that you express yourself to God. Tell Him what you need. Praise Him for His provision.

No matter what effort it may take, get to Jesus today!

EXPECT TO RECEIVE

When Jesus saw their faith . . .

MARK 2:5

The men who brought their palsied friend to Jesus were men of faith. They didn't just have faith. They had an active, alive, relentless faith. They had faith in action.

I have to admit, I really LIKE the four men who were carrying the man with palsy to Jesus. They were not ordinary believers. They were *radical*. They weren't about to let anything get in the way of their receiving from Jesus what they wanted to receive. They had come to get a blessing and they weren't going home until they got it.

When you go to church, make a commitment to yourself that you aren't going to go home until you have received from God what you need and want to receive from Him. Say to yourself . . .

I'm not going home until I come out of the bondage I'm in.
I'm not going home until I'm delivered from the pressure I feel.
I'm not going home until I get the blessing I need.
I'm not going home until I release the unforgiveness, discouragement, anger, or resentment I feel.

Open yourself up to every bit of the power of Christ that is present.
Draw out the power of Christ that's in the singing.
In the preaching.
In the teaching.

In the praying.

In the communion.

In the giving.

In the loving.

Don't shut yourself off to any of the power of Christ that is flowing toward you. And if there's no *power* of Christ Jesus in your church, get to a place where His power *is* flowing freely.

I have no use for dead churches. I have too many things that I'm fighting to come into a sophisticated arena where everybody is acting like intellectual, spiritual elitists and Holy Ghost yuppies. I need the power of God to be at work in my life every day!

I want to be in such powerful services that if I have any demons whatsoever trying to cling to me, the very power of praise and worship will shake them off. I want to be under the anointed preaching of God so that as the Word of God goes forth, it will deal with any issues in my heart that need to be changed. I need to be in the presence of an anointed ministry that will cause tears to well up in my eyes and confront me with the hard issues that I have been refusing to face, but need to face, so I can truly be set free of all influences of evil that are aimed at my destruction.

Go to where the power of God is being manifest. Open yourself to receive God's power and presence. Expect with your faith that God *will* fill you to overflowing.

Put your faith into action today. Go to God
and expect to receive from Him.

TEAR AWAY ALL HINDRANCES

They uncovered the roof where he was: and when they had broken it up,
they let down the bed wherein the sick of the palsy lay.

MARK 2:4

When the four men who were carrying the palsied man arrived at the house where Jesus was preaching, they couldn't get in. They went up on the roof, but there was no opening there. They had to uncover the roof—peeling away the roofing material to create their own "door" through which they could let down their friend. Nothing about bringing this man to Jesus was easy. They had to make it happen.

The roof was a hindrance to them, but they didn't let a mere roof stop them.

What is hindering you today from getting to Jesus?

It might be your temper . . .

It might be your loneliness . . .

It might be your frustration . . .

It might be your childhood.

Tear the roof off! Get to Jesus—whatever it takes.

Who told you that you couldn't get a job?

Who told you that you couldn't have a good marriage?

Who told you that you couldn't get free of drugs?

Tear the roof off! Believe God can do it.

If you are bringing another man to Jesus, you are going to run into all kinds of hindrances.

He hasn't been to church in twenty years.

He won't go with you. He is too strung out on dope to know what's going on. He's not in a condition to go with you.

He's too angry to hear your invitation. Don't try talking to him now.

He's too involved with crime to give it up. Don't endanger yourself.

Tear the roof off! Don't let fear or pride stand in your way. Get that man to Jesus.

I don't know what "roof" separates you or someone you love from Jesus. Whatever it is, it *can* be removed. It can be torn away.

As these men were working on the roof, they were only a matter of feet away from Jesus. They were very close to their miracle. They were not about to be denied.

You are close to your miracle today. Get to Jesus no matter what it takes. Don't let anything stop you.

Don't give up. Jesus has a miracle for you and for those you love. Get to Jesus. His power is sufficient for every need.

GIVING A NAME TO THE FATHERLESS

He said unto the sick of the palsy, Son . . .

MARK 2:5

The Bible doesn't give us the name of the man with palsy. In many Bible stories, we not only have the man's name, but we have his father's name. For example, we know that the blind man in Jericho was Bartimaeus, son of Timaeus. (See Mark 10:46.) When a person's name and father's name are given, the implication is that the person is important. This palsied man was a no-name boy. We don't know his name. We don't know his father. For that matter, he may not have known his own father.

Fathers in the Bible give their sons status, a place in the society. They give them their identity. Today—as then—if a boy doesn't have a father, he doesn't have full status. He doesn't have a full identity.

When I look at our society today, I see thousands upon thousands of young men who are fatherless. They group themselves together because they don't belong to a group called family that is led by a leader called father. When I was a boy, my friends and I were afraid to walk into a group of men who might be standing on a street corner. We'd give them a wide berth. Now I see grown men who are afraid to walk into a group of boys. They go out of their way to avoid them.

Fatherless boys are very often called by their problem, not their names. They are labeled just as this man was labeled—"sick of the palsy." He was identified by his condition.

Troublemaker.

Dope-head.

Gang-banger.

Homosexual.

Convict.

Rapist.

Fatherless boys become known for their condition, their predicament, their past actions.

We, as Christians, must go get these fatherless boys. It may take four of us to reach one boy, but we must go get them and bring them to Jesus.

And what did Jesus call this man who was called by everyone else as the one who was "sick of the palsy"? Jesus called him "son." He saw beyond this man's problem and looked into his person. He spoke to him, giving him a name that gave him a relationship. Jesus gave this man an identity, even before He forgave his sins and healed his body!

In calling this man "son," Jesus was taking upon Himself the role of "father." We must do the same.

We must not wait until the fatherless boys we encounter are cleaned up, singing in the choir, or leading the Bible study. Jesus called this young man "son" while he was still sick. He didn't condemn him for what had caused his palsy. He didn't say to this man . . .

You shouldn't have dated that girl.

You shouldn't have hooked up with that gang.

You shouldn't have taken that first drink.

You shouldn't have smoked that first joint.

You shouldn't have gone into that pool hall.

You shouldn't have . . .

No. Jesus loved him as he was. He entered into a relationship with him while he was still sick and in sin.

Neither did Jesus put any qualifications upon His relationship with this man. He didn't say to him . . .

If you'll clean up your life . . .

If you'll agree to do things my way . . .

If you'll stop . . .

If you'll start . . .

No. Jesus loved him without qualification, without condition.

We are called to do the same.

I tell my sons, "You are strong . . . handsome . . . vibrant . . . able . . .

resourceful . . . intelligent *men*, not wimps. You are able to take a licking and keep on ticking. You are *somebody!* As God's child, you don't ever have to be lonely, destitute, desperate, or empty. You never have to be jealous of anybody. You are rich soil and fertile ground for a great harvest of blessing."

I have told my daughters repeatedly that I am their first date. I am the one who takes them out to nice places and buys them pretty dresses and shows them a good time. I'm the one who shows them the example of how a man should treat a woman with courtesy and manners. I'm the one who tells them that they are special, beautiful, and lovely in spirit. When they get to be dating age, their dates are going to have a tough act to follow. My daughters are accustomed to affection and praise and kindness; a young man would have a very tough time slapping my daughter and then trying to convince her that she deserved it. She'd likely say to him without any hesitation whatsoever, "I don't *think* so. My daddy told me otherwise."

Tell your children who they are to you, and who they are to God. Do the same for your spiritual sons and daughters.

Every child needs an identity. Every child needs a daddy.

Identify a boy or young man today whom you can love and help as a spiritual son. Bring that young man to Christ. Don't put qualifications, conditions, or condemnation on him. Love him as Jesus loves him. Call him "son."

FROM THE INSIDE OUT

*[Jesus said], Why reason ye these things in your hearts? Whether is it
easier to say to the sick of the palsy, Thy sins be forgiven thee; or to say,
Arise, and take up thy bed, and walk? But that ye may know that the
Son of man hath power on earth to forgive sins . . . I say unto thee,
Arise, and take up thy bed, and go thy way into thine house.*

MARK 2:8–11

Jesus first healed this young palsied man on the inside—down deep
where nobody could see any manifestation whatsoever that he had been
healed. So often, we bring a man to Jesus and then we say to ourselves,
"Nothing happened." We are looking for signs on the outside. We don't
know what Jesus is doing on the inside of that man, or what Jesus has
already done to heal him where he hurts the most.

We say, "He doesn't really know Jesus. He's not really saved. If he was
saved, he'd. . . ."

We say, "He didn't get delivered. If he was delivered, his life would be
cleaned up."

The reality, however, is that God may very well have accomplished a
definitive work on the inside of that man. In *God's own timing*, He will also
do the outer work.

God heals the man . . . and then He heals the man's marriage.

God saves the soul . . . and then He deals with the man's addiction.

God delivers the man . . . and then He addresses the issue of the man's
finances.

God deals with the inner man . . . and then He gives the promise, delivers the gift, and creates the new identity and reputation.

God doesn't heal our circumstances until He first heals us so we don't destroy the new circumstances He creates! Believe that God is at work in the ones for whom you are praying . . .

to whom you are witnessing . . .

for whom you are believing . . .

and with whom you are ministering.

Believe for both an inner healing and an outer restoration.

Never dismiss or discount God's ability to work in ways that may remain a mystery to you.

PICKING UP YOUR SICKBED

And immediately he arose, took up the bed, and went forth before them
all; insomuch that they were all amazed, and glorified God.

MARK 2:12

Once the Lord has established Himself as Lord over your spirit, He seeks to establish Himself as the Lord over your life. He anoints you, calls you, and leads you into service. He gives you the strength and energy and ability to carry the very thing that once was the mark of your sickness.

Once Jesus had healed this man and raised him up from his sickbed, this man raised up his sickbed and carried it away.

When this palsied man was forgiven and healed by Jesus, he had a bed—but the bed no longer had him. True deliverance is when you have control over the thing that once controlled you. You can control your temper, when once your temper ruled you. You can control your spending habits, when once your lust for things had control over you.

You can control the wandering eye that once was always looking for a new woman to conquer.

Your problem may remain, but it isn't bossing you. It isn't in control of you. You are in control of it.

And to whom does the Lord often call you to minister?

To a person who is in the very condition you were in before you were brought to Jesus! It is to that person that your witness is the most effective because you can say with authority, "I once was lost just like you. But now I am found. I once was blind. But now I see. I once was lying paralyzed and out of control in a sick condition just like you, but now I am healed. Jesus made the difference for me. And He can and will make the difference for you."

From what has God delivered you?
To whom, then, is He calling you?

LIFT UP YOUR HANDS

Thus will I bless thee while I live: I will lift up my hands in thy name.

PSALM 63:4

I have a young son and when he was learning to walk, he didn't walk with his hands down by his side, but with his hands raised straight up. That position apparently gave him a sense of balance he didn't feel when he had his hands down.

When we raise our hands in praise, we find a new balance for our spiritual lives. We are better able to walk, regardless of the circumstances that may be in our way or which direction our path takes us.

No matter how tired I might have been when I got home at night, if my young son came toward me, toddling along with his hands raised up in the air, I couldn't help but pick him up. Even if he was stinky, if he grinned at me with that cute grin of his, I had to pick him up. I'm his father. He's my son. I couldn't help but pick him up and hold him close.

The same for our heavenly Father. He responds to our uplifted hands of praise. He picks us up. He carries us through the places that are too hard for us to walk through. He holds us close and whispers in our ear how much He loves us.

No matter how stinky we may be in our sin, if we will only look toward Him, He picks us up and forgives us. He calls us "son."

You may be wounded . . . but you're still His son.

You may be hurt . . . but you're still His son.

You may be in sin . . . but you're still His son.

He wants to lift you up and heal you so that you can lift up whatever it was that once held you down.

Praise Him today. Lift up your heart, your voice, and your hands to Him.

Reach up today to the One Who is already reaching down to you—
your heavenly Father.

T.D. JAKES

T.D. JAKES SPEAKS TO MEN!

INTRODUCTION

Few church leaders are ministering God's message of restoration and masculine identity to the needs of men today like T. D. Jakes. Bishop Jakes' biblical message on the true nature of manhood is a clarion call to the church.

We have tried to capture some of T. D. Jakes' most inspiring manhood messages in this convenient quote book. Whether it is read at home or during a break at work, it is our hope that these bite-size nuggets of wit and wisdom will encourage men everywhere to celebrate their manhood—with T. D. Jakes!

You must eat from the garden of your own thoughts. So don't grow anything you don't want to eat.

If there is anything worse than the rage, the frustration, and the other negative things that come out of us, it is the things that do not come out! Festering wounds are dangerous wounds.

Within every man dwells the little child who preceded him. Manhood is rooted in childhood. Many of the thoughts you and I have today come from our early experiences as children.

We court disaster when we carry childish perceptions into adult relationships.

You will never understand the man I am on the outside until you have touched the child within me.

There is no room in the kingdom of God for macho men trying to impress one another with their collection of "toys" or "possessions." It doesn't matter whether these toys are cars, biceps, girlfriends, church members, or certificates of deposit. There is no room for this power struggle.

Our handicaps—whatever form they may take—keep us from reaching our potential and fulfilling our dreams.

Even our failures as Christian men are successes! They represent the miracle that you and I survived!

In desperation, we make permanent decisions about temporary circumstances.

We can no longer allow our past to destroy what God has for us in the present.

Only Jesus can walk us through the barrier of time to invade our
past. There, He can make us comfortable with our uncomfortable
parts and at peace with our frailties and brokenness.

You can never become what you want to be until
you can drop who you used to be.

The greatest and most lethal weapon the enemy
can ever challenge you with is YOU.

Thousands of men once believed they could never cheat
on their income tax or their wives. But they did.

When you do not assess the potential of sin within,
you will not pray against it. This will inevitably
leave you vulnerable to the attack of the enemy.

Who are you when nobody is looking? That is the real you.
Who are you really?

God has given you a marvelous gift. He has given you life.
What are you going to do with it?

God's way is to tell it like it is. He doesn't put a bandage on
your infected wound—He demands that the problem be dealt with.

God has commanded me to tell you that *you are not who others say
you are!* . . . You are more than other people's opinions. Why
should others name you, determine who you are, and set
the limits of your success?

This is not the day for the sniveling, weeping, weak, limp-wristed,
emasculated man. This is the day for the leaping, jumping, rejoicing,
resourceful man! Leap out! God has a plan for you.

Men, you are more than your childhood. You are more than your past. . . . You are a prince, and you don't even know it!

If you face your past because you want your future, God will open up the windows of heaven and pour you out a blessing!

Christian man, you are a prince, and the devil knows it. That's why he's been trying to assassinate you.

The enemy knows what you can be, and he wants to destroy you before you become what God said you will be.

It is time for men to pray. It is time for us to go to war as men, as princes of God. There are hands holding this book right now that will not be here next year if someone doesn't pray for them.

The turbulence of change can be overpowering. Satan does not want men to change. So if you are going to have peace in the process, you must guard your heart and mind with prayer.

Change isn't cheap. It will cost you a "death to the old" in order to experience a "birth to the new."

We need to celebrate our manhood from our first entrance into adulthood—to the end of our "grandfather phase." We need to receive instruction about our God-given responsibilities. We need to celebrate who we are in God's plan.

There may be a lot of people who don't want to give you a chance to change. But God is not like people. Every morning that you open your eyes and fill your lungs with air, God gives you another chance to change.

David didn't rely on his own strength, ability, or skill. He didn't claim to be a mighty warrior or a great tactician. He just claimed to serve a mighty God! His strength came from *knowing who God is.*

David tapped into the true source of manhood. His strength didn't come from male hormones or his male-dominant culture. It flowed from God's supernatural source.

David showed us the right way to love true friends. He openly loved Jonathan, without any taint of homosexuality. We're so uptight that we can't even touch one another—except for a slap on the rear after a great play on the football field.

We need to model masculinity before our sons and help them celebrate their developing manhood.

True manhood doesn't flow from the natural,
it flows from God's supernatural source.

A true man inspires manhood in others.

One absolute prerequisite to the celebration of manhood is
that there must be a *lion and a lamb* in every man.

Jesus Christ was both God and man, lion and lamb.
The art is to have both and know when to be which.

Generations are waiting to taste the fruit of
your manly obedience and determination today.

Our challenge as men is to overcome our reputation for being unable or unwilling to recognize problems in our relationships.

The greatest triumph in any man's life can be reduced to a mere monument of bitter rejection received through a withering remark or icy glance from a jealous wife.

Many times relationships arrive at their demise because we fail to discern problems before they escalate to emergencies.

It is normal to expect your priorities and needs to change with time and maturity. But if you fail to keep your wife abreast of the changes within you, don't be surprised or upset if she continues to give you what you used to need and wonders why it isn't working anymore.

Tragedy comes to our marriages when we fail to *discuss*
our discouragement rather than argue about guilt.

There is a difference between discussion and argument. A discussion
airs the issues, but an argument alleges charges and appoints blame.

Many times the fear of rejection has closed down the hearts of men
because they are traumatized and paralyzed by its pain.

We surround ourselves with images of success
to hide our secret fears.

The greatest problem that can arise in our marriage is when we
decide to become "marital missionaries." A marital missionary
is a man who thinks he is called to change his wife—
rather than to understand her!

Men are master at giving things. Where we have big problems is
when we are asked to give *ourselves!* The real truth is that
your wife doesn't need more things—she needs *you!*

If you believe in the sovereignty of God, as I do, you know that
God can make a bad decision turn out good. He can make a
miracle out of a mistake.

You don't have to be a perfect performer. You don't even have to be a
"ten." You just have to be a man. Your wife doesn't need to be a
perfect "ten" either— or a "convert" to your image. She just has to be
a woman, a genuine woman of God.

Cleaning up the messy problems of real-life men will force us to get
personally involved with foul-smelling issues we don't even like to
discuss. It is a laborious process, but *we need men who will loose men.*

If we want to touch men, then we must learn how to "adopt"
one another. Some men desperately need to be fully accepted
because they need to experience a relationship they never
had in their childhood.

If you want to climb from the mediocre to the supernatural, find
someone who is doing what you want to do and do it with them.

People can never give you what they have not received.

The greatest investment you can make is an investment in people!
That's what God did. He invested His Son in humanity,
and reaped the harvest of the church.

If you have achieved any level of success, pour it into someone else!
Success is not success without a successor!

The greatest compliment you can give a father is
to catch what he gave you and carry on!

If you feel you have outgrown your need for a father, then at least be
a father. Somewhere there is a desperate young man whose natural
ties are broken. Bind him and train him. Teach him and pour into
him all the things you want to say to the next generation!

Our Savior keeps His commitment to men who have been discarded
and buried by others. He is a God of relationship, and His creation
can never escape its need for intimacy with its Creator.

The same confident men who are so tough and brash and brawny elsewhere—these master negotiators of the workplace find themselves nervous and anxious about facing the 110-pound woman who waits for them at home!

Men have merely *reacted* long enough. Now it's time to *act*.

God wants strong men who lead
instead of weak men who only follow.

Many men are wrestling with inner fear. Most of us are afraid of intimacy and feelings. Masculine emotions have become the twenty-first-century version of "Pandora's box." We don't know all that is in there, but we have a feeling we had better not let it out!

Man of God, *you have been robbed*! The enemy has stolen the warm, giddy feeling of excitement out of your heart! Do you want it back? Fight for it! Recall the soft songs, light those fragrant candles, take those long walks of longing, and once again murmur passionate words in your mate's ear. Take back what the enemy is trying to steal from you.

It is *tragic*. Most men assume God doesn't love fallen and fearful men as much as men who "have it all under control."

You can't have genuine friendships if you hide your true self.

If you hide your true self from your friends, they will only love *what you do—not who you are*!

Most of your jobs and relationships have been built on your personal performance and achievement, but God's call is not like that. All He wants is you.

Jesus was the Only One who was willing to die to be your Friend!

Once you understand that God is committed to you,
loneliness is impossible.

Many men struggle with commitment because
we seldom see it in others.

The hand of God is warm and tender, yet firm and strong. It is there
for every dark night, for every tainted secret, and for every wounded
marriage! God wipes away the hidden tears we never allowed to fall.

Each stage of life has its own challenges and potential. Somewhere
ahead of me —in yet another stage—is the smile of contentment
that I will display if I have handled this stage correctly.

If you want some good advice, don't take
the opinions of others too seriously.

Whoever comes after you should have it easier than you did
because blessed people always leave a blessing!

Teach your children wisdom. Teach them how to make and
handle money without worshiping it!

Excellent leadership always works itself out of a job!

Stagnancy is the enemy of progression.

How can we condemn abortion and shun women
with illegitimate children?

How can we condemn divorce and fail to teach and
practice restoration for damaged marriages?

Do you realize that we all don't heal at the same rate? You may be
healed, but that doesn't mean your wife, your children, your
employer, or your parents have been healed as well. It may be time
for you to show the same patience they once showed you.

Remember to comfort rather than criticize.

The wisest of men are those who recognize their need to change.

Have the courage to face the uncertainity of
new beginnings with a deep commitment to succeed!

Most Christian men pray like wimps and brag like warriors. The
truth is that real spiritual warriors are men who pray.

Don't avoid prayer because you think you are not articulate or
expressive. The stumbling, bumbling words of a tear-stained heart
ring out louder in the spirit realm than the finest resonating
voice of an orator.

Prayer is a compliment to God. It is an admission that we
believe in His competence to deal with the issues.

Your greatest message to your son is the one he sees,
not the one he hears.

Man of God, *I dare you to kneel down and pray!* Don't ask God to fix "them"; ask Him to fix you, and He will heal the land.

Obedience is the highest form of praise.

I am my wife's resting post and my children's compass.
If I do not affect my family in a positive way, then
my presence in the home is a disgrace to God!

I want to set a standard of excellence that is so high I won't be afraid
for my daughters to marry "someone like their father."

God will give you miracle after miracle if you are a praying man
with a goal, an agenda, and faith in His name!

There *are some things you give to no one but God.* Always reserve the deepest and innermost portion of your heart and trust for God.

Tell the enemy, "I am a man of prayer.
I will be knocked no lower than my knees!"

Giving is an opportunity to share the fruits of your undeserved blessing with a deserving God who has been gracious to you.

Resurrection changes the way you react to fear and death.
It doesn't mean you will never fear again. It simply means
you will forever react to fear differently.

Survival breeds confidence.

God never says "if" when He talks about your destiny.

The devil is deathly afraid of a *loosed man*!

Jesus told Simon, "When thou art converted, strengthen thy brethren." A loosed man always reaches back for others.

Although God had made a wonderful place for Adam to live, the man remained less than complete. He needed a woman. Keep in mind, though, that she completed his *purpose,* not his *person.* If you're not complete as a person, marriage will not help you.

As a father, I have found that I have a ministry of hugs. When something happens, and I really can't fix it, I just hug them.

Christ is not an impotent, weak, unresponsive, incompetent force. He is a God of power. He is revolutionary. He is life-changing. He is able to affect circumstances and situations.

We need to send a signal that reverberates across the world. Our Lord is not dead! He has all power in His hands! And when His people get together—not only can we rent auditoriums— we can buy them!

You cannot legislate love. Don't look to the White House. Don't look to the ballot box. Don't even look to the Church House. Look to getting on your knees before God.

Whatever you are involved in ought to feel the effect of your presence because of your likeness of God.

When you decide to help somebody, you won't have to carry them forever. Just get them to Jesus.

David said, "When my heart is overwhelmed, *lead me to the rock!*"

Men have an appointment with a miracle. The Spirit of the Lord wants to do a work in our lives.

Have you been in church so long that you've forgotten what you came for?

What has happened to this generation? When I was a little boy, we were afraid to walk into crowds of men. Now men are afraid to walk into crowds of boys.

Our healthy God looks at a wounded man and says, "You're still
My son. You blew it. You messed up and did a whole lot of things
you shouldn't have done. You said some things you shouldn't
have said and hurt some people you shouldn't have hurt.
But you are *still My son.*"

Real deliverance is when you take control of
the thing that had control of you.

Even if you've messed up, and other folks don't want to touch you,
if you will just raise your hands and begin to worship your God,
He will pick you up.

The move of God cannot be contained. It can be criticized and
frustrated, but it cannot be contained.

It's not that people who don't tithe don't want to give, it's that
they have no discipline. They never give God what is right,
they give God what is left.

Even if you don't have money and can't give, don't despise
an offering. If you can't sing, you don't despise the choir.
So don't despise an offering. Lack of money is only
a temporary circumstance.

You better plan on getting old, because you either do it or die.

A blessed man is in authority and under authority.

No woman wants to be in submission to
a man who isn't in submission to God.

A man who cannot rule his own spirit is like a city without walls. A man with no walls will let anything in.

If you want God to bless you, you need a plan. It will not be enough just to pray about it. Work toward your goals and what you're praying about. Faith without works is dead.

When your life is on hold and you think you're waiting on God, I've got news for you. You're not waiting on God, He's waiting on you.

I want to send a message to you, my brothers and my sisters, and I want you to understand something quite clearly: Christianity is not the white man's religion, it's not the black man's religion, it's not the Hispanics' religion, it is *all men's religion*.

Christianity is not for wimps. It's for *real* men.

Man was the only thing in creation that God touched to create.

Faith for the believer is what gasoline is for an automobile.

God is the Master Architect and Master Builder. He never
gets confused about what is planned or how it is to be built.
When He built you, He built you for maximum efficiency
and optimal performance.

God has a way of taking people who have been forsaken by men and
raising them up. In fact, God *prefers* such individuals, because
when they get into a place of power, they are not arrogant like
those who think they deserve to be there.

God's grace and mercy have brought you through.
Quit acting as if you have made it on your own.

A tremendous amount of power is released when we praise.

When you take God's thoughts and enter into praise, you become like a battering ram against the strongholds that Satan has erected in your mind.

Whatever we worship is what we ultimately end up serving.

It's not enough for us to go to church together. We're not really brothers until we can laugh and cry together.

It is the nature of a fallen man to hide from God. But when a man hides himself from God, he loses himself.

Trusting God with your successes isn't really a challenge.
The real test of trust is to be able to share your secrets,
our inner failures and fears.

Mutual enhancement comes into a relationship where
there is intimacy based on honesty.

We need heroes today. We need someone to believe in and look up
to. We need role models and men whose shadows we may stand in,
men who provide a cool, refreshing place of safety away from
the despair of our oppressive society.

We are suffering from an eroding *sense* of family,
not just from an eroding sense of family values.

We need to understand that God is able to repair the broken places.
All He requires of us is to expose where those broken places are.

It takes great courage to exemplify total honesty with God.

When we discover our own limitations, we become eligible
to discover the all-sufficiency of God.

The call of God is a high calling. Yet it has been answered by lowly
men who have had the discernment to see a God high and lifted up.

There can be no fulfillment where there is no passion.

Jesus Christ, the greatest lover the world has ever known,
gives Himself openly and unashamedly.

His love is exemplified in His coming,
but is consummated in His dying.

Undirected passion becomes a spawning bed for perversity and
dankness. It is *what we do with what we feel* that controls
the direction of our lives.

There is nothing more hollow than empty words and lofty clichés
that have no real meaning or compassion in them.

Do you know that many times your *thoughts* need to be healed? We
must understand that modern medicine can heal many afflictions of
the body, but only God Himself can heal the mind.

One of the great challenges of our walk with God is to resist
the temptation to allow what happened in the past determine
who we are today.

Thoughts are previews of coming attractions.

As we hear the thoughts of God,
His thinking becomes increasingly contagious.

In a world where people seem void of commitment and become so
easily distracted, it is comforting to know that God won't
give up on you.

More Insight
From T.D. Jakes

In *Life Overflowing*, T.D. Jakes powerfully teaches from the book of Ephesians, where you'll discover "unsearchable riches" of what it means to live in total consecration to God. Here in one volume you have all the key teachings from Bishop Jakes's SIX PILLARS FROM EPHESIANS series:

- Loved by God
- Experiencing Jesus
- Intimacy With God
- Life Overflowing
- Celebrating Marriage
- Overcoming the Enemy

When you rely on the Word of God and the power of the Holy Spirit, you will experience a life that's "exceedingly abundantly" above all you could ask or think.